D1522134

The Two Faces of Ionesco

The Two Faces of Ionesco

by

Rosette C. Lamont

and

Melvin J. Friedman

The Whitston Publishing Company
Troy, New York
1978

Library of Congress Catalog Card Number 76-51038

ISBN 0-87875-110-6

Printed in the United States of America

For Henri Peyre,

teacher, colleague, and friend.

FOREWORD

by Henri Peyre

Ionesco is the most paradoxical and probably the most enigmatic of today's French authors. The supreme badge of recognition, the Nobel prize, has not yet gone to him, but all the honors that France can bestow have come to that master of mockery: decorations, election to the Academy, delivering addresses at teachers' conventions, being exalted, or demeaned, to the rank of a classic in school textbooks.

He began writing for the stage because he hated the theater and was determined to kill it through ridicule and parody. Others meanwhile around him were monotonously voicing their challenge to the hypocrisy inherent in language and their hostility to psychology. He quietly undertook to reinstate language in its pristine nobleness through greater honesty in its use and inventive freshness. He lent a metaphysical dimension to psychology. While French authors around him deemed it fashionable to adopt a new orthodoxy, supposedly revolutionary, invoking idols worshipped by Russia, China, Cuba and other lands addicted to the cult of personality, Ionesco retained a free mind. Not for him any form, Fascist or anti-Fascist, bourgeois or leftist, of Rhinoceritis! "All writers have attempted to do propaganda", he remarked; "the great ones are those who have not succeeded at it."

Ionesco appears in the eyes of some, and perhaps in his own, as the most pessimistic of French writers today, but for another Rumanian, Cioran. Neither Camus nor Malraux has been haunted so persistently as Ionesco by the omnipresence of death. Anguish has preyed upon him more harrassingly than upon Kierkegaard or Sartre. His business, he stated with simplicity, is none other than "universal misfortune." But he is endowed with too much humor to ever dramatize himself or to pose as a healer of human woes. If man is, according to the age-old definition, the animal that laughs, he is even more, Ionesco contends, the animal that creates. Through scores of plays, one novel, essays as pungent and suggestive as any in our time, he has remained an inexhaustible creator.

Rosette Lamont, the shrewdest and most perceptive interpreter of Ionesco in Europe and America, and Melvin Friedman known in France for his *Configuration Critique de Samuel Beckett* which was published by Chicago University Press as *Samuel Beckett Now,* have ingeniously gathered here a series of chapters by diverse hands which illuminate all the conflicting aspects of that enigmatic personality. Their introduction, and Professor Lamont's own essays in this volume, brilliantly written, unravel the thought, the technique and the complexities of Ionesco's work. A fervent student of Jarry, of the contemporary theatre in Paris, New York and Moscow, equally at home in three or more literatures, Professor Lamont has been, from the very first, the dramatic critic who has won America over to an intelligent appreciation of Ionesco. In this volume, her study of the dramatist's latest play to date, *L'Homme aux valises,* stands as a model of courageous and enlightening appraisal of an immediately contemporary work. Her enthusiasm is contagious. Her gift as an "animator" of academic and non academic audiences is extraordinary. Together with Professor Friedman, she has persuaded several of the most distinguished writers on literature in this country and abroad, eminent essayists, and the great historian of religion, Mircea Eliade, to contribute to this volume. A valuable bibliography adds to its usefulness. A significant personal essay by Ionesco himself, here translated "Why do I write?", answers with candid straightforwardness the very questions which posterity wishes could have been asked Molière, Musset, Jarry, or O'Neill. This book takes its place among the most revealing critical works written from a variety of angles on any living writer.

PREFACE

I

People do not know how to take Ionesco, what to make of him: Is he a prankster laughing at us, with us, at himself alone? Is he "dead serious" as in *Exit the King,* an exploration of the apprenticeship of dying? Is his sense of the comic that "laughter through tears" characteristic of many great humorists: Swift, Gogol, Chekhov? Or does this man cry out in anguish, pity for his fellow man, fear for the very survival of humanity, a cry wrested from what Artaud calls the "anarchy of humor"? To all these conflicting questions the answer is an emphatic "yes."

Ionesco is Janus faced: one side is *l'enfant terrible,* heir of his compatriot Tristan Tzara and the Dadaists, claiming to belong to the "cabaret school of literature"—be it that of the Cabaret Voltaire—and tracing his genealogy to the Marx Brothers and Charlie Chaplin, the other is the philosopher-king, denouncing tyranny in its various incarnations, diagnosing *rhinoceritis* whether of the Right or Left, but also transcending politics is an attempt to reach the source of the sacred. It is this thirst for purity, for the absolute that brings the philosopher back to the child allowing us to see that the two faces of Janus are aspects of the same head.

Like Wordsworth, the Surrealists and their followers felt that "the Child is father of the Man." Every moment of life is a miracle; for example, as Breton remarked: "Isn't it miraculous that when we take a warm bath we don't dissolve in the water like a piece of sugar?" To recapture an abstract purity, to see the theatre as a mirage, and the stage as the space where the impossible begins, a playwright must dare become once again the child he was. Back in France as an adult after thirteen years spent in Rumania, Ionesco thought he would add a third living language to his two native tongues. He embarked on the *Assimil* method of English conversation, but, as he began to recite the lines of dialogue, it seemed strange to him that people had to explain to one another that the ceiling was above their heads, the floor under their feet, that the days of the week were Monday-TuesdayWednesdayThursdayFridaySaturdaySunday, that they were English, a family by the name of Smith, living in their English home with their English daughter and their English maid, eating English food. Ionesco did not succeed in acquiring the English language, but he felt the floor move under his feet, the ceiling swim overhead. Faint, dizzy, nauseous, he was forced to lie down. The would-be student had become a philosopher-child, king of the absurd, the creator of a new genre, the Metaphysical Farce.

Ionescoland is peopled by headless great men, mustachioed maidens to marry, brides with three noses, grooms hatching over-size eggs that yield both our consumer society and the engines of its destruction. It is not so much of an anti-world as one parallel to our own. Once we have willingly suspended disbelief, we find that it is regulated by rules as strict as those of the so-called real world. "I am a realist, nothing else," Ionesco likes to affirm. It is only what the playwright calls "the cholesterol of the mind" which prevents us from seeing that the outside is in, the inside out. In his conclusion to the new edition of *Notes and Counter Notes* Ionesco says: "Modern psychology teaches us that man does not adapt himself to the real, but that he reconstructs reality, that by looking and touching he reconstitutes a world, gives it shape: interpretation and creation are identical phenomena, to know is to invent."

For him, as he so often says and writes, nothing is actual; there is only the veil of appearance which must be rent. Only then can we become "synchronic with thought" (*Découvertes*), and begin to invent a language which will translate the original world, the world of "before" which is that of thought itself. "All is language in the theatre," Ionesco stated in a radio interview. Words, gestures, props, objects are all aspects of language, the semantics of the new theatre. But language itself is only an approximation of the original metaphysics of astonishment, the basis of ethics. "It seems to me we have not progressed much beyond this intuition of childhood," Ionesco writes in *Découvertes*.

History, Hegelianism, Marxism, Existentialism, these are the dry bread of abstract though. Only poetry, the astonished consciousness of the world, can nourish man. Too many people give in to the illusion that one must act upon the world, change it, or divine its inevitable changes. One must create the world instead of altering it, says the artist. And what is more, what all the isms ignore, is that the world is there, ready to be read and recreated. Ideologies, are, as Talleyrand knew, merely a question of dates. So-called facts lie, and are made to deceive, but "invention is the opposite of lying since it unveils and rebuilds." (*Découvertes*). Above all, Ionesco does not seek to be "original," or strange in his literature, he wants to capture "the expression of origin." (*Découvertes*). His ancestors, he claims, are Job and King Solomon, men who knew, and experienced in their flesh the fact that all is vanity.

To preach and teach through characters set upon the stage, extensions on one's ego, is a supreme form of vanity. There is, however, another type of theatre, mythical and therefore universal. Ionesco despises the didactic stage, but he allows himself to be open, receptive, so as to be invaded by these strange presences, phantoms of the past and future, archetypal images. In this sense he is a primitive, a child, a witness. The latter, however, reveals Ionesco's second face, the suffering mask of an acute consciousness of man-made evil. The passionate champion of Russian dissenters, the friend of Israel which he considers the true socialist state, the admirer of the independent form of mind born in the America of the Revolution, Ionesco has increasingly come to voice his opinions in the press, and is at work on a book of *pensées* of a political, moral nature. If one had to situate him in a line of thinkers, it would be on the latitude of Pasternak, Solzhenitsyn, Amalrik, Siniavsky, Elie Wiesel, Saul Bellow. More committed to public statements than Samuel Beckett, Ionesco no longer avoids confrontations with limousine leftists ("les gauchistes du seizième arroundissement"), cliché-ridden structuralists, and, in general, the intellectual establishment of Paris. Like Bellow's Charles Citrine, the narrator of *Humboldt's Gift,* the dramatist has diagnosed this "Curious moment in the history of human consciousness when the mind universally awakens and democracy originates, an era of turmoil and ideological confusion, the principal phenomenon of the present age."

As a young man growing up in Rumania, the dramatist learned to recognize the signs of political and intellectual fascism. *Rhinoceros* was born from the feeling that a time might come when we would remain the only human left in a society of wild beasts. *Macbett,* a late play, is a cartoon version of the knowledge that absolute power corrupts absolutely. It has become increasingly apparent that Ionesco is not a prankster but a man with metaphysical concerns, the most profound one being with man's inhumanity to man. Those who have sought to reduce his attitude to some political school of thought have had to blind themselves to the complexities of the dramatist's personality and attitude. Those who would have liked to dismiss him as a dreamer found his stance irreducible. In today's world of black and white allegiances, the two faces of Janus are paradoxically less clearly defined; one is the hesitant mask of the child-like anti-hero, the other the pensive mien of the contemporary hero in spite of himself. The latter, like Odysseus, cannot rejoice or glory over slain men, he is groping for a new vision of man's fate, a principle of cosmic justice.

Ionesco the child has led us to Ionesco the man. The latter, in turn, will take us onto that transcendent plane where the innocence of his fervor, of what we call his courage, permits us to see into ourselves. For us as for him what we were and what we have become is perhaps a fusion of seemingly disparate selves, travelers along Everyman's path.

II

The present collection acknowledges the two faces or aspects of Ionesco: the child-like prankster and the mature artist. All the essays, except for *"Hunger and Thirst:* A Conversation with Simone Benmussa and an Analysis," were written especially for this volume. The techniques of the contributors vary widely as does their subject matter. Some critics in *The Two Faces of Ionesco* look at Ionesco's texts with the care and scrupulousness of the New Critics; others are more interested in giving his work a broader context and setting it in confrontation with other dramatic forms. There is virtually no overlap among the essays in the collection; the subjects treated are as various as the critical approaches used.

Mircea Eliade is concerned with Ionesco's religious dimension and his substantial grounding in religious texts. He usefully discusses the role of "light experiences" and "light symbolism" in both the personal life of the dramatist and in his work. Eliade, the greatest living historian of religions, sees Ionesco as behaving somewhat like a *"homo religiosus"* yet insists upon his "serene detachment from any institutionalized form of religion."

Germaine Brée devotes much of her attention to studying three plays of the 1960s: *A Stroll in the Air, Exit the King,* and *Hunger and Thirst.* She brings these dramatic works in close juxtaposition with Ionesco's essays of that decade; she explains how they offer valuable skeleton keys to Ionesco's sensibility.

Rosette Lamont, Bruce Morrissette, and Michel Benamou all discuss neglected phases of the *oeuvre.* Lamont looks closely at the two children's tales—which she considers "a kind of pre-literature"—and tries to link them with the plays. Morrissette concentrates on the unpublished *La Nièce-épouse* which he finds to be "an amusing scherzo in which the master Ionesco employs with practised hand many of his most characteristic techniques and develops with considerable cunning a number of implicit themes of a semi-serious nature." Benamou speaks of his collaboration with Ionesco on the textbook, *Mise en train*—which contains twenty of Ionesco's dialogues. He explains how these dialogues "touch the limits of language" and how they help inform the techniques of the plays. All three of these critics demonstrate how Ionesco's seemingly marginal gestures illuminate the central preoccupations of his work.

Alexandre Rainof looks outside Ionesco's work, at certain film figures and film techniques of the 1920s and 1930s, to explain Ionesco's movement away from "verbal language" and his "constantly greater emphasis on visual metaphors."

Irving Malin, Robert Champigny, and Simone Benmussa each concentrates on a single text. Malin studies the autobiographical *Fragments of a Journal* in systematic detail and finds that "it can stand alone as an impressive work of art." It does more for Malin than merely give pieces of a man's life: it "contains his attempt to *organize himself through language.*" Champigny concentrates on the "strong reflexive aspect" of *The Chairs.* Benmussa looks closely at *Hunger and Thirst* as she de-

pends on intermittent comments by Ionesco himself. She makes
the telling assertion about this 1966 play: "The theme of encirclement, of asphyxiation, dominant in Ionesco's entire theatre,
reaches its greatest intensity in *Hunger and Thirst*."

Roy Swanson, John Fletcher, and Edith Kern all fall back
on critical strategies readily identifiable to students of Comparative Literature. Swanson points to "Ionesco's classical antecedents in, specifically, Greek tragedy" and sets up a lineage which
accommodates a variety of playwrights from Aeschylus and
Sophocles through Shakespeare to Beckett, Ionesco, and Pinter.
Fletcher brings together for close scrutiny Ionesco's *Victims of
Duty* and Pinter's *The Birthday Party;* he notices a variety of
similarities but insists that there is no likelihood of influence.
He ends with side glances at Albee's *Who's Afraid of Virginia
Woolf?* and a variety of other contemporary plays. Edith Kern
describes Ionesco's uneasy relationship with Brecht and his
supporters and remarks rather tellingly that "even in his contradictions and in his insistence upon his right to be contradictory Ionesco shows an amazing kinship with Brecht and the
Brechtian conception of theatre." She decisively proves her
point by applying Brechtian *Verfremdung* to *Macbett.*

In her study of *L'Homme aux valises,* Ionesco's most recent play, Rosette Lamont shows that the two faces of Ionesco
are in reality the double aspect of the artist's Janusian nature.
Through the prism of Jungian psychoanalysis, and his poetic
exploration of Surrealism's discovery of the importance of the
world of dreams and of the reveries of childhood, Ionesco concretizes upon the stage a voyage into the hidden, atavistic self.
On the vertical level, the play is a plunge into the subconscious,
on the horizontal, it is a political allegory. The restless traveler
returns to the country of his forefathers, now a cruel police state
where he is confined to a hospital/insane asylum in which beds
are made available through systematic euthenasia. In *L'Homme
aux valises,* metaphysical farce and political satire are fused
through the magic of the mature artist's ability to look with the
astonishment of a child at the surface of things, and beyond, into
that zone of the sacred which is familiar to the primitive, the
poet and the mystic.

These essays convince us that Ionesco's work is entirely of
a piece. Every time he puts pen to paper—whether composing a

dialogue for a textbook, or writing a children's story, or respond-
ing to an interviewer, or contributing to an autobiography-in-
progress, or writing a play—he is adding significantly to an *oeuvre*
which is among the most realized and complete of any we have
from a contemporary.

III

All that seems missing from the canon is a novel. Ionesco
accommodated this need by publishing *Le Solitaire* in 1973
(translated as *The Hermit,* by Richard Seaver, in 1974). This
novel reveals the second face of Ionesco we have been speaking
of—the writer with metaphysical concerns who never ceases to
worry about Montaigne's *l'humaine condition.*

Berenger, the principal character of Ionesco's *Rhinoceros,*
remarks to his friend Jean: "I just can't get used to life." This is
precisely the difficulty with the narrator of Ionesco's first novel,
The Hermit. He has the financial means, however—thanks to an
inheritance from an American uncle—to give up an unappetizing
job and retreat to an apartment in the Paris suburbs. He submits
to his flirtation with idleness at the age of thirty-five. He reminds us a bit of Huysmans' Des Esseintes (*Against the Grain*) as
he plans certain future activities: "To have your apéritif in a
different café every day, now that could be a real voyage of discovery. Trying a new drink every day would be, too."

Idleness, it turns out, suits him no better than work. His
world-weariness keeps getting the better of him and boredom,
frustration, and nausea (three of his favorite words) take over.
He gets a temporary reprieve when a waitress, Yvonne, moves in
with him, but their brief liaison is marred by his silences and his
depressive habits. He becomes increasingly a recluse and finally
barricades himself in his apartment when a revolution threatens
to destroy his neighborhood. He emerges an indeterminate
period later ("Time went by. Months went by. Years maybe.")
to find himself and the world grown older and wearier.

It is tempting to use adjectives like "existential" and "absurd" when speaking of Ionesco's narrator. Indeed his vocabulary favors turns like "nausea of nothingness," "nausea of the
infinite," and "metaphysical anxiety." He seems to have much

in common with Sartre's Roquentin (*Nausea*) and Camus's Meursault (*The Stranger*). Yet, in the end, he is an authentic unique, very much a child of Ionesco's imagination. This is the Ionesco who admitted in his memoir, *Present Past, Past Present:* "I have a tendency, almost always, to be against my time, to be swimming against the stream." *The Hermit* and its narrator-hero surely appear to be going against the grain of contemporary notions of fictional technique and characterization.

The narrative itself—unlike most recent fiction—proceeds in an unbroken, strictly chronological line. The first-person story teller, who remains unnamed, painstakingly describes every detail of his existence. He spares us nothing: he supplies us with the titles of the books in his library (fortunately, they are not very numerous); he gives us the menu of the various meals he eats in his favorite restaurant; he offers an almost verbatim transcription of a telephone conversation he has with a philosophy student. This is not to suggest that his narrative habits at all resemble the cataloguing procedures we have grown accustomed to in the novels of contemporaries like Samuel Beckett, Alain Robbe-Grillet, Nathalie Sarraute, Michel Butor, and Claude Simon. *The Hermit,* on the contrary, relies on conventional and even old-fashioned devices—which acknowledge the importance of character, plot, and theme.

Aside from the narrator's almost clinical insistence on detail, he has a tendency to connect every happening in the outside world, however casual, with his own psyche. He makes the crucial observation at one point: "or rather, what was going on outside was going on in me. The outside was beginning to reflect the inside." His classic French case of *ennui* makes him turn increasingly inward and concern himself more and more with self ("What is this 'I'? Does it exist?") and with consciousness.

This narrator has a genuine gift for aphoristic turns: "There was still a measure of joy possible, if you stood aside and simply watched the madding crowd."; "When one is not a great philosopher, one should not philosophize."; "I know that the world is always and indefatigably virgin." If he had heeded the wisdom of certain of these maxims, he would probably have accommodated himself better to living in the world. But his man, Ionesco seems to be telling us, can turn elegant phrases but is incapable of transforming theory into practice.

He is not unlike the characters in Ionesco's plays. Indeed a knowledge of the drama is very helpful in understanding certain of the fictional strategies at work in *The Hermit.* Ionesco's almost unique ability to turn reality into phantasmagoria and nightmare, with no warning, gives readers the same chilling sensation in his first novel that theater-goers have been getting for some time from *Rhinoceros, The Lesson,* and *The Chairs.* The crankily precise way that the narrator of *The Hermit* chooses to spend his days scarcely prepares us for the vagueness which surrounds the revolution and the uncertainties about time following the moment he locks himself in his apartment. There is nothing in the language of this narrator either to suggest a change; it maintains a monotonous sameness and is syntactically correct and coherent from first to last.

We must end by questioning the credibility of this narrator who describes himself on one occasion as "the constant dreamer." His increasing confusion about reality makes us doubt his reliability. For example, after the waitress' departure he is never sure whether her name is Yvonne or Marie. When he begins to examine the causes of the revolution, the best he can come up with is: "The fact was, I didn't understand the first thing about why they were fighting. But I had to assume there was indeed a reason."

Some of these questions are answered by Ionesco himself in the text of a lucid lecture given in 1976 on a tour through Europe. "Why do I Write?" is a brilliant summing up of his career. It is particularly suitable for this book of essays since it shows that the dramatist is aware that he owes his *Weltanschauung* to his ability to preserve the child's wonder at the core of the mature artist's apprehension. It is a deeply moving text, confessional in tone, a kind of literary last will and testament.

If Ionesco posed a question in *Present Past, Past Present:* "Who is there who can distinguish reality from a mirage?" he does seem to provide a key in "Why Do I Write?" Mirage is the essential part of the artist's reality. Mirage is the hidden face of the moon which will be revealed to us if we travel in the wake of "the man with bags", crossing with him the invisible line of the equator of the mind.

Rosette C. Lamont
Melvin J. Friedman

TABLE OF CONTENTS

ACKNOWLEDGMENTS

Acknowledgment is made for use of the following material:

For quotations from *Entretiens avec Eugène Ionesco* in the essay, "Eugène Ionesco and 'La Nostalgie du paradis'," by Mircea Eliade (Paris: Editions Pierre Belfond, 1966).

For quotations from *Découvertes,* by Eugène Ionesco, in the essay, "Father of the Man," by Rosette C. Lamont (Geneva: Editions d'Art Albert Skira, 1969).

For quotations from *Entretiens avec Eugène Ionesco* translated by Rosette C. Lamont, in the essay, "Father of the Man," by Rosette C. Lamont (Paris: Editions Belfond, 1966).

For quotations from *Notes and Counter Notes,* by Eugène Ionesco, in the essay, "Father of the Man," by Rosette C. Lamont (New York: Grove Press, 1964).

For quotations from the unpublished play, "La nièce-épouse" by Eugène Ionesco in the essay, "A 'lost' Play by Ionesco," by Bruce Morrissette (Eugène Ionesco and the anonymous owner of the manuscript).

For the lecture, "Pourquoi j'écris" ("Why Do I Write?"), by Eugène Ionesco (Eugène Ionesco).

For a quotation from "Le Langage universel d'Eugène Ionesco," by Branco Vuletic in the essay, "Ionesco and the Film of the Twenties and Thirties," by Alexandre Rainof (*Studia Romanica et Anglica Zagrebiensia,* No. 13 (1961), pp. 102-103).

For permission to reproduce "Chez la Boulangère" ("The Face of the Future") in translation and to quote from *Mise en train* (dialogues originaux de Eugène Ionesco, avec la collaboration de Monique Callimand), in the essay, "Philology Can Lead to the Worst," by

Michel Benamou (New York: The Macmillan Company, 1969 and Eugène Ionesco).

For permission to reproduce, in slightly modified form, Part III of the Introduction by Rosette C. Lamont and Melvin J. Friedman (*The New Republic*, 7 December, 1974, pp. 26-27).

For quotations from *Fragments of a Journal*, by Eugène Ionesco, in the essay, "The Fragments of Eugène Ionesco," by Irving Malin (New York: Grove Press, 1969; London: Faber and Faber, 1969).

For quotations from Simone Benmussa's *Ionesco*, in the essay, "Designation and Gesture in *The Chairs*," by Robert Champigny (Paris: Seghers, 1966).

For quotations from *Découvertes*, by Eugène Ionesco, in the essay, "Ionesco's Later Plays: Experiments in Dramatic Form," by Germaine Brée (Geneva: Editions d'Art Albert Skira, 1969).

For quotations from *Notes and Counter Notes*, by Eugène Ionesco, in the essay, "Ionesco's Later Plays: Experiments in Dramatic Form," by Germaine Brée (New York: Grove Press, 1964; Paris: Gallimard, 1964).

For quotations from *Fragments of a Journal*, by Eugène Ionesco, in the essay, "Ionesco's Later Plays: Experiments in Dramatic Form," by Germaine Brée (New York: Grove Press, 1969).

For a quotation from *Aesthetic*, by Benedetto Croce, translated by Douglas Ainslie, in the essay, "Ionesco's Later Plays: Experiments in Dramatic Form," by Germaine Brée (New York: Noonday Press [Farrar, Straus and Giroux], 1960).

For quotations from *Modern Tragicomedy, an Investigation into the Nature of the Genre*, by Karl S. Guthke, in the essay, "Ionesco's Classical Absurdity," by Roy Arthur Swanson (New York: Random House, 1966).

For quotations from *The Pattern of Tragicomedy in Beaumont and Fletcher*, by Eugene M. Waith, in the essay, "Ionesco's Classical Absurdity," by Roy Arthur Swanson (New Haven: Yale University Press, 1952).

For quotations from *The Theatre of the Absurd* by Martin Esslin. Copyright © 1961 by Martin Esslin. Used by permission of Doubleday and Company, Incorporated.

For a quotation from *Eugène Ionesco,* by Leonard C. Pronko, in the essay "Ionesco's Classical Absurdity," by Roy Arthur Swanson (New York: Columbia University Press, 1965), by permission of the publisher.

For quotations from *Notes and Counter Notes* by Eugène Ionesco, in the essay "Ionesco's Classical Absurdity," by Roy Arthur Swanson (New York: Grove Press, 1964).

For quotations from *Joe Egg,* by Peter Nichols, in the essay "Ionesco's Classical Absurdity," by Roy Arthur Swanson (New York: Grove Press, 1967).

For quotations from *Metatheatre,* by Lionel Abel, in the essay, "Ionesco's Classical Absurdity," by Roy Arthur Swanson (New York: Hill and Wang/Farrar, Straus and Giroux, Incorporated, 1963).

For a quotation from "The Theatre of the Absurd Reconsidered," in *Reflections—Essays on Modern Theatre,* in the essay, "Ionesco's Classical Absurdity," by Roy Arthur Swanson (New York: Doubleday & Company, Incorporated, Copyright © 1969) used by permission of the publisher.

For a quotation from *Découvertes,* by Eugène Ionesco, in the essay, "Ionesco's Classical Absurdity," by Roy Arthur Swanson (Geneva: Editions d'Art Albert Skira, 1969).

For quotations from *Amédée, The New Tenant, Victims of Duty,* by Eugène Ionesco, in the essay, "A Psychology Based on Antagonism: Ionesco, Pinter, Albee, and Others," by John Fletcher (New York: Grove Press, 1958).

For quotations from *The Birthday Party* and *The Room,* by Harold Pinter, in the essay, "A Psychology Based on Antagonism: Ionesco, Pinter, Albee, and Others," by John Fletcher (New York: Grove Press, 1968).

For quotations from *The Caretaker, The Homecoming, The Birthday Party,* by Harold Pinter, in the essay, "A Psychology Based on Antagonism: Ionesco, Pinter, Albee, and Others," by John Fletcher (London: Eyre Methuen Ltd.).

For excerpts from an interview with Harold Pinter by Jean Blakewell, in the essay, "A Psychology Based on Antagonism: Ionesco, Pinter, Albee, and Others," by John Fletcher (*The Listener*, November 6, 1969).

For quotations from *Notes and Counter Notes,* by Eugène Ionesco, in the essay, "*Macbett* in the Light of *Verfremdung*," by Edith Kern (New York: Grove Press, 1964).

For quotations from *Conversations with Ionesco,* by Claude Bonnefoy, in the essay, "*Macbett* in the Light of *Verfremdung*," by Edith Kern (London: Faber and Faber, 1970).

For quotations from *L'Homme aux valises; Fragments of a Journal; Notes and Counter Notes; The Killer; The Lesson,* by Eugène Ionesco, in the essay, "*L'Homme aux valises:* Ionesco's Absolute Stranger," by Rosette C. Lamont (New York: Grove Press).

For quotations from *Découvertes,* by Eugène Ionesco, in the essay "*L'-Homme aux valises:* Ionesco's Absolute Stranger," by Rosette C. Lamont (Geneva: Editions d'Art Albert Skira, 1969).

For a quotation from *Memories, Dreams, Reflections,* by C. G. Jung, ed. Aniela Jaffe and translated Richard and Clara Winston, in the essay, "*L'Homme aux valises:* Ionesco's Absolute Stranger," by Rosette C. Lamont (New York: Vintage Books/Random House; Alfred A. Knopf, Incorporated, 1965).

For the two photographs of Eugène Ionesco by Beverly Pabst (Stockbridge, Massachusetts, 1969).

For quotations throughout from British editions of *Macbett, Maid to Marry, Hunger and Thirst, Victims of Duty,* and *Notes and Counternotes,* we are grateful to John Calder (Publishers) Ltd.

For permission to reproduce Rosette C. Lamont's translation of "Hunger and Thirst: A Conversation with Simone Benmussa and An Analysis" from *Ionesco* (Paris: Seghers, 1966).

INTRODUCTORY REMARKS TO EUGENE IONESCO'S "WHY DO I WRITE?"

by Rosette C. Lamont

Eugene Ionesco's 1976 lecture, "Who Do I Write?" can be called a summing up of his life and of his career as a dramatist. It reveals with greater clarity than that already achieved in his confessional journals his life-long dependence on a moment of mystical revelation which occurred in his childhood when his mother, finding life in Paris very hard at the end of the First World War, sent the boy to live for a couple of years with a kind peasant family in the tiny village of *La Chapelle Anthenaise.* There, at the Old Mill, the eight year old boy discovered an idyllic, pastoral existence, and experienced a wholeness, a sense of security hitherto unknown to him. He seemed to have forgotten his early apprehension of mortality at about the age of four when, having questioned his mother about death, he extracted from her the acknowlegment of the latter's universality. The scene, as he told it to Claude Bonnefoy, remained imprinted on his mind:

> I was sitting on the floor, she was standing in front of me. I can still see her, with her hands behind her back, leaning against the wall. When she saw me sobbing—because all at once I broke into tears— she kept on looking at me, disarmed, powerless. I was very frightened. Particularly when I thought, she would die someday; that haunted me. Did I fear her death more than my own.

At the Mill, however, "everything was joy, everything was presentness," as he writes in *Fragments of a Journal.* The boy's universe was complete, and he himself seemed to dwell at the living core of the mandala, until "a centrifugal force" projected him out of "immutability into the midst of things that come and go, and come back and go away for good." Suddenly, as he once explained in the beginning of a talk given at Lausanne in

November 1954, "a curtain, an impassable wall" stood between
him and himself, "matter (filled) every corner." Like Adam and
Eve, he was swept into whirling space, into death-dealing time.
It was perhaps as if Proust had lost the taste of *la petite madeleine,* never to recapture it again. Art, for Ionesco, as for Proust,
is the quest of *le temps perdu.* For the dramatist it is also
l'espace perdu, and, above all, *la lumière perdue.*

It is not an exaggeration to say that Ionesco, the child,
experienced a mystical state which continues to haunt Ionesco,
the adult, the mature artist. For the latter, the way to recapture
the initial illumination, at least in part, is to write. This is the
statement Ionesco makes in the text published here. Above all,
he longs for the paradisiacal light of the cosmos of his childhood.
As Gershom G. Scholem explains in his *On the Kabbalah and Its
Mysticism:*

> Because mystical experience as such is formless, there is in principle
> no limit to the forms it can assume. At the beginning of their path,
> mystics tend to describe their experience in forms drawn from the
> world of perception. At later stages, corresponding to different levels
> of consciousness, the world of nature recedes, and these 'natural'
> forms are gradually replaced by specifically mystical structures. Near-
> ly all mystics known to us describe such structures as configurations
> of lights and sounds. At still later stages, as the mystic's experience
> progresses towards the ultimate formlessness, these structures dissolve
> in turn.

If one could compare Ionesco to that rabbi of the Academy of
Caeserea who felt that the Holy Scriptures were like a house with
many rooms, but that the keys to these chambers were not the
right ones, an apprehension mirrored closely by that of a writer
truly steeped in Jewish mysticism, Franz Kafka, one ought perhaps to study another influence on Ionesco's understanding of
his primordial vision, that of the Byzantine mystics he read when
he returned to Rumania to join his father who had separated
from his mother. It is from these readings, according to an unpublished* essay by Ionesco's friend Mircea Eliade, "Eugene
Ionesco and 'La Nostalgie du Paradis'," that the dramatist culled
the image and theme of light. As Eliade explains, the light experience brings mystics out of time and history, projecting them
into a transcendental world. Thus, Ionesco's aesthetic is closely
tied to the behavior of the *homo religiosus.* Although the

dramatist is not devout in a traditional sense, his *Weltanschau-ung* is that of a man of faith, or at least of a child of faith.

"Why Do I Write?" is a tremendously important text; it brings final proof of the philosophical depth of Ionesco's think-ing, and shows that his *oeuvre,* diverse as it may appear, follows a line, or curve, always true to itself, and its initial revelation. The dialectic in the *corpus* of his works is between the existential in-justice of death, that of the body and of the human conscience, and the remembrance of an infinite oneness. Both of these polar apprehensions fill one with astonishment at our situation in the world. Adults tend to lose that sense of wonder, but art-ists, who are often able to preserve the freshness of the child's re-actions, never stop to question the universe in which they are im-mersed. An artist is a living question, as is every one of his works.

Ionesco has often been accused of political conservatism. In this essay, he faces once again this indictment. He reveals the narrowness of the commitment expected of him. There is the wonderful story of Mr. Panigel, a member of the Communist party, who summons him and his colleague-dramatist Jean Vauthier. The "boys" are offered to place their budding talents in the service of a ready-made ideology. What is implied is that this will not only provide them with subject matter but with a built-in audience. Neither one of the young playwrights allowed himself to be lured. It is not easy to preserve one's independence in any country, but in France, where dramatic and literary criti-cism is often prejudged—Marxist critics such as Bernard Dort know in advance that they cannot like Ionesco's latest play—lack of adherence to a group opens one to virulent attack. A po-liticized, laicized society is unable to comprehend Ionesco's freedom which, according to Eliade, has "religious" dimensions.

Nor is Ionesco a pessimistic writer, as has been affirmed by those who obviously never read him. In "Why Do I Write?" this notion is irrevocably dispelled, for the dramatist states in no un-certain terms that he creates in order to communicate his "daz-zlement with the very fact of existence." Thus, a work of art in general, and a play in particular since it can be seen as a kind of rite, opens up a view of the infinite. Ionesco's mystical sub-stantiality makes him kin to the great Kabbalists of Medieval Languedoc. And did he not, himself, claim as his ancestors

King Solomon and Job?

*Published herein, page 21 et seq.

WHY DO I WRITE? A SUMMING UP

by Eugene Ionesco

I am still asking myself this question. I've been writing for a long time. When I was thirteen, I wrote my first play, at about eleven or twelve I was writing poems, and I was all of eleven when I started my memoirs: two pages of a school notebook. It isn't as though there was a lack of things to say. I know that at that time I still had a clear recollection of my early childhood, when I was two or three years old, a time which has now become the memory of a memory of a memory. Seven or eight was the awakening of love; I was deeply attracted by a little girl of the same age. Then, when I was nine, there was another, Agnes. She lived eight kilometers from the Mill of the Chapelle-Anthenaise where I spent my childhood, a farm at St-Jean-sur-Mayenne. I made faces to make her laugh, and laugh she did, closing her eyes, revealing dimples, and tossing her blond hair. What has become of her? If she is still alive, she must be a fat peasant woman, perhaps a grandmother. There would also be other things to tell: the discovery of the cinema, or the magic lantern; my arrival in the country, the barn, the hearth, and old man Baptiste with his missing thumb on the right hand. Many other things: the school, the teacher, old man Guéné, the priest, Durand, the tippler, who returned dead drunk from his rounds of the farms of the *commune*. Everywhere he went they'd give him cider, or pear brandy.

Then there was my first confession when I said yes to all the priest's questions because I couldn't make out what he was saying—he was muttering under his breath—and it seemed better to take upon myself imaginary sins rather than to let any slip by. I could have spoken of my little friends, Raymond, Maurice, Simone, and of the games we played. But all this required training which one acquires later. We speak of our childhood when we're no longer in it, when we no longer understand it very well.

Of course, we also fail to understand what we are when we are children, but, at any rate, I was conscious of being alive when I lived in the Mayenne, I lived in happiness, joy, knowing somehow that each moment was fullness without knowing the word fullness. I lived in a kind of dazzlement. The first rift occured when I had to leave the Chapelle-Anthenaise. But with time the light dimmed, and now I realize I was not suited to being a farmer, ungifted as I am for manual labor. Some of my school pals from the *école communale,* Lucien, Auguste, have become wealthy farmers. To me, however, it seems that they lead quite a hard life, and that there's little play left in their daily existence. They cast an indifferent eye on frolicking children. Perhaps I might have been the village teacher but my only vacations would have been school holidays which are not real holidays for adults.

One of the real reasons for which I write must be to find once again the marvellous element of childhood beyond daily life, joy beyond drama, freshness beyond hardship. Palm Sunday, when the tiny village streets were strewn with flowers and branches, was a transfiguration under the April sun. On religious feast days, I would climb the narrow, rocky path, guided by the church bells, and the church itself would appear little by little, first the top of the bell tower with its weathercock, then the whole steeple outlined against the blue sky. The world was beautiful, and I was conscious of it, everything was fresh and pure. I repeat: it is to find this beauty again, intact in the mud, that I write literary works. All my books, all my plays are a call, the expression of nostalgia, a search for a treasure buried in the ocean, lost in the tragedy of history. Or, if you prefer, what I am looking for and seem to find from time to time, is light. This is my basic reason for writing literature, and for having nourished myself by it. Always in search of this light, its presence beyond the shadows a certainty. I write in the night, in anguish, by the brief flicker of humor. But this is not the light I'm seeking, not that lighting. I want a play of intimate confession, or a novel to remain shadowy until one issues into the light. In my novel, *Le Solitaire (The Loner)*, as one comes out of a long moral tunnel, one is greeted finally by a dazzling landscape with the morning sun shining on a flowering tree, a green bush. In *Hunger and Thirst,* Jean, the wanderer, sees a silver ladder rising from the earth into the azure of the heavens, and in *Amédée or How to Get Rid of It,* the hero flies up in the direction of the Milky Way. In *The Chairs,* however, the characters have but a dim recollection of a church standing in a luminous garden, then the light fades and the play opens into the void. And so on.

Most of the time these images of light, quickly fading, or, on the contrary seeming to arise naturally at the end of a lengthy journey, have not been willed into existence but found. Or, if they appear in the conscious mind, it is because they first came to me in dreams. I mean by this that in my plays, or my written meditations, I have the feeling of embarking on a voyage of exploration, of groping my way through a dark forest, in the middle of the night. I do not know whether I will ever reach my goal, or even if a goal exists. I proceed without a clear outline, and the end comes of its own accord. It can be an awareness of failure, as in my last play, *L'Homme aux valises,* or of success providing that the end resembles a new beginning.

I am in fact seeking a world which has recovered its virginity; I would like to repossess the paradisiacal light of my childhood, the glory of the first day, an untarnished glory, and of an intact universe which would appear before me as though it were new born. It is as though I wanted to witness the event of creation before the Fall, looking for it within myself, as if attempting to swim up the stream of History, or within my characters who are other incarnations of my self, or who are like those others who resemble me in their quest, conscious or not, of an absolute light. It is because they have not mapped out a road to follow that my characters wander in the dark, the absurd, in incomprehension and anguish. It has often been suggested that I speak a great deal of my anxieties. I rather think that I refer to those of human beings caught in the grayishness of daily existence, or in misfortune, people who mistakenly believe that they are prisoners of the impasses of history and politics, but who, as a result, become ready victims of exploitation, repression and wars. To return to what I way saying, I would like to stress that the state of childhood, and a certain intensity of light are indissolubly fused in my mind. All that is not light is anguish, sinister shadows. I write to find anew this light and communicate it to others. This light is at the outer edge of the absolute which I lose, and find again. It is also astonishment. I see myself in my childhood photos, eyes wide open, amazed by the very fact of existence. I haven't changed. The primordial wonder is still part of me. I am here, I've been put here, surrounded with all of

this and all of that. I still don't know what happened to me.
I've always been deeply touched by the beauty of the world.
When I was eight, and then nine, I lived two months of April,
and two months of May I will never forget. I ran along a path
edged with primrose, gamboled through fresh green meadows,
full of an indescribable joy of being. These colors, this dazzling
light, haunt my mind so that when I say that the world is a prison I am not being truthful. In the Spring, I recognized the colors,
the beauty, the light of a paradise whose memory I have kept.
Even now, in order to escape from my anguish, I place myself
marginally, peering with profound attention at the world, as
though I were seeing it all for the first time, on the very first day
of consciousness. Standing back, away from the world, I contemplate it as though I were not part of it. Then it may still
happen that I will feel transports of joy. Wonder having reached
its zenith, I no longer doubt anything. I feel certain that I was
born for eternity, that death does not exist, that all is miraculous. A glorious presence. I am grateful then to witness this
Manifestation and participate in it. And since I participate in
this particular Manifestation, I will take part in all the Manifestations of the divinity, for all eternity. It is at such moments, beyond the tragedy and anguish of the world, that I am certain of
being fully, truly conscious. I recover the age when I would
walk, hazel stick in hand, among primroses and violets, and the
sweet smells permeating the light of spring. The world and I
were just beginning. Yes, it is to speak of my wonder that I
write. But joy is not always part of wonder, or rather I am
rarely sufficiently astonished to reach this kind of joy, this
ecstasy. Most of the time the sky is dark, most of the time I
live in anguish, used to feeling anguish, habituated to the habitual. The click which illumines everything happens with increasing
rarity. I try to remember, I attempt to hold on to the miracle of
light, and at times I succeed, but with age it becomes increasingly
difficult. The passing years of personal history are like the
stormy, tragic, demoniacal centuries of universal History. A
tumultuous past, thick as memories, or as the collective memory
of the world separates me, and all of us, from the beginning. We
live inured to anguish and misfortune, and if on occasion I perceive that the world is a celebration, I also know, as all of you
do, that it is misery.

There was to begin with the initial amazement: the conscious awareness of existence, an astonishment which I might call

metaphysical, a pure surprise experienced in joy and light, free of any judgment brought to bear on the universe, the kind of astonishment which I recover only at moments of grace, in themselves extremely rare. Then a second type of amazement was grafted onto the first, the ascertainment that evil exists, or perhaps more simply that things are bad. This discovery that evil is among us, that at this moment it gnaws away at us, destroying us, preventing that we take cognizance of the miraculous, as though it were not part and parcel of the miracle of existence, is a frightful knowledge. Thus, the joy of being is strangled, submerged by misfortune which is as inexplicable as existence, tied to existence. Misfortune is a profound enigma. This theme has been debated by countless philosophers, theologians, sociologists. I myself will not dwell on this insoluble problem. I simply want to state that as a writer universal misfortune is my intimate, personal business. I must transcend evil in order to reach, beyond evil, not happiness, but a transient joy. In a naive, awkward way, my works are inspired by evil and anguish. Evil has squelched my joy. It is my circumambient atmosphere, and yet it continues to amaze me as does the light. It weighs more heavily than the light. I feel its weight upon my shoulders. In my plays I did not seek to discuss it, but to show it. The fact that it is inexplicable renders all our plans, all our acts absurd. This is what I feel as an artist. I found the existential enigma acceptable, but not the mystery of evil. And what is all the more unacceptable is the fact that evil is law, and that human beings are not responsible for its existence. But of course it suffices to look at a drop of water under a microscope to see that cells, that microscopic organisms, fight among themselves, kill and devour one another. What takes place on the level of the infinitely small, happens at every level of universal greatness. War is indeed the law of life. That's all it is. All of us know this, but we no longer pay attention. If only we were to be conscious of it, to even give it some thought, we would realize that this is not the way things should be, that life is impossible. It is already puzzling to be squeezed between birth and death, but to be forced to kill and be killed is inadmissible. The existential condition is inadmissible. We live in a closed economy; nothing comes to us from outside, and we are forced to devour one another. Go in peace and eat each other. I have the feeling that creatures are not in complete agreement with this state of things. We make one small gesture and precipitate the catastrophic end of protozoan worlds, dig in our shovels and destroy a nation of

ants. Every gesture, every movement, be they insignificant, pro-
voke disasters, catastrophes. I walk through this meadow without thinking that all the plants in it struggle for vital space, and
that the roots of these magnificent trees, by reaching deeper in
the earth, bring about suffering, tragedies, kill. Every step I take
also kills. And so I say to myself that the beauty of the world is
a deception.

Later in life, at about fifteen or sixteen, when we are all
disciples of Pascal, without necessarily having read Pascal, but
simply by looking at the stars, I was seized by the vertigo of
infinite spaces. The infinitely small is even more vertiginous than
the infinitely large. To be unable to conceive a limitless world,
to be unable to imagine the infinite, is our fundamental in-
firmity. Nor do we really understand what we are doing. We
are made to do things we do not understand, of which we are not
responsible. For a superior intelligence, we are all ridiculous wild
beasts, tamed to perform meaningless acts in a circus, performing
them with no understanding of what they are. We are being
mocked; we are someone's plaything. If at least we could know.
we are plunged in darkest ignorance, doing the opposite of what
we think we're doing, not masters of ourselves. Everything
eludes our control. We make revolutions to institute justice and
freedom. We institute injustice and tyranny. We are dupes.
Everything turns against us. I have no idea if there is meaning or
not, if the world is absurd or not, for us it is absurd, we are absurd, we live in the absurd. We were born deceived.

Condemned to know nothing, except that tragedy is universal, we are now being told that death is a natural phenomenon, that suffering is natural, that we must accept it because it
is natural. This is no solution. Why is it natural, and what
does natural mean? The natural is the incurable, something I
refuse to accept; it is a law I deny, but there is nothing one can
do, and I am in the trap of what appears to be the beauty of this
world. Still, there is one thing we can be conscious of: all is
tragedy. To explain this by original sin is no explanation. Why
was there original sin, and did such a thing really exist? What is
far more extraordinary is that finally each and every one of us
is conscious of universal tragedy. Also that each of us is the
center of the universe, each human being lives in a state of
anguish he cannot share with billions of other human beings who
nevertheless experience the same anguish. Each one of us is like

Atlas who bears alone the full weight of the world. And yet, they tell me, I can discuss this with a friend who will not necessarily murder me, I can go this evening to a concert, or a play. To hear what, see what? The same insoluble tragedy. I can go on to a good restaurant for a fine meal, and I will eat animals they have killed for it, and vegetables whose life span I interrupted. What I can do is not think of it. But let's watch out, for the same menacing force weighs upon our lives. We will be killed by other men, or germs, or on account of a psychic inbalance. There are moments of respite, short recesses at the expense of others. I realize of course that I am proferring the most banal of statements. At least one calls them banalities, when they are fundamental truths which people try to push aside in order not to think of them and go on living. We are told that we musn't be obsessed by things, that it is abnormal that things should obsess us. It seems to me that what is abnormal is that things should not obsess us, and that a thirst for life, a desire to live put our consciousness to sleep. We are all metaphysically alienated. Unconsciousness is added on to our alienation.

In these conditions, a man I call conscious, a man for whom these elementary truths are present, can he accept to go on living? I have a friend, a philosopher of despair, not at all insensitive, who lives in pessimism as in his natural element. He speaks a great deal, is a brilliant conversationalist and a jolly person. "Modern man," he likes to state, "fiddles with the incurable". That's exactly what he does. Let's do likewise. We live on various levels of consciousness. Since there is nothing we can do, since we are all doomed to die, let's be merry. But let's not be duped. We ought to keep, in the background of our consciousness, what we know. And we must also come out with it to set people on the right path. First, let's try to kill as little as possible. Ideologies do nothing but prompt us to murder. Let's demystify. It is now obvious that colonial empires have been erected, and massacres perpetrated in the name of Christianity and love. Other colonial empires are being formed at the price of even greater slaughter perpetrated in the name of justice and human fraternity. It is essential to come to the realization that so called ideologies are nothing but convenient masks used by those who yield to the explosion of the irrational or extrarational forces of crime inscribed in the very fibers of our nature. If there is a battle to wage, let it be against criminal instincts which find alibis in ideologies. If we cannot avoid massacring plants and animals, let us at least stop killing human beings. Neither philosophies, nor theology, nor Marxism have been able to solve the problem of evil, nor to explain its presence. No human society, above all not the communist one, has succeeded in averting or even diminishing it. Wrath is everywhere. Justice is not equity, it is vengeance and punishment. If the evil perpetrated by men upon one another undergoes a change of aspect, it remains fundamentally the same in its deepest nature.

Thus, I have written also to ask myself this particular question, to probe this mystery. It is the theme of my play, *The Killer*, in which the hero questions the assassin to ask him, in vain, what are the reasons for his hatred. Hatred must have excuses; it has no reasons. A murderer kills because he cannot help himself, without motive, with a kind of candor and purity. By killing others, we murder ourselves. To live beyond good and evil, to consider a thing to be beyond good and evil, as Nietzsche wished, is not possible. He himself went mad with pity when he saw an old horse slump down and die. There is pity then, not Eros but Agape. But charity is grace, a gift.

There is perhaps one way out still; it is contemplation, the wonder in the face of the existential fact as I said earlier. This might be, after all, a way of being beyond good and evil. I know it is difficult to live in the state of astonished wonder when one is serving a life sentence, undergoing forced labor with machine guns turned upon you, or simply having a toothache. Still, let us live in that state of wonder to the extent that it is possible. The richness of creation is infinite. No man resembles another, no signature is alike. One can never find two men with the same fingerprints; no one is anyone other than himself. This fact can also plunge you into amazement. It is also a miracle. In America, modern men of science have transcended atheism. Psysicists, mathematicians, researchers in the natural sciences believe they know that creation has a finality, a plan, that it is the grand design of a conscience which directs it. No individual can be born for nothing. If there is a final plan to the universe, then there must also be some kind of plan for the individual, and for every particle of matter. We must keep faith. This too will pass. The world may be merely a gigantic joke played by God on man. That's what the protagonist of my play, *A Hell of a Mess*, comes to realize at the end of it when he bursts out laughing; his whole life has been spent questioning himself and the mystery of creation, and all at once he sees that it's all been a terrible gag. I have no doubt been inspired by the story of a Zen monk who, in old age, having spent his whole life in search of a key, the seed of an explanation as to the meaning of it all, receives an illumination. Looking about himself with new eyes, he exclaims: "What deception!" and cannot stop laughing. I'm also thinking of an Italian film whose title I have forgotten along with the name of the director. I saw the film long ago, right after the Second World War. It showed German soldiers occupying a convent. Italian partisans attack the convent and the Germans leave, except one, more absent minded. He wears glasses, must be an intellectual. Alone in the convent, he is chased by a knife—wielding partisan who pursues him into the very chapel. This place will not prove to be a sanctuary. In his precipitous flight, the German knocks down a statue of the Virgin, then a cross bearing a tormented, bloody Christ. The Italian catches up with the soldier, and knifes him in the back. He falls. He looks about him, as though seeing the world for the first time in all its horror, takes off his glasses, and asks out loud: "Why, but why?" and dies. Here also there's a kind of illumination, and this ultimate question is in fact an ascertainment. This is the first and the last time that this man has thought about the world, and he has come to the realization of existential horror. Why this horror, why the absurdity of horror? This question can be posited from the very birth of consciousness, as it can also at the end of our existence. But throughout our life we are all plunged in horror as though it were the understood state of affairs, without ever questioning it. We are so used to things as they are that it is the act of questioning which seems absurd, when, in reality, what is senseless is not to question. Thus, to posit this fundamental question is already an illumination. It is at least the full realization of the basic problem: why horror?

I repeat that I don't have the feeling that I have said things that are new, but rather that I experienced intensely two contradictory apprehensions: the world is at once marvelous and atrocious, a miracle and hell, and these antithetical feelings, these two obvious truths, constitute the backdrop of my personal existence and my oeuvre. I said at the beginning of this lecture that I was wondering why I wrote. When I analyze myself I come up with a temporary yet substantial answer. I write to give account of these fundamental truths, these absolute questions: why existence, or rather how, and also how is evil possi-

ble, and how does it fit in with the existential miracle. I write
to remind people of these problems, to make them aware of
them so that they watch out and never forget. It is enough if
they remember it from time to time. Why not forget, but, on
the other hand, why not remember? We must be conscious of
our destiny in order to know how to situate ourselves in relation
to others, and to ourselves. Our social awareness flows out of
our metaphysical consciousness, out of our existential intuition.
By not forgetting who we are, where we're at, we will understand ourselves better. A human fraternity based on the metaphysical condition is more secure than one grounded in politics.
A questioning without a metaphysical answer is far more authentic, and in the end useful than all the false and partial answers
given by politics. Knowing that each individual among billions
is a whole, a center, and that all the others are ourselves, we will
be more accepting of ourselves, that is to say, for it is the same
thing, of others. We must consider that each one of us, paradoxically, is the world's navel. Thus, every individual will be able
to acquire a greater importance, we, ourselves, a lesser one, with
the greater one being accorded to the others. We are, at one and
the same time, unimportant and very important, and our destiny
is identical. New human relationships can spring from this
awareness. It is the feeling of amazement and wonder in the
face of the world we contemplate, tied to the intuition that
everything is at the same time suffering, which can constitute
the fundamental basis of human fraternity, and of a metaphysical
humanism. As Jean Paul Sartre wrote in *No Exit,* hell is other
people. The others are us, we could answer. If we cannot make
our common existence a paradise, we can nevertheless transform
it into a less thorny, disagreeable passage.

The theatre that some of us have written since 1950 is
radically different from *boulevard* theatre. In fact, it is its
opposite. Contrary to *boulevard* theatre which is free of problems and questions, and is entertainment, ours, despite its humor,
its derisive snicker, is a theatre which puts in question the totality of human destiny, of our existential condition. Whereas
popular theatre puts consciousness to sleep since it neither dis-
turbs nor reassures, we have been told that we are disquieting,
and that since there is good dose of disquiet in the world already,
it would be nice not to increase our problems, at least for a time.
But this time passes quickly and we find ourselves face to face
with our anguish. Personally, *boulevard* theatre increases my

anguish more than anguish. It is unbearable, so empty and useless does it seem. But as to us, we do not want to chase anguish
away. We try to make it familiar so that it can be surmounted.
The world can be comical, or derisory, it can also seem tragic,
in any case it isn't funny. Nothing is funny.

Nor do we write political theatre, or, at least, not purely
political. Politics seem to me to be also entertainment, a horrifying kind of entertainment, but entertainment nevertheless. That
is to say that politics cannot be detached from metaphysics.
Without metaphysics, politics do not express a fundamental
human problem. They constitute in such case a limited, secondary activity, stripped of ultimate implications. Two centuries
of politics and revolutions have instituted neither liberty, nor
justice, nor fraternity. Politics offer no answer to the fundamental questions: who are we, where do we come from, where
are we going? They are maintained within strict limits, cut away
from transcendental roots. Metaphysics have also been unable to
offer definitive answers, and such is the case of science, and the
philosophy of sciences. The only possible answer is the question
itself. It reactualizes within our consciousness the certainty of
our fraternity in ignorance, beyond social class, beyond the
barriers of our fundamental identity, beyond the differences
between human beings. This consciousness cannot cancel out
anguish, but it is able, as politics are not, to stop provoking wars
and massacres. Politics are alienation, and can be experienced
only as the analyzable, or unanalyzable reflection of the passions which direct them, dominate them, making us into pup-
pets. Political theatre can bring only a very limited illumination.
Ideological theatre is inferior to the ideology it wishes to illustrate, and of which it is the tool. Since political theatre reflects
ideologies familiar to us, it is tautological. For a century, and
above all in the last fifty years, it has rehashed the same themes.
Thus, political theatre makes us as unconscious metaphysically
as *boulevard* theatre. We must depoliticize theatre. Political
theatre can teach us nothing new.

I would not be telling the whole truth if I were to affirm
that the reasons I have just given are the only ones which im-
pelled me to write. Many of the latter came to me in stages, as
I progressed in my career in the theatre and found myself confronted by the diverse theatre guides, masters of the mind,
directors of human conscience who came forward to give me pro-

per orientation. I also met along the way recruiters of committed art and theatre. Some twenty years ago, or more, Jean
Vauthier and I were summoned by a Mr. Panigel whom we did
not know. After slight hesitation, we accepted his invitation.
Mr. Panigel was a member of the Communist party, at that time
extremely pro-Stalin. He addressed us in the following terms:
"Boys, you have a bit of talent, but no ideas. You can't write
theatre without ideas. I'll instruct you. It is I who will provide
you with ideas. We'll meet periodically, and I will teach you how
to write." Obviously, we never returned to see this gentleman.
At about the same time, or perhaps a year later, Bernard Dort
wrote a lengthy article, a whole page in *L'Express* on Adamov
and on me. Our two photographs illustrated the text in the
paper. What did Dort say in his article? It appeared that, as he
saw it, both of us had done until then good negative work: we
had criticized bourgeois or petty bourgeois society, which was
fine but not sufficient.—Of course, this sort of criticism was the
least of my own concerns, but this was not clear from the piece.
—The latter went on to say that Adamov and I had a good deal
of talent, and that we could become the two greatest men of
contemporary theatre. One condition had to be fulfilled. No
more negative criticism, from now on we had to make positive
statements or we would suffer the consequences of having nothing to say. To renew ourselves, to become adult writers who have
reached their majority, there was only one possibility: become
committed writers. One spoke a lot of commitment at that time.
It was essential to take part in the social, political struggle.
We had to create a revolutionary theatre, not only in form, but
in content, and in underlying intent, for this was commitment.
To become committed did not mean to opt for the cause you
were interested in, but simply to become a card carrying, militant
member of the Communist party. Only this was commitment
and nothing else. Our theatre had to become one of Marxist
instruction. Such was the new definition of popular theatre:
to educate the masses in this particular way, not even solely in
Marxism, but rather train them to follow the orders of the day.
The latter, issued by the governments of the countries of Eastern
Europe to the intellectuals of these countries, from which independent thinkers wish to escape, and do so, at the price of enormous personal sacrifice, are the very one the occidental ideologues wanted to impose on us. In France, as in England and Ger-
many, the opposition, or rather the ideological fashion brought
to bear, or attempted to exercise a veritable form of censorship. I

felt that I belonged to a minority, crushed between bourgeois convention and the new ideological convention. I was alone, in disagreement with everyone, ill at ease, deprived of a spiritual family. Of course, I did not give in. Adamov did not resist; he accepted commitment, converted to an elementary kind of Marxism and Brechtianism and was applauded by the ideological critics. But he did not receive the plaudits of the public. A minority of bourgeois thinkers, who thought of themselves as revolutionary, people with no contacts with humanity at large, were his only supporters. Arthur Adamov denied his early plays and lost himself as a writer and an artist. I know that at the end of his life he regretted this action.

The young bourgeois, reactionary by nature, now no longer young but still intent on indulging in literary criticism, believed they were getting "close to the masses," to the will of the masses, and that they would teach the proletariat what the proletariat is supposed to be. But we know that for them, "the masses" and "the proletariat" were nothing but abstract ideas. They never worked in factories, nor in the fields; all they knew were society's *salons.*

I myself wrote committed plays. Such a one is *Rhinoceros,* as is *The Killer,* and a number of others, in spots. Only, I did not commit myself in the direction desired by the ideologues. I pointed out the existence of evil in a thousand different societies, in thousands of different aspects. The ideologues held this against me. From that time on they began to write both in newspapers and in literary reviews that my works were worthless, that I had been untrue to myself whereas in reality I was listening to myself alone. Because I was not in agreement with them, because I had not obeyed them, they decreed that I had no talent, and that they were bitterly sorry to have mistakenly attributed some to me earlier on. They went so far as to attempt to take back what they had published about me, declaring, as Bernard Dort did in the course of a lecture delivered on a trip through Europe, that I had been given "too much importance" when, in actual fact, it was he who had at first lavished this attention upon me. But let us leave for some other time these personal polemics despite their curious insight into what goes on behind the curtain not of a theatre, but of literary criticism in general, and dramatic criticism in particular, at least that of contemporary critics who are never objective being much too passionately involved. One can make mistakes when one is passionate about objectivity, but one makes conscious mistakes, or lies to oneself, when the passions have ideological orientation. Thus, it must be said that if one accords "too much importance" to anything these days, it is to contemporary criticism.

I would like to return to the first impulses which propelled me to write. I have said that I wanted to communicate my dazzlement by the very fact of existence, then, after the apprehension of the existential miracle, that of horror and evil, and finally, as I explored existence in detail, I had ideas to express. But, in order not to withhold anything, I must add the gratuitous joy of writing, of inventing, the delight of imagining, and telling things which never happened to me. In short, the joy of creation, that is to add to the universe things which were not there before, to add on a small universe, or universes, to the universe. Isn't it true that each writer, each artist, each poet wishes to imitate God, doesn't he wish to be a little God who can create gratuitously, without reason, in sport, because he is free and in a way that is totally free?

When I went to the *école communale,* the older children of the next class would tell me about the strange and difficult homework they had to do: composition. They had to write stories, or improvise upon a theme. I was impressed, and I decided that it must be very hard indeed, but very beautiful. I couldn't wait to try it myself. For most of my school friends this was the worst of chores. For me it held a mystery. Finally, the following year, as I graduated from one class to the next, I was put to the test of composition. We had just had a village fair. We were asked to write about it. I described an imaginary fair, with bits of dialogue. I got the highest mark, and the teacher read my composition out loud in the classroom. What seemed to impress him most was that the story was in dialogue form, contrary to all the others. The teacher congratulated me for inventing dialogue, which, he said to me, had been invented long ago. I went on writing more compositions, always with the same sense of joy. Since we were not assigned enough compositions in class I began to write stories, just for myself. I can say that I've been a writer since the age of nine, that is to say since forever. A born writer. I've never been able to do anything but literature. Literature gave me great pleasure, my own and that of others. I also began to love paintings, those that tell stories, like Breughel for example where there are country fairs with lots of people, or Canaletto where you can see unreal looking people walking through the unreal town of Venice, a whole life, a universe taken from reality but become imaginary, and then Dutch interiors, ancient portraits where the quality of the art work is deepened by the documentary, human quality. Yes, there's a whole world which may be real or not, a world which used to fill me with nostalgia for things which could have been, or had existed once but were no longer there, worlds offered yet defunct. And I wrote to offer worlds in turn, possible worlds, other possible worlds. So, it was in childhood that I experienced the purest pleasure of writing, and that my vocation came to the fore. The miracle of the world was such that I was not only dazzled by it, as I have just said, but that I wanted to imitate this miracle by making miracles of my own. Creation.

Thus, it is in this dazzlement before the world, in this astonishment at the thought of the marvel of the world, and in the joy of invention that I find the fundamental, conscious or semi-conscious, or subconscious reasons for writing, for artistic creation. The other reasons, more adult, therefore less pure, less naive, came later. When I entered the ring of polemics, I began to answer, to explain, to explain myself, to deliver messages and anti-messages, but always I went on questioning, for it is this interrogation above all things which is closest to the impulses of childhood.

There is one more reason which you must guess since it is not only that of artists but of each and everyone of us: to do everything so that the world I have seen, the people I have known, the landscape of my childhood and other landscapes I saw later, would never be forgotten, lost in nothingness. One writes to perpetuate all this, to perpetuate oneself, to triumph over death. We are here with our paintings, our music, our poems, our books, in search of a kind of immortality. One writes in order not to die completely, not to die at once, since everything perishes in the end. And I believe that among all these reasons, the two strongest are the following: to allow others to share in the astonishment, the dazzlement of existing, in the miracle of this world of ours, and to shout to God and to other men our anguish, letting it be known that we existed. All the rest is secondary.

Translated by Rosette C. Lamont

EUGENE IONESCO AND
"LA NOSTALGIE DU PARADIS"

by Mircea Eliade

Asked by a journalist what he was doing to eliminate social inequalities and political injustice, Eugène Ionesco answered: "Je ne prétends pas que mes pièces vont sauver le monde!". As he made explicit in that interview, and on many other occasions, Ionesco does not believe that the goal of an artistic creation is to foster political education. On the contrary, in his opinion, a politically oriented theater, even that of Brecht, becomes an instrument of propaganda and, in the last analysis, a new dogma no less intolerant and tyrannical than the old dogmatic systems.

However, Ionesco is the first to deplore the fact that the theater cannot "save the world"; meaning salvation, in the *religious,* and not the *political,* sense of the word. He would be happy to know that there is a "soteriological theatre", able to communicate revelation, and thus modify the human condition. But he doubts that such a "soteriological theater" will ever be possible. Instead, he hopes that his plays will help his contemporaries to forget, at least for a few hours, the oppressive "historical moment", and thus to break through the automatisms, the clichés and the ideological opacities of everyday life. In other words, he is anxious to see the spectators recover the blissful spontaneity of their own imaginations. He repeatedly emphasized the decisive role of imagination, not only for what is usually called mental health, but, what is more important, for the new quality of life brought forth by an active and creative imagination. "Imaginer, c'est construire, c'est faire, créer un monde... A force de créer des mondes on peut 'recréer' le monde à l'image des mondes inventés, imaginaires".[1]

Most of the products of imagination have a "religious"

significance. That is to say, they are related to primordial *excellence* a religious dimension.[2] A historian of religions cannot fail to notice the variety and vigor of religious symbols in Ionesco's works. Of course, a number of them are employed outside of their traditional settings; nevertheless, their original intentionality is not completely lost. Such is the case, for example, for symbols of ascension and flight, or those of "paradise" and the labyrinth. It is interesting to note that Ionesco places the labyrinth in opposition to "paradise". For him, the labyrinth is an exemplary image of Hell. "Le labyrinthe, c'est l'enfer, c'est le temps, c'est l'espace, c'est l'infini, alors que le paradis au contaire est un monde sphérique, entier, où 'tout est là', ni finitidue, ni infini, où le problème fini-infini ne se pose pas".[3]

The traditional religious symbolism of the labyrinth is unusually complex and discourages any hasty formulation. Nevertheless, the "infernal" elements recovered by Ionesco are indisputable. But in his personal understanding of the labyrinth one misses another important factor, namely its initiatory function. Entering and successfully traversing a labyrinth, without being lost in its mazes, is tantamount to a *descensus ad inferos* followed by a triumphant return to our world; thus constituting a successful initiation.[4] For Eugène Ionesco, the labyrinth represents exclusively an *Inferno,* accumulating all the terrors of spatial and temporal infinity ("c'est le temps, c'est l'espace, c'est l'infini"). Standing in contrast is Paradise, a "spherical world", a totality in which finitude and infinity are definitively transcended.

It is difficult to specify to what extent this *description* of the paradisiacal beatitude was influenced by Ionesco's readings of the Byzantine mystics.[5] Already as a young man, in Rumania, he had perused certain mystical and theological authors,[6] and in France, after 1940, he considerably widened his horizon. He read not only Pseud-Areopagytus, and some of the Greek Fathers, but also Cusanus, Buber, the Upanishads, many Buddhist texts and *The Tibetan Book of the Dead.* Occasionally one can discover in certain plays the effects of his readings. Thus, for instance, *Le Roi se meurt (Exit the King)* reflects the powerful impressions left by *The Tibetan Book of the Dead* and the *Brhadaranyaka-Upanishad.* One cannot really speak of "influences", though, but only of the renewal of Ionesco's imaginary universes through his creative encounter with exotic and traditional religious worlds.

Whatever might *have been the impact* of Ionesco's theological readings on his description of "Paradise", there can be no doubt about the authenticity of his personal experience. His "Paradis" was the time he spent in the country, at La Chapelle Anthenaise, when he was eight, nine and ten years old. In his Diaries, and in the *Entretiens (Conversations)* with Claude Bonnefoy, he repeatedly evokes that lost beatitude. "A La Chapelle Anthenaise, le temps n'existait pas. Je vivais dans le présent. Vivre était grâce, joie de vivre.[...] Une plénitude; une symbolisation, si je puis dire, du paradis. Ce lieu est toujours pour moi comme l'image d'un paradis perdu".[7] Leaving La Chapelle Anthenaise was, for him, equivalent to a "rupture avec le paradis".[8]

A happy childhood is frequently remembered as a "Paradisiacal" existence, but what is noteworthy in Ionesco's case is the significant rôle played by these early experiences both in his life and in his *oeuvre*. More or less unconsciously, he was somehow able to recover, at least in part, and only for a few blessed moments, that primordial beatitude, the lost Paradise of La Chapelle Anthenaise. For him, those were "jours de plénitude, de bonheur, de lumière".[9] Ultimately, Ionesco relates the ideas of perfection, serenity, clarity, and beatitude to a rather mysterious presence of light. The first French authors he admired—Valéry Larbaud, Charles du Bos, Flaubert, Alain Fournier—all have in common "un style de lumière". He specifies: "Chez tous, j'ai retrouvé cette présence de la lumière", that is to say the light of his "propre vision d'enfance".[10] He confesses, however, that he does not know what corresponds to this light. "Evidemment, il ne faut pas tout de suite lui donner une signification mystique, mais je voudrais savoir ce qu'elle vent dire au point de vue psychologique, pourquoi j'en ai besoin, pourquoi, chaque fois que j'ai le sentiment qu'il y a de la lumière, je deviens heureux".[11]

Indeed, for him, "la lumière, c'est le monde transfiguré". Such an expression brings to mind the idiom of the Byzantine mystics, particularly the Hesychasts and Gregory Palamas in discussing the Light of the Transfiguration on Mount Tabor.[12] But for Eugène Ionesco this "miracle" is part of our world: "C'est, par exemple, au printemps, la métamorphose glorieuse du chemin boueux de mon enfance. Tout d'un coup, le monde acquiert une beauté inexplicable".[13] Such a "transfiguration" may occur any time and in any circumstances. He relates an experience, when he received the visit of a friend, a pessimist, who was depressed by the meaninglessness of life, and the ugliness and dreariness of everything, including Ionesco's apartment. "A l'époque, j'habitais un rez-de-chaussée, rue Claude Terrasse. Ma fille était encore un bébé et nous n'avions pas beaucoup de place, nous avions mis son linge à sécher dans la maison". And suddenly he noticed a glorious illumination of every object in the room. "J'avais eu l'impression que le linge, sur la ficelle, était d'une beauté insolite, le monde vierge, éclatant. J'avais réussi à le voir avec des yeux de peintre pour ses qualités de lumière. A partir de là, tout semblait beau, tout se transfigurait".[14]

Commenting on Claude Bonnefoy's observation, that in his *oeuvre* the theme of light is opposed to what may be called the theme of sinking in the mud and slime[15], Ionesco admitted that these two contradictory themes reflect his antagonistic modes of being: "Je me sens ou bien lourd ou bien léger, ou bien trop lourd ou bien trop léger". For him, "le thème de la condition malheureuse se traduit[...] par la lourdeur et par l'épaisseur".[16] In contrast, as we have seen, beatitude is connected to light and spontaneity.

His decisive experience, though, which he utilized in *Tueur sans gages (The Killer)*, took place in a Rumanian provincial town, when he was 17 or 18 years old. The description deserves to be quoted integrally. "C'était en juin, vers midi. Je me promenais dans une des rues de cette ville très tranquille. Tout d'un coup j'ai eu l'impression que le monde à la fois s'éloignait et se rapprochait, ou plutôt que le monde s'était éloigné de moi, que j'étais dans un autre monde, plus mien que l'ancien, infiniment plus lumineux; les chiens dans les cours aboyaient à mon passage près des clôtures, mais les aboiements étaient devenus subitement comme mélodieux, ou bien assourdis, comme ouatés; il me semblait que le ciel était devenu extrêmement dense, que la lumière était presque palpable, que les maisons avaient un éclat jamais vu, un éclat inhabituel, vraiment libéré de l'habitude. C'est très difficile à définir; ce qui est plus facile à dire, peut être, c'est que j'ai senti une joie énorme, j'ai eu le sentiment que j'avais compris quelque chose de fondamental; que quelque chose

de très important m'était arrivé. A ce moment-là, je me suis dit:
«Je n'ai plus peur de la mort». J'avais le sentiment d'une vérité
absolue, définitive. Je me suis dit que lorsque, plus tard, j'aurai
des tristesses ou des angoisses, il me suffirait de me souvenir de
ce moment-là pour retrouver la sérénité, la joie. Cela m'a soutenu
un certain temps. A présent, ce moment-là, je l'ai oublié, je veux
dire que je m'en souviens bien un peu, mais que ce n'est plus
qu'un souvenir, comment dire, théorique... Je me souviens pour
m'être répété, avoir voulu me remémorer ces moments. Je ne
les ai plus jamais «vécus». Oui, ce fut une sorte de moment
miraculeux qui a duré 3 ou 4 minutes. J'avais l'impression qu'il
n'y avait plus de pesanteur. Je marchais à grands pas, à grands
bonds, sans fatigue. Et puis, tout d'un coup, le monde est
redevenu lui-même, il l'est toujours, ou presque. Le linge qui
séchait dans les cours des petites demeures provinciales ne
ressemblait plus à des étendards, à des oriflammes, mais vraiment
à du pauvre linge. Le monde était retombé dans un trou".[17]

Without being a literal recovery of the "paradisiacal" state
of his childhood at La Chapelle Anthenaise, this experience can
be considered equally important for Ionesco's life and *oeuvre*.
The encounter with the light is accompanied by a sense of joy
and serenity, the certitude of eternity ("Je n'ai plus peur de la
mort"), the revelation of the absolute truth and the impression
of deliverance from the law of gravity. Experiences of light
occur frequently in the history of different mysticisms as well as
in religiously ignorant, or indifferent, individuals. It is particularly the latter case that is relevant for our topic. A number of
books and monographs are devoted to such "spontaneous" (or
"natural") experiences of light.[18] Although of a great morpho-
logical variety, all these "spontaneous" light experiences contain
some basic features in common: they come suddenly and un-
expectedly; they are accompanied by the feeling of joy, happiness, peace and confidence, or by an intellectual illumination
quite impossible to describe; they reveal a fundamental unity,
purpose and meaning of the world and of human existence, an
Urgrund where contraries are reconciled. Some experiences may
give the impression of taking place outside—or beyond—time;
others seem to develop in time, the light continuously changing
its colors (for instance, from bluish smoke to a violet haze and
finally to a blinding golden incandescence).[19] Another common
element is the sense of being born again, of *incipit vita nova*, of
an "existential mutation" or of being "saved". And what is

more, in many cases the subject's life was radically and permanently transformed.

We will not discuss in any detail the differences, which are important, between these "spontaneous", "natural" light experiences, and those of the mystics belonging to various religious traditions. There is not only a question of *intensity* (for instance, the dazzling light that blinded Saint Paul on the road to Damascus, or the terrific vision of Arjuna in the *Bhagavad-gita*) but also one of dissimilarity between the light revealed as divine, personal presence, and the light which discloses an *impersonal holiness*. But we do not need to extend this comparative analysis. What should be noted is that ultimately each "mystic"[20] values his experience of the light according to his own theological (or philosophical) presuppositions. Nevertheless, whatever the nature and intensity of a light experience, such an experience always evolves into a religious experience: as it brings an individual out of his profane universe or historical situation, and projects him into an entirely different world—"transcendent" and "holy". Whatever his previous ideological conditioning, the light produces a break in the subject's existence, revealing to him—or making clearer than before—the world of spirit, of the sacred and of true freedom.[21]

These few remarks may help to estimate the role of light experiences and light symbolism in Ionesco's personal life and in his *oeuvre*. From the "paradis" of La Chapelle Anthenaise, to the sudden irradiance of a dusty street in a Romanian provincial town, to the illumination of that crowded room in *rue* Claude Terrasse, there is a secret but impressive continuity. Eugène Ionesco could not doubt that *there is* Being, absolute truth, beatitude and freedom (in every sense of this term). He never emphasized the religious dimensions of his experiences and nostalgias, but in his conversation with Claude Bonnefoy he did not disregard a religious vocabulary ("paradis", "monde transfiguré", "péché originel", "résurection", etc.). In a certain way he feels, and he behaves, *naturaliter,* like a *homo religiosus.* The creative imagination, the "play" and what has been called his "humour et fantaisie", are in the last analysis equivalent expressions of that prodigious *freedom,* which is not only political, social and spiritual, but also includes deliverance from the physical sense of weightiness. It is probably this profound understanding of the "religious" dimension of freedom—the freedom experi-

enced in the fabulous and inexhausible "play"[22] of the imagination—that explains Ionesco's serene detachement from any institutionalized form of religion.

NOTES

1.   Claude Bonnefoy, *Entretiens avec Eugène Ionesco* (Paris: Editions Pierre Belfond, 1966), p. 106.

2.   Eugène Ionesco speaks of "archétypes", using this term both in the neoplatonic (paradigms, exemplary models) and in the Jungian sense (structures of the collective unconscious).

3.   *Entretiens,* p. 45.

4.   The initiatory function of the labyrinth has been acutely analyzed by W. F. Jackson Knight, *Cumaean Gates. A reference of the sixth Aeneid to Initiation Pattern* (Oxford, 1936). *Cf.* also Paolo Santarcangeli, *Il libro dei labirinti. Storia di un mito e di un simbolo* (Firenze: Vallecchi, 1967).

5.   He states that among the books which influenced him are those of the The Byzantines of the XII, XIII and XIV centuries, and the Hesychasts: *cf. Entretiens,* p. 32.

6.   Like so many Rumanian writers of his generation, Eugène Ionesco was, in the '30s, attracted by the Byzantine spirituality and the eastern-orthodox traditions. For a number of intellectuals, such preoccupations were part of their endeavour to connect modern Rumanian culture to its "autochthenous", i.e. "oriental", roots, in order to counterbalance the powerful influence of Western, particularly French, culture. However, by 1936-38, this concern for the autochthonous tradition became an ideological slogan of the right wing movements, and Ionesco lost his interest in the "reactualization" of eastern-orthodox spirituality.

7.   Claude Bonnefoy, *Entretiens,* p. 13.

8.   *Entretiens,* p. 18. When Ionesco contrasts the labyrinth to Paradise, "where the problem of finitude-infinity does not arise" (*Entretiens,*

p. 45) he adds: "C'est ce que me semblait être La Chapelle Anthenaise: un lieu désangoissant".

9. *Entretiens*, p. 11.

10. *Entretiens*, pp. 31-32.

11. *Entretiens*, p. 32.

12. *Cf.* Mircea Eliade, *Méphistophélès et l'Androgyne* (Paris: Gallimard, 1962), pp. 73 ff. (= *Mephistopheles and the Androgyne*, New York: Sheed and Ward, 1965, pp. 61 ff.).

13. *Entretiens*, p. 33.

14. *Entretiens*, p. 34. In part, this experience is reflected in *Tueur sans gages*. "An premier acte, Bérenger entre dans une cité radieuse. Il découvre un monde transfiguré qui avait été défiguré; il retrouve le paradis après avoir quitté la ville pluvieuse, après avoir quitté le monde des limbes" (*Ibid.* p. 35). Ionesco specifies that, for him, "radieuse" means "rayonnante".

15. On the social plane, this corresponds to alienation; *Entretiens*, p. 33.

16. *Entretiens*, pp. 41-42.

17. *Entretiens*, pp. 36-37.

18. The most notable is R. M. Bucke, *The Cosmic Consciousness* (Philadelphia: Innes and Sons, 1901). See also Warner Allen, *The Timeless Moment* (London: Faber, 1946); R. C. Johnson, *The Imprisoned Splendour* (New York: Harper, 1953); J. H. M. Whiteman, *The Mystical Life* (London: Faber, 1961), pp. 25-45; M. Eliade "Expérience de la lumière mystique" (in: *Méphistophélès et l'Androgyne*, pp. 17-94; E. T. *Meph. and the Androgyne*, pp. 19-77); id., "Spirit, Light, and Seed", *History of Religions*, XI, 1971, pp. 1-30. Some relevant psychedelic-mystical experiences of preternatural light have been brought to the discussion by R. E. L. Masters and Jean Houston, *The Varieties of Psychedelic Experiences* (New York: Holt, Rinehart and Winston, 1966), pp. 307 sq.

19. *Cf.* W. L. Wilmhurst, *Contemplation*, pp. 142 sq. quoted in R. C. Johnson *The Imprisoned Splendour*, pp. 306-07.

20.   We use this term in its broadest sense, i.e. including the shamans, medicine-men, yogins and all species of contemplatives and ascetics.

21.   *Cf.* Eliade, *Méph. et l'Androgyne,* pp. 91 ff. (= E. T. pp. 69 ff.).

22.   It is not without significance that the sanskrit word *lila*—meaning "play", especially cosmic play—has been explained by the root *lelay,* "to flame", "to sparkle", "to shine". The term *lelay* may convey the notions of Fire, Light or Spirit. Indian thought seems then to have detected a certain relationship between, on the one hand, cosmic creation conceived as a divine game, and on the other, the play of flames. Likewise, in the Christian tradition the "flame" is the exemplary epiphany of Spirit (as in *Acts* II, 3-4, where the Holy Ghost appears to the disciples in the form of tongues of fire); *cf.* Eliade, *Méph. et l'Androgyne,* pp. 37 ff. (= E. T., pp. 36 ff.).

FATHER OF THE MAN

by Rosette Lamont

> I cannot start from a beginning, dawn, childhood, to reach something
> else, an end. Actually I do not wish, do not hope to do so, it does
> not interest me. What interests me is the seed. That is why I always
> retrace my steps, returning to the beginning of beginnings. I have
> learned nothing since the age of seven or eight.[1]

In *Découvertes,* Ionesco's self-illustrated Journal published
by Skira in the new series, *Les sentiers de la création,* the dramatist affirms the superiority of the child over the adult. "When
one says childish, it sounds pejorative," he explains, "but men
are infantile, not child-like. If one wants to find the meaning of
something beyond sense or through nonsense, we must return to
the very beginning [...] The 'why' of the child is one of integration, of acceptance. Serenity, for me, does not belong to matur-
ity. It belongs to extreme youth, to childhood. It is joyful acceptance of being, of existence. [...] The adult 'why' is weighty;
it falsifies, disguises. [...] Whenever I find again my child-like
newness, the 'why' allows me to rest in wonder and in joy, because that question [...] does not require an answer, being itself
its own answer."[2]

Together with this record of early impressions, Ionesco has
published two* tales for children under three. It is not surprising
that the man who claims to have stopped learning after the age
of seven has wished to recapture in story telling that seminal
moment of discovery. It is a time when all objects are as amazing
as the appearance of Martians on our planet. The self must be
distinguished from the non-self. Toes can be touched, brought
up to the mouth, bringing with them, so to say, the foot, the leg,
parts of the self yet not the self. There is the problem of classi-
fying daddy, mummy, the locomotive, the cat, rain, a mechanical
mouse. Without yet knowing the names of things one thinks

things about things. This recognition constitutes a kind of pre-language. To call a hat "bi, ba," a dog "bo," daddy and mummy, "baba," and express amazement by the sounds "bi, bo, ba, bu," is an act of creation. Thus the child is a poet. And thus the poet, in order to create, or rather re-create the cosmos, must become once again a child. "Imagination," said Ionesco to Claude Bonnefoy, "is not escape. To imagine is to build, to fashion a world."[3] The creator is as free as God. He becomes God's rival.

Conte Numéro 1 and *Conte Numéro 2* are the stories of Creation and Designation. Deceptively simple, on the surface, the tales appear to be a kind of pre-literature. Written in 1969 and 1970, they could be the work of a Ionesco who recalls dimly that he has become Ionesco, a writer who is convinced that "to create literary texts one must of course have forgotten all literature."[4] What we are left with is an archetypal truth, the stuff of myths and fables.

Conte Numéro 1 is a cosmological fable about the victory of imagination. As we open the beautifully designed book, with the Etienne Delessert illustrations, we see Josette, the tiny hero-ine of both stories, climbing out of a box in the shape of the Arabic numeral 1. The act is about to begin. We are then told that Josette is a big girl, thirty-three months old. This of course lets us know that the story is written for children under the age of three, but it seems, by the very emphasis on the number 3, to suggest a mystical numerology. For the Christian, thirty-three cannot fail to suggest the perfect age of Man, the age of Christ at his death and that of all men after the Last Judgment. After we accept the astonishing fact that the child's age is given to us in months rather than years, we cannot fail to make the association with the above. Clearly, this children's story will deal with the absolutes of life, death and resurrection.

We find Josette waiting, in the morning, at her parent's door. She would like to wake them, as she does every morning. This is the dawn of creation, and the child is fused with the early light. In this Garden of Eden before the awakening of Adam and Eve, Josette is also the only animal, or perhaps the animal kingdom in one, for we are told that she tries to push the door open "like a little dog." Unable to do so, she calls out, and this call wakes the sleeping couple.

Until paragraph two, Josette seems free of ontological roots. She comes first. It is as though her call created the parents till now absent in the heavy sleep of time. They pretend not to hear for, as the teller of the tale informs us, they are weary. Their sleep is not a natural state, it is the exhaustion of sophisticated adults given to an excess of *divertissement.* Not only have they indulged and over-indulged in the pastimes of grown-ups: theatre and restaurants, but they have even stolen the prerogatives of childhood having also attended the "guignol." Thus, their sleep is a guilty, sinful state. They are slothful. "It isn't nice for parents!"

Society seems to agree with Josette as the maid, a symbol of the outside world, barges in, carrying a tray loaded with breakfast foods: café-au-lait, sugar, fruit juices, croissants, toast, butter, orange marmelade, strawberry jam, eggs sunny side up, and ham. The announcement of meat is followed by that of the flesh of their flesh: "And here's your daughter." The maid seems to be serving breakfast between the social slice of post-cards and morning paper, and the biological one of progeniture. In perfect Ionesco fashion, objects and people are equated.

The "morning after" is hardly a good time to think of food. Father and Mother, feeling nauseous and gaseous as a result of having added a midnight supper to their dinner—we are told that "after the guignol" they went to another restaurant—reject the maid's offerings. Though they refuse to eat, we, the readers, are treated a second time round to the complete list of breakfast dishes, a device which forces us to empathize with the sensation of being "stuffed." There is, however, a very revealing difference between list number one and the second list: the strawberry jam, we are now told, is not strawberries at all, it is oranges. Thus, society lies in its offering of traditional breakfast menus. Not only does this passage echo the opening lines of *The Bald Soprano* ("We've drunk the soup, and eaten the fish and chips, and the English salad. The children have drunk English water. We've eaten well this evening.") based as we know on phrases from the conversation manual Ionesco used to study English, but it reminds the Ionescologue that once again we are not concerned with "real" people but with structures of the mind, myths or mechanisms, or both. The maid is not a real maid, but a cliché, like the breakfast menu.

"Give all this to Josette," says the Father to the Maid, "and when she's through eating, take her back to us." The act of eating in itself carries no taint. In one of his *conversations* with Claude Bonnefoy, the dramatist says about his first play: "I wished to express the astonishment I felt before this extraordinary act: eating."[5] Despite this assertion it is clear that Ionesco's attitude in this regard is ambivalent. In *Victims of Duty* his protagonist is forced to chew and swallow great pieces of dry bread. In *Hunger and Thirst,* once Jean has assuaged his needs he becomes the slave of the monks who seemed at first to be generous hosts, and the monastery is revealed to be an inferno. Seduced by Roberta of the Three Noses, Jack admits to loving the family dish of potatoes and bacon. Food, like love, is a lure and a trap. "I do not like mouths," Ionesco once said, "they are greedy, made for eating. Bodies are pure, not mouths." In the case of Josette, food is substituted for love. The parents go on sleeping while the little girl seeks consolation in eating "mummy's marmelade, daddy's jam, both parents' croissants." Consuming parental substance, little Josette is called an "ogress" by the maid. The latter reverses the well-known saying by adding: "Your belly is as big as your eyes!"

By calling the child "ogress" the maid disguises the fact that she, the symbol of society, is the real cannibal. Children are not usually *baba yagas* in folk tales. They are eaten by the cannibalistic witch. We find a clue to Ionesco's mythic pattern in his conversation with Bonnefoy on the subject of individuality as against social function. "What is sad about today's society is that the person is fused and confused with his or her function, or perhaps one should say the person is tempted to identify himself or herself totally with that function; the function does not acquire a human face, it is rather man who loses his human aspect, becomes dehumanized."[6] The dramatist adds: "Man is thus devoured by social machinery. The mechanisms of society render social life monstrous; society becomes an ogress."[7] Under the pretence that the child must not get sick from overeating, the maid drinks the parents' coffee, eats the fried eggs, the ham, adding to the devouring of future life (eggs) and flesh (ham), last night's rice pudding.

Unaware that their substance is being consumed, Daddy and Mummy are sound asleep. "They snore." Now that they have refused nourishment their sleep is innocent, profound. In a sense they are purged and thus ready to receive their child. We are made aware that a *rite de passage* has taken place when Josette steps into the bedroom announcing: "Daddy, Jacqueline (the maid's name) has eaten your ham." Granting absolution, Daddy, now the High Priest of his household says: "That's all right." He is now ready for the highest function, that of story telling.

"Tell me a story, daddy," says Josette. He will comply while Mummy is asleep. At this point, it is important to note that this noble activity takes place during the mother's "absence," sleep being a form of absence. Women's liberation notwithstanding, Ionesco is not a feminist. We must remember, however, that he is the father of a daughter he worships, Marie-France. The family triangle, Father Mother Daughter, is one of the basic structures of his dramaturgy, either in its direct aspect as in *A Stroll in the Air,* or *Hunger and Thirst,* or its more disguised form as in *Exit the King* (the Old Queen and the Young Queen), *The Lesson* (the Professor, the Student and the Maid). Thus, in the act of story telling and story listening, a new couple is formed, a spiritual pair. The act is a sublimation, or a symbolic representation of *copulation.* The result will be the creation of a world.

We are now going to be given a story within the story. As in the case of a play within a play, a frequent device in Ionesco's comitragedies, the mirror effect brings us closer to a reality beyond the real. Ionesco always claims that the reality of the imaginary world is superior to the banal, everyday reality we accept without a question. The child is the only human for whom there is no difference between these levels of reality since all is new, all is equally amazing. It is the child within the man who writes poetry, who trusts the reality of the dream world. The love fusion between Daddy and Josette allows the grown man to return to a blessed state of fresh awareness. Led by the young virgin, the *pater familias* will walk backwards into primordial time. He will then do what every creator must, start the cosmos spinning.

Daddy's story begins like all fairy tales: "Once upon a time there was..." The story will be about a little girl, but she must be different from Josette, the listener. She will be called Jacqueline, like the Maid, but she will not be the Maid, not even as a child.

"It was not Jacqueline. Jacqueline was a little girl."

No sooner is the One created than she multiplies. "Her Mummy's name was Madame Jacqueline. Little Jacqueline's daddy was called Monsieur Jacqueline." There are two sisters also called Jacqueline, two boy cousins, Jacqueline, two girl cousins, Jacqueline, and an aunt and uncle Jacqueline. Not only does this family remind us of that of Roberta of the Three Noses and of her fiancé Jack, but it echoes the last section of that play when Roberta decides that it is more practical to designate all things by the single word: *cat.* "Cats are called cat, food: cat, insects: cat, chairs: cat, you: cat, me: cat, the roof: cat, the number one: cat, number two: cat, three: cat, twenty: cat, thirty: cat, all the adverbs: cat, all the prepositions: cat. It's easier to talk that way." Roberta's language is the Neo-Spanish of *The Lesson.* But, if, according to the Maid of the Mad Professor: "Arithmetic leads to philology, and philology leads to crime," the only criminal act of the story teller will be the turning of One into the Many. It is after all, according to the dramatist himself, "an abdication of lucidity, of freedom in favor of the organic."[8]

Ionesco, however, never stops at the organic. The wild proliferation of matter gains momentum, affecting the inanimate world as well. In *The Future is in Eggs,* the huge ova hatched by Jack, the bourgeois husband, yield indiscriminately "valets and masters, diplomats, knitting wool, leeks and onions, bankers and pigs." The chorus of proud parents chants: "Production, production!" Here also the Jacqueline aunt and uncle have friends whose name is Jacqueline. The latter have Jacqueline children, a girl who has three dolls, each named Jacqueline, and a boy whose pal, also Jacqueline, has toy soldiers and wooden horses called, of course, Jacqueline.

Comic acceleration is one of Ionesco's most common scenic devices. He himself realizes that he owes something to Bergson's theory expressed in *Le Rire* as well as to Feydeau's practice of a similar rhythmic structure. Laughter springs from the discovery that "something mechanical has been superimposed upon the living," explains the philosopher. Ionesco's characters, emptied of all psychological realism, together with the props which constitute their universe are propelled onward, towards some final, apocalyptic dissolution. Creation means destruction since *eros* and *thanatos* are one. The whirlwind of chairs, coffee cups in *Victims of Duty,* pieces of furniture in *The New Tenant* is as suggestive of the flux of matter as of the void. Ionesco tells us that his ultimate ambition in *The Chairs* was to fill the stage with a "massive void."[9] With the wild acceleration of production we seem to spin closer and closer to the final bang which ends Ionesco's film, *Anger.* There, everything starts in the most benign fashion. People smile at each other, greet one another politely. The world seems set to continue forever. A fly in somebody's soup sets off the irreversible chain of events. The anger of one becomes the wild rage of the many.—We are reminded of the assassination at Sarajevo.—Quarrels grow into strikes, demonstrations, street battles, revolutions, wars. "There is a mechanism in human passions which transcends initial intentions,"[10] says the playwright in his discussion of his scenario. The mechanisms of hate so easily stirred cannot be as easily stopped. The planet bursts.

Thus, we understand the danger inherent in Daddy's story. It may be the tale of creation, but if it is allowed to continue on its course it can become that of the world's end. *The Bald Soprano* was supposed to end with the actors picking up machine guns and shooting down the audience. Those who accuse Ionesco of being "un petit bourgeois" do not realize the violence which exists at the core of his work. Here, in this gentle story for little children, the wild unleashing of events is not allowed to take place, though when one looks at the Delessert illustrations one is made aware of how faithfully the artist interpreted the secret thoughts of the author. The museum or zoo of monsters created by Daddy is peopled by winged pigs, fish whose intestines dart out like tongues, beaked and crested insects, eyeless lions, totemic dragon flies. Delessert has concretized and set on paper the mobile architecture of Ionesco's nightmarish universe. The proliferation of horrifying mutations is interrupted by the second intrusion of the Maid who has come to fetch little Josette to take her along marketing. The presence of the symbol of society, her diurnal, banal concerns put a halt to the wild imaginings which threaten ordinary existence. This is indeed the situation of Ionesco, the poet, when faced with the necessities of daily life. As Josette leaves, Daddy and Mummy fall asleep again. Actually, Mummy never awoke. We are told once again that they are weary from their round of activities. This sinful state condemns them to absence from the world of daylight.

In the outside world where Josette goes shopping with the
Maid the child meets another child. The other girl is accompanied by her parents. Clearly, the latter are a different breed
from the dreamers Josette has left at home. The ones shopping
are proper, bourgeois parents who do not overindulge and are
therefore able to go smoothly through the routine of daily
chores. "Do you want to play with me?" questions Josette.
And she asks in all innocence: "What's your name?" The answer: "Jacqueline" sets Josette upward into the lunar regions of
the fantasy world. Her reaction is as instantaneous, as determined as that of Apollo rising over the crackling combustion of
a million drops of oil. "I know...your daddy's name is Jacqueline, your little brother is called Jacqueline, your doll is called
Jacqueline, your gramp is called Jacqueline, your hobby horse is
called Jacqueline, your house is called Jacqueline, your chamber
potty is called Jacqueline." At this point Delessert's illustrations
show a hugh mountain in the shape of a little girl. An infinite
procession of tiny Jacquelines makes its way along a winding
road, up the slopes of the huge cosmic shapes of The Jacqueline.
It is obvious that Daddy's story has taken over the world, that
indeed a new cosmos has been created. Little Josette has been
infected with the madness of imagination. It is of course, for
Ionesco, a sublime kind of folly. To Bonnefoy he explains:
"Each work of art is unique, a world, a cosmos."[11]

For society at large the individual, inner world is a scandal—
in its etymological sense of stumbling block. No sooner has
Josette released this proliferation of images that all in the shop
turn in her direction, staring at this tiny monster with wide,
frightened eyes. In the Delessert illustration all eyes have become one gigantic eyeball supported by collective legs so that it
looks like a huge, Kafka bug.

The Maid has the concluding speech, however, and she
seems to calm the crowd by saying: "It's nothing at all, don't
worry, it's only those silly stories her daddy tells her." But does
the Maid reject the stories, or is she actually a kind of shield,
perhaps even an accomplice? In the illustration she appears all
of a sudden as a hieratic figure, a finger raised to her mouth. On
the middle finger she wears a large ring, and when one looks at
what it represents one sees the portrait of the philosopher
Descartes. The Maid's apparent rejection of the world of imagination as "silly" would appear to be a continuation of Cartesian-

ism in France. From Ionesco's *Rhinoceros,* we know how the
dramatist feels about Cartesian logic. In Act I of that play, the
Logician demonstrates a syllogism: "All cats die. Socrates is
dead. Therefore Socrates is a cat." In the course of that absurd
demonstration, Jean, contrapuntally, reverses Descartes' *cogito
ergo sum* when he tells his friend, the shy, insecure Bérenger:
"You don't exist, my dear Bérenger, because you don't think.
Start thinking then you will." We must recall, however, that
Jean's preaching ends with his becoming a rhinoceros while his
modest friend retains his humanity to the end. For Ionesco as
for Shakespeare men who think too much are dangerous, or at
least particularly vulnerable to the germ of ideologies, to rhinoceritis. As to the learned Logician he cannot even help the
crowd in the public square determine whether the rhinoceros
they have just seen in their quiet streets is Asiatic or African,
single-horned or bicorned. The scientist does not trust his senses
and finds no answer in his mind, Jean does not trust himself.
Can the Maid at the end of the story be trusted? Is she not,
like her counterpart in *The Bald Soprano,* Sherlock Holmes?
What special truth does she have access to? Is she not a kind of
double agent, seeming to voice the feelings of the crowd, cover-
ing at the same time the illicit but all-important activity of myth
making, story-telling?

    In the case of Ionesco's two *Contes,* it seems that we must
take the books as a whole, which means that the Delessert drawings are an important, often revealing part of the story. As we
look at the final page of *Conte Numéro 1,* we no longer see
Jacqueline the maid, but the Jacqueline of Daddy's tale. She is
as large as the cosmic mountain a few pages back. With her
wide-set Minoan eyes, her finger raised to her lips symbolizing
silence and final mystery, she is transformed from a household
fixture into a divinity. This metamorphosis is not unlike that
suffered by the shrewish Queen Marguerite in *Exit the King.*
There also, the shrill, prosaic, profoundly annoying Old Woman
becomes at the end all three Fates in One, a wise goddess who
will teach the frightened King how to set aside his mortality.
Thus, Jacqueline the maid, the intruder in the bedchamber,
the food bringer and food shopper, the symbol of every day
life and of society, testifies to the triumph of imagination since
she herself is transformed into a great figure, a protectress of the
most private and yet the most universal of all activities. And indeed, Ionesco would say, that the poet transmutes society. The

cosmic world, parallel to our own, the spiritual universe created
by the tender couple, Daddy-Josette, will in the end convert the
one we take for real till that new planet must, in turn, be changed by the next poet who dares to dream the dream of a child.

Conte Numéro 2 constitutes the logical next step after the
creation of a world. It is a parable of the intellectual activity of
Designation. Ionesco's attitude towards this expression of the
mind is ambivalent, and the tale reflects the oscillations of the
divided mind. As an artist whose medium is words, Ionesco
must feel God-like in inventing vocabulary or new structures.
The artist is God's rival. The dramatist has even stolen from
God the power to make the Word flesh. Ionesco admits to
Bonnefoy:

> What is stranger than strange is to realize that one has created char-
> acters. When I saw people of flesh and blood studying my text, be-
> coming the Fireman, the Maid, the Smiths, the Martins, later the
> King or the Queen, the Old Man and Semiramis, I found it astonish-
> ing. Even now, when I am used to it, I am still amazed. It is so
> strange to see an imaginary world take on flesh. I have always ex-
> perienced a kind of anguish at this sight. I felt I had substituted
> myself for God.[12]

As a sensitive man, wary of the dryness of the intellect, Ionesco
sees all verbalization as a demonic occupation. In a sense, the
writer is not only God's substitute, but an anti-God. The process
of naming turns the One into the many, breaks the wordless
harmony of creation, shatters holy silence, introduces us into
world history and time. Satan, "le rusé doyen," as Baudelaire
called him in his "Epigraphe pour un livre condamné," is responsible for the "vaporation du Moi." (Baudelaire, *Mon coeur
mis à nu*, I.) For Ionesco as for Baudelaire, one of the poets he
admires the most, the Fall is "l'unité devenue dualité." (*Mon
coeur mis à nu*, XXXIII) To seek *son semblable* is a form of
prostitution for "l'homme de génie veut être *un*, donc solitaire."
(*Ibid*, LXV) Solitude is the greatest luxury, says Ionesco, the
kind of creative solitude which leads to contemplation, reflection. He would agree with Proust, another one of his "beacons",
that friendship is merely a form of cowardice. He decries "the
solitude amidst crowds, a kind of promiscuousness, the need to
be at all times outwardly with others."[13]

The friendship of words is one of the most subtle temptations, a cardinal sin as elusive as Pride. Man, the name giver, is a
fallen creature, and the only escape is through a poetic sabotage
of language. Robbed of their so-called "real" meaning, dyna-
mited, sapped, metamorphosed, words can regain once more
their original freshness, their state of grace. The poet and the
child alone can operate this transformation.

Taking again the book as a whole, *Conte Numéro 2* begins
with a picture of a flower from which we see issuing little Josette
thrusting out a hand puppet of a red devil with a long, pepper-
mint-striped, snake-like, green tongue. The tale about word-
making is about to begin.

If *Conte Numéro 1* started with a feast, its sequel opens
with a fast. We are told that on this occasion Josette's Daddy is
up bright and early. He has slept soundly since he did not go to
restaurants the night before. Nor has he eaten that Alsatian dish,
favored by all sophisticated Parisians, but denounced by their
physicians as indigestible, *choucroute garnie.* Josette's father
seems in fact to be paying for the excesses listed so many times
as to constitute the *leitmotiv* of the first tale. The family doctor
has put him on a strict diet.

A fasting man has a clear, sharp mind which allows him to
exercise the lucidity required for name giving. No sensual haze
obscures his faculties. If the night and the bed are the realm
and *locus* of imaginative creation (see Marcel Proust), the clear
light of day in which all things stand out, each separate from all
the others, is the element of the rational processes. In *Conte
Numéro 2* the mythic world of dream is replaced by the finite,
chronometric sphere of the nomenolative intelligence.

Always faithful to the spirit of the text he illustrates,
Delessert shows us a huge cat, its tiny, pink tongue licking its
chops. In its paw it holds a tiny mouse which seems certain of
not being eaten. Daddy's abstinence and continence seems to
have pervaded the universe of his household. So has the peculiar
sense of time which infects the waking hours. The pupils of the
feline eyes are tiny clocks; the time is five after seven. In the
back of the picture a wall clock registers the same time. Daddy
and Josette stand under the clock. No one else seems to be
around.

Once again Mummy is absent, but this time it is not escape through sleep, it is a real departure. We are told that she has gotten up early and has left to go shopping. She is not "in bed", nor is she "under the bed". She is gone. This she could do because, like Daddy, she has abstained from their usual round of sinful indulgences: "She did not go to the restaurant, she has not been at the *guignol,* she did not go to the theatre, she has not eaten *choucroute.*" She is pure.

Because Mummy is also fasting she can be described by the Maid as a being not made of flesh, a flower. She has stepped out wearing her flowered hat, her flowered stockings, her flower print dress and coat. She was carrying a bouquet of flowers. Jacqueline says that all of Mummy is flower-like: "her eyes are two flowers (violets or periwinkles?), her tiny pink nose is just like a flower, and she has flowers in her hair." She is indeed the flower from which Josette is seen emerging with her demonic hand puppet on the frontispiece.—Little girls, as is well-known, come out of roses, while boys are found in cabbages.—Josette's mother thus described by Jacqueline, the symbol of society again, is the perfect poetic cliché, a *concierge* version of a Ronsard sonnet.

Flowers may be decorative but their heady perfume is disruptive to the serious activity of Designation. Mummy is not only dispensable, she is definitely *de trop,* structurally speaking, and although she will be allowed to return at the end, at this moment the truly creative couple is formed once more, Daddy-Daughter.

Alone with her father in the apartment, Josette dares go into his study. She finds him on the telephone speaking and smoking. Is it the smoke, associated with the fires of Hell, or the banalities of business conversation, or his anger at being constantly harassed that makes his face devil-red in the Delessert illustration? In fact, as we look at his profile, we realize that he resembles Josette's hand puppet. The answer to this question cannot be found perhaps in *Conte Numéro 2,* but a perfect explanation can be culled from one of Ionesco's most important plays, the one where, in fact, he tried to recapture a certain quality of light, a glow that he associates with his memories of three happy years spent in the country at *La Chapelle Anthen-*

aise, The Killer.

Ionesco often says that critics have not understood this play. In the First Act, the protagonist, Bérenger, wanders into an unknown part of his city and finds a magnificent combination of modern architecture and gardens. The whole is pervaded by a magic light, the light he associates with his childhood. Later, he will discover that this ersatz paradise, the creation of careful engineering, is nevertheless haunted by the absurdity of evil. An elusive killer systematically destroys the inhabitants of the "radiant city." But prior to this discovery, Bérenger is deeply moved by what Ionesco calls "a disfigured world now trans-figured."[14] Having left behind the grey streets of the First Circle, the modern town, the hero has a brief glimpse of the paradise of his early years. At that time, even the mud of a country road shone like gold. The glow came from the store-house of a child's sensitivity. The world was then a wheel, softly turning around its centre, the child. The latter lived in a tiny village, a kind of perfect nest. His house was an old mill, standing at a crossroads. Time did not seem to exist then. "I lived in the present," Ionesco explains, "and just to be alive was a state of grace, perfect joy."[15] He recalls a Sunday morning, walking to the village church:

> I can still see a blue sky, and in that sky, the church steeple. I can
> still hear the church bells ringing. There was sky and earth, the per-
> fect marriage of the two. I believe a school of psychoanalysis, the
> Jungian, says that we suffer from feeling within us the separation of
> heaven and earth. At that moment in my life I experienced the union
> of the two spheres.[16]

Whenever Ionesco thinks back on that blessed time it is in terms of certain colors, "a blue, virginal, pure,"[17] and a quality of light. In *The Killer*, Bérenger tries to explain to the Architect the euphoria he experienced at the sight of "the radiant city", com-paring it to those memories of childhood or early adolescence:

> It happened five or six, ten times perhaps in my life. Often enough,
> though, to fill to overflowing Heaven knows what secret reservoirs of
> my mind with joy and conviction. [...] The last time I must have been
> seventeen or eighteen, and I was in a little country town. [...] I was
> walking along a narrow street, which was both old and new, with low
> houses on either side, all white and tucked away in courtyards or little

gardens. [...] it was fine, not too hot, with the sun above, high above
my head in the blue of the sky. [...] I was deeply aware of the unique
joy of being alive. [...] Suddenly the joy became more intense, breaking all bounds! [...] The light grew more and more brilliant, and still
lost none of its softness. [...] It's as if there were four suns in the sky.

While the protagonist of *The Killer* pours out his heart to the
Architect, the latter continually keeps on speaking on the telephone. It does not seem to the scientist-businessman that he
cannot reconcile the two activities: "I'm attending to my files,
and to you too..." he says reassuringly. This creates, however,
some amazing quid pro quos. The Architect on the telephone
communicates to some company that "the supplies have run
out." Bérenger, thinking of his spiritual situation echoes: "I'm
afraid they have."

   The telephone is the instrument of the planner, the scientist, the businessman. These are the natural enemies of the poet,
the allies of Satan. Bérenger's mystic vision of "four suns in the
sky," passes unnoticed by the Architect who says right after:
"Hullo? Have you seen my secretary today?" It is also on the
telephone that the unfortunate Académicien is faced with his
utter demise. Having failed the baccalaureate examination which
he had to take over again because of a "gap" in his diploma
which invalidates all his subsequent honors, the Academician
clutches at the last straw before facing infamy, he calls his friend,
the President of the Republic, only to hear him say: "I can't
speak to you. My mummy doesn't let me make friends with
students at the bottom of the class." The world of childhood in
Ionesco is never far removed.

   In *Conte Numéro 2* it is Daddy who is telling his interlocutor not to bother him any more with telephone calls: "You
annoy me, Sir. I don't have a second to lose." The business-like
tone is initself an ironic contradiction. The last part of the
statement is the cliché expression of a busy man. We will soon
discover, however, that Daddy considers business activities as a
waste of his time. He is in the business of nonsense making, of
poetry. This will be revealed in this very scene with the subversion of the word telephone. Josette asks: "You're speaking on
the phone?" Daddy hangs up and says: "It's not a telephone."
Josette cannot believe her ears, and retorts: "But it is a telephone. Mummy told me so. Jacqueline told me so." Daddy

continues to deny it stubbornly: "Your mummy and Jacqueline are mistaken. Your mummy and Jacqueline don't know how it is called. It is called cheese." With this renaming of a familiar object the social order is subtly subverted. The familiar at once acquires a character of strangeness. We can no longer take for granted any of the objects that surround us. Jacqueline and Mummy are the representatives of society, and of its order. Unnaming the telephone, renaming it cheese is a profoundly antisocial act. The man too busy to talk on the telephone is at last exposed. Even his fast was a mask; his purity assumed but not real. He is an anarachist, a poet.

Were Josette a grown-up instead of a child, she would be seized at that moment with the dizziness which forced Ionesco to lie down when the text of *The Bald Soprano* began to run away with itself and the comedy he was writing turned out to be "the tragedy of language." Here is the experience as Ionesco tells it in his *Notes and Counter Notes:*

> Unfortunately the wise and elementary truths they [the Martins and the Smiths] exchanged, when strung together, had gone mad, the language had become disjointed, the characters distorted; words, now absurd, had been emptied of their content and it all ended with a quarrel the cause of which it was impossible to discover, for my heroes and heroines hurled into one another's face not lines of dialogue, not even scraps of sentences, not words, but syllables or consonants or vowels!...
>
> ...For me, what had happened was a kind of collapse of reality. The words had turned into sounding shells devoid of meaning; the characters too, of course had been emptied of psychology and the world appeared to me in an unearthly, perhaps its true, light, beyond understanding and governed by arbitrary laws.[18]

For a child the whole world is strange, and therefore Josette accepts Daddy's statement quite readily. The difficulty as she sees it is of a practical nature: If the telephone is to be called cheese what is to happen to cheese? Daddy solves this instantly: "Cheese is no longer cheese. It is called music box." This second step precipitates the collapse of the edifice of social conventions. Caught in the whirlwind of his unbridled imagination Daddy cannot stop: "The music box is called carpet. The carpet is called lamp. The ceiling is called floor. The floor is called ceiling. The wall is called door." This list which is, as it should be, on a separate page, marks the turning point of the tale. Structurally, one could say that is is the moment of destruction. Daddy-Dionysos is setting fire to the temple and the city of Thebes. Having dismissed the world at large in the person of the invisible interlocutor on the telephone, Josette's father proceeds to dynamiting our planet. But, on the next page we are told that Daddy then begins to teach Josette the true meaning of words. In French the sentence reads: "Et papa apprend à Josette le sens juste des mots." The adjective "juste" suggests not only correct or true but also fair. With the introduction of the idea of justice, we realize that the principle of disorder has been quelled. The nihilistic phase has run out its course, and a new order is being ushered in.

On the surface, the proliferation of word change seems to continue, but the sentences have acquired a quiet, dignified rhythm. The passage has a peacefully didactic tone to it: "The chair is a window. The window is a pen. The pillow is bread. Bread is a scatter rug. Feet are ears. Arms are feet. The head is the behind. The behind is the head. Eyes are fingers. Fingers are eyes." In this enumeration, only the last two sets have reliably become opposites of one another, just as on the preceding page the floor and the ceiling had exchanged meaning and place. It is not surprising that by the same token the head shifted to the back of the body and the behind is promoted to the dignity of ruling man. In Ionesco's absurd universe the average man seems indeed to think with his *derrière*. But the sarcastic tone is quickly softened by the poetic transposition of fingers and eyes. To see through touch is the prerogative of the blind seer, the sensual poet. The sense of sight is cold, objective. He who recognizes the universe through touch truly enters into intimate communication with his surroundings. The *voyeur* becomes the lover.

Nor is Josette confused by Daddy any longer. She recognizes him as the lover of words and of the things around them. The seed of imaginative, free thinking is deeply planted in the fertile soil of the child's mind from which will spring a new vision of the world, gratuitous, fantastic and joyful:

> I look through the chair while eating my pillow. I open the wall, I walk with my ears. I have ten eyes for walking, ten fingers for looking. I sit with my head on the floor. I put my behind on the ceiling.

When I've eaten the music box, I spread jam on the scatter rug and have a delicious desert. Take the window, daddy, and draw me pictures.

In the Delessert illustration we see a man's hand, holding a pencil, or perhaps a pen. The hand is drawing arrows which direct us to turn the page. In the center of the book the two facing pages are all drawings. The striking difference between these illustrations and the ones in the rest of the two stories lies in the fact that they seem to be reproductions of children's drawings. Josette's mind is doing the guiding of the adult's hand. A perfect union of the grown-up and the girl-child has been effected, but here the child is indeed father (or perhaps it would be more accurate in this case to say mother) to the man. Once again we find the Delessert illustrations to be a profound and subtle interpretation of Ionesco's text and of his hidden thoughts. It must also be noted that this particular set of drawings resembles the child-like, surrealist illustrations that Ionesco himself made for the Skira volume of his childhood reminiscences, *Découvertes.*

Doubt, however, casts a brief shadow over Josette's mind: "How does one call pictures?" Daddy answers in the style of Ionesco's Professor in *The Lesson:* "One musn't say 'pictures' but 'pictures'." This is an echo of the latter's philological theories about the close relation of all languages which necessitates careful pronunciation. The Professor, a Father figure gone mad and incestuously lustful, mounts an attack against the Pupil in the form of a statement about the elusiveness of all sound and meaning:

I was very young, little more than a child. It was during my military service. I had a friend in the regiment, a vicomte, who suffered from a rather serious defect in his pronunciation: he could not pronounce the letter f. Instead of f, he said f. Thus, instead of "Birds of a feather flock together," he said: "Birds of a feather flock together." He pronounced filly instead of filly, Firmin instead of Firmin, French bean instead of French bean, go frig yourself instead of go frig yourself, farrago instead of farrago, fee fi fo fum instead of fee fi fo fum, Philip instead of Philip, fictory instead of fictory, February instead of February, March-April instead of March-April. Gerard de Nerval and not as is correct—Gerard de Nerval, Mirabeau instead of Mirabeau, etc.

As we can see the vicomte's disturbance infects the rest of the alphabet, turning the v of victory into an f which suggests a lethal German accent, and slipping further from February to March, corrupting the months of the year, the history of French literature in the person of the mad poet Nerval, and history itself, or perhaps sapping the foundations of Paris' famous bridge. It is revealing to note that the Professor's acquaintance with this profoundly disturbing man goes back to the time when the academic was "little more than a child."

Like the Professor, Daddy, an outwardly conventional man, is initiating his pupil-daughter into the elusive world of Neo-Spanish, the esperanto of absurdists. The reduction of All to the One constitutes a synthesis, a reaching for the Absolute, a quest Ionesco found both slightly grotesque and yet touching when he met with it in one of his university professors in Rumania who proposed to "measure exactly, quantitatively, the specific quality"[19] of any work of art. By affirming that "pictures" are "pictures", Daddy puts a halt to the diabolic dialectic of name shifting. A prelude to synthesis can be found in the child's creation of a world based on the unorthodox classification of the father. The surrealist description, logical within itself, based on the novel set of designations implies its own, poetic ordering. This accomplished, however, all further doubts must be nipped in the bud before they are given the chance to set the newly formed universe spinning once again toward final destruction. True synthesis, however, depends on the reconciliation of the intellectual principle of the anti-word promulgated by the devil-like, red-faced Daddy when he first called the telephone cheese, and the "natural" or at least ordinary life force anchored in the acceptance of cliché descriptions. Jacqueline, the Maid, the symbol of the life force returns at that very moment. Josette, running to her, communicates with breathless excitement her newly gained knowledge: "You know, Jacqueline, pictures are not pictures. They're pictures." As at the end of *Conte Numéro 1*, the Maid dismisses such strange imaginings as silly talk. Yet, this time, she echoes Daddy's designation while seeming to contradict it: "But no, child, pictures are not called pictures. They're called pictures." One cannot escape from the All, particularly when it has become the One.

An argument begins between Daddy and the Maid, the quarrel of *animus* with *anima*.

-That's what Josette told you.

-No, says Jacqueline to Daddy, she says the opposite.

-No, says Daddy to Jacqueline, it is you who says the opposite.

-No, you.

-No, you.

-You both say the same thing, says Josette.

The child is best equipped to notice and declare that opposites are one and the same thing. The child brings about the final synthesis.

In the Delessert illustration, we see Daddy, now white-faced and calm looking, facing a red-faced Jacqueline. The words they speak are issuing from their mouths, concretized as a double-forked rainbow. The ends of that divided rainbow penetrate the large, plump body of a huge white dove behind and above the speakers. Josette, waving the white flag of peace, is seen astride the dove. A single rainbow, the result of the inner joining of the separate rainbows, issues from the top of the little girl's head, rising to join a majestic, cosmic rainbow which runs across the top of the page.

On the next and last page of *Conte Numéro 2,* we have Mummy's return. She has chosen the right moment to reappear, and in fact Ionesco states it in exactly these terms in French: "Voilà maman qui arrive comme une fleur." *Arriver comme une fleur* means to arrive in good time and implies that the person who has come in is strangely innocent of the events that preceded his or her arrival. A pun is intended since Mummy is the *concierge* cliché for Beauty and Nature. She is described as entering with "flowers on her flowered dress," the perfect Flora, or Proserpine. It seems indeed at the end of the story that a certain kind of Hell, that of intellectual destruction, has been affronted, passed through, transcended. Because the seeds of creation have been sown in Mummy's absence, the rites of Spring can take place. We find out that Mummy did not go shopping when she stepped out so early. Queried, she reveals that she was picking flowers. The time of synthesis, of the reconciliation of opposites, of the rainbow, is the season of the daughter of Demeter.

It is not in the nature of Ionesco's tales, however, to end on a romantic, or sentimental note. It will be Josette who will have the last word in *Conte Numéro 2.* What the girl child will say will be beautiful but strangely ambiguous. "Mummy, you have opened the wall." It is as deceptively kind a statement as the Maid's dismissal of Josette's imaginings is falsely conciliatory. We saw that the Maid at the end of *Conte Numéro 1* becomes a kind of accomplice who by keeping her cool actually covers up the subversive activity of world making or remaking. In the same way, Josette seems to compliment her mother, to describe her as a divinity who has stepped through walls. It is true that there are no walls for the goddess of the Underworld and of Nature's rebirth. She travels freely down into the depths, and back to the joyful surface of our planet. Yet Nature and the bourgeois order are natural allies. Mummy, as far as Jacqueline is concerned, is more apt to come through a door, like everyone else. When she visits mortals this divinity takes on the attributes of an ordinary woman. So, perhaps Josette's words are less a description of Mummy's action than a suggestion that while she was out another couple was formed, and that this couple forged a new vocabulary. Now that the mother is back, and order re-established, the accomplices, Daddy-Daughter, the dreamers, will still communicate above the heads of all the others in that secret code which is the language of their love and their freedom.

Conte Numéro 1 and *Conte Numéro 2* form the panels of a diptych whose theme is the triumph of imagination. Under the absurdist surface one can detect some of the great myths of human character. As to Josette, the issue of her parents, she is a metaphor for the artist's work, yet unlike either one of them, strong and pure in her newness, welcoming the world, and giving it back to itself renewed, resurrected. If the child is father of the man as Wordsworth said, then the work of art is the generatrix of humanity.

*Ionesco has published two additional children's tales.

NOTES

1. Eugène Ionesco, *Découvertes* (Geneva: Editions Albert Skira, 1969), p. 78. All quotations from this book are translated by the author of this essay.

2. *Ibid.*, pp. 79-80.

3. Claude Bonnefoy, *Entretiens avec Eugène Ionesco* (Paris: Editions Pierre Belfond, 1966), p. 106. All quotations from this book are translated by the author of this essay.

4. *Découvertes*, p. 110.

5. *Entretiens*, p. 71.

6. *Ibid.*, p. 17.

7. *Ibid.*, p. 18.

8. *Ibid.*, p. 159.

9. *Ibid.*, p. 84.

10. *Ibid.*, p. 126.

11. *Ibid.*, p. 53.

12. *Ibid.*, p. 103.

13. *Ibid.*, p. 136.

14. *Ibid.*, p. 35.

15. *Ibid.*, p. 13.

16.   *Ibid.*, p. 14.

17.   *Ibid.*, p. 15.

18.   Eugène Ionesco, *Notes and Counter Notes* (New York: Grove Press, 1964), p. 179.

19.   *Entretiens*, p. 20.

A "LOST" PLAY BY IONESCO:
La Nièce-épouse

by Bruce Morrissette

Writers on the works and career of Eugène Ionesco have referred to the presentation by Jacques Poléri at the Théâtre de la Huchette in September, 1953, of seven one-act plays or sketches, including *Le Salon de l'automobile (The Motor Show), La Jeune Fille à marier (Maid to Marry)*, and *Le Maître (The Leader)* (all subsequently published), as well as *Le connaissez-vous, Le Rhume onirique, Les Grandes Chaleurs*, and *La Nièce-épouse*, all four of which, as Martin Esslin writes in *The Theatre of the Absurd* (p. 106), "appear to be lost, the manuscripts having gone astray."

Whatever may have happened to the other missing plays, *La Nièce-épouse* passed in manuscript form into the hands of a private collector shortly after 1953. The collector has permitted me to microfilm the manuscript, and the present article is based on a print-out from this microfilm. The autograph manuscript, signed by Ionesco (who adds his then current address, 38 rue Claude Terrasse, Paris XVIe), consists of 28 numbered pages, a title page, and 3 unnumbered pages containing additions to be inserted at three points in the text. One of the unnumbered pages contains a pen portrait by Ionesco of an actor's face, or perhaps a self-portrait.

Written as it was with Ionesco at the height of his innovative verbal powers and comic inventiveness (only a year or two after *The Bald Soprano, The Lesson, Jacques*, and *The Chains, La Nièce-épouse* has the air of a brilliant improvisation by a relaxed and self-confident master of the genre. While depending in great part on word-play and manipulation of phrases, the sketch is nevertheless rich in stylized dramatic situations with those thematic and archetypal overtones that audiences had sensed beneath the surface absurdity of dialogue and action in the earlier plays.

La Nièce-épouse is termed, on the title page, a "sketch juridique." The cast of characters is listed "par order d'entrée on schène" as —

> Le vicomte —
> Le valet —
> La vicomtesse —
> Le babaron —
> La babaronne —
> Maître Cucupibi —

Immediately apparent, along with the legal reference to a "Maître" Cucupibi, is the principle of comic verbal generation by syllabic repetition, reminiscent of stuttering, or of the composition of certain "secret" languages (like *javanais,* with its "Pavarlavez-vavous javavavanavais?", its transformation of a word like Comtesse into "Comtouilledemédeuzesse," and the like). Even Maître Cucupibi's name, when it first appears, is changed by an overstroke from "Cupibi" to "Cucupibi," to reinforce the procedure.

Especially skillful is the way in which Ionesco leads immediately into his systematic use of parasitic syllables. Instead of introducing them by brute force or preconception, Ionesco makes them emerge from the phonetics of ordinary, quite banal speech. Thus the "vi" of *vicomte* proliferates in the opening sequence into the following exchange:

> (Le vicomte entre.)
>
> *Le valet* (entrant, un plateau à la main). Bonjour, monsieur le vicomte! C'est une belle journée qui s'annonce, monsieur le vicomte.
>
> *Le vicomte.* Hier, il faisait vilain!
>
> *Le valet.* Aujourd'hui, il fera vibeau!
>
> *Le vicomte.* Mon verre de Vichy, Victor!

> *Le valet* (lui présentant le verre sur le plateau).   C'est du Vittel, monsieur le vicomte.

> *Le vicomte.* Alors, je n'en reprends pas! [...]

> *Le valet.* Monsieur le vicomte voudrait-il m'accorder deux heures cet après-midi [...] pour accomplir mon devoir de citoyen? Je dois aller voter.

> *Le vicomte.* Mon ami, depuis le temps que vous êtres à mon service you n'avez donc pas appris que le valet d'un vicomte ne vote pas? Il vivote!

Thus syllabic echolalia is transformed smoothly and ingeniously into punning social criticism, after which the opening variations on the "vi" sound subside (following the valet's "Vivoilà la vicomtesse" as he leaves the stage), and the playwright initiates the main development of the play, on the theme of the legalities of a "niece-wife."

The entrance of the Vicomtesse, as the valet departs, introduces a scatological note, as if to prepare for the pétomanie of later portions of the play: she hurls at the valet a "Crotte!" which he receives with a ceremonial bow, murmuring, "Crotte— crotte, oh, madame, merci!" To the Vicomte, who asks if she has slept well, with nice dreams, she replies with one of those Ionesco *non-sequiturs,* in which the mundane is treated with elaborate seriousness, that she has dreamt of washing one of her feet, the left one, nearest the heart. This unlikely transitional element is quickly utilized to lead, with artificial suspense depending on pure verbal echoes, into the theme:

> *Le vicomte.* C'est un bon signe. Votre bon coeur vous porte chance. D'ailleurs, ma chère épouse, votre rêve sera exaucé. J'ai la joie de vous annoncer une excellente nouvelle. Laquelle!

> *La Vicomtesse.* Laquelle?

> *Le valet* (apparaissant et se retirant de dos). Laquelle?

> *Le vicomte.* Laquelle? Oui, laquelle?

> *La vicomtesse.* Laquelle?

> *Le vicomte.* J'ai pris une décision à votre égard... Voulez-vous être ma nièce?

> *La vicomtesse.* Oh! quelle bonne surprise! Certainement, je veux bien. Je vous suis reconnaissante. Vous avez été le meilleur des maris...

> *Le vicomte.* Je saurais être aussi le meilleur des oncles. (Ils s'embrassent.)

At this juncture, the valet announces a visit from the "ba-baron" and the "ba-baronne." The Vicomte asks that they be shown in; as the Vicomtesse heaps further insults upon the valet, the latter asks the Vicomte what his father would have thought of his referring to his wife as his niece, as the Vicomte now does; and the "vi" by-play resumes:

> *Le valet.* [...] Que dirait votre père?

> *Le vicomte.* Un vicomte n'a pas de père, il a des vipères! [...]

> *La vicomtesse.* On vous expliquera plus tard.

> *Le valet* (au vicomte).   J'y compte, monsieur le vicomte, j'y vi-compte, vivement!

Though the Baron and the Baronne are designated in the *dramatis personae* by the composite terms "babaron" and "babaronne," as they are in all the ensuing passages of dialogue (the two words are written both with and without a hyphen), the hand-written marginal indications of speakers employ the conventional Baron and Baronne, as if to reinforce the distinction between the level of "normal" reality ("Baron" and "Baronne") and that of the stylized verbal universe of the play ("ba-baron," "ba-baronne"). On the arrival of the guests, ceremony and ritual are mocked in the words and actions of mutual salutations. The Baronne emits with each bow "un bruit sec en provenance du fondement." From asides exchanged, it becomes obvious that the Baron is or has been the Vicomtesse's lover. He is extremely displeased with the news that she is now to become the Vicomte's niece, and has difficulty substituting for his angry aside, "Merde! Merde!" a mere "Crotte de bique," pronounced "avec suavité." Hiding his feelings, he congratulates the Vicomte, whispering a question to the Vicomtesse:

> *Le baron.* [...] (A l'oreille de la vicomtesse). Mais, ma chère, vous
> l'avez envoûté? Comment avez-vous réussi?
>
> *La vicomtesse* (à l'oreille du baron). Grâce à la synchronisation des
> sexes!
>
> *Le baron* (à l'oreille de la vicomtesse). De quels sexes?
>
> *La vicomtesse* (au baron). Des miens!

The Baron then expresses his doubts as to the legality of
this elevation in rank, leading thus into the main development of
the sketch, which exploits in typical paradoxical Ionesco fashion
the vagaries, illogicalities, and contradictions of the law. The
Vicomtesse views the Baron's objections as an envious attack on
her new situation, and says in his ear, "Canaille! Tu veux te
venger! Tu n'auras plus mon corps!" To which the Baron replies, "Que veux-tu que j'en fasse, tes sexes sont synchronisés...
et surtout, depuis que tu es sa nièce, on ne peut plus le tromper."
The Vicomte insists that he will not take back his word: "Elle
sera donc ma nièce illégitime, si je ne puis faire autrement." The
valet announces Maître Cucupibi, whom the Vicomte identifies
as "notre meilleur avocat"; delighted, the Vicomtesse jumps with
joy. With absurd seriousness, the Baron warns, "Ne sautillez
plus, vous pourriez vous essouflesser!"—while the admiring valet
murmurs, "Quelle souflesse!"

The entrance of Maître Cucupibi shows Ionesco's customary
inventiveness in creating comic anti-theatre with an undercurrent
of critical seriousness. In the old-fashioned system of the well-
made play, entrances were surrounded by suspense, usually at
the novel of plot and the psychology of the characters. All this
théâtre de boulevard dramatic maneuvering is replaced in *La
Nièce-épouse* by a kind of puppet-show stylization, in the midst
of which one remark constitutes a satire of dramatic structure,
while another makes it clear that the popping in and out of
Maître Cucupibi mocks the mechanical rituals of the legal profession:

> (Maître Cucupibi montre sa tête par la porte du fond.)

Maître Cucupibi. Coucou! (Il disparaît.)

La vicomtesse (admirative). Il est étonnant!

(Maître Cucupibi réapparaît par la porte à droite, toujours seulement la tête et disparaît aussitôt.)

Maître Cucupibi. Coucou!

Le baron. Pourquoi fait-il ça? Il n'est pas un chien.

Le vicomte. C'est pour préparer son entrée.

Le baron. Pourquoi la prépare-t-il ainsi?

Maître Cucupibi (même jeu, porte de gauche). Coucou!

Le vicomte. Il ne peut pas faire autrement. Il est avocat. On les oblige, au palais.

At last, Maître Cucupibi, clothed in his legal robes, enters "pour de bon, cette fois." Among the salutations is an audible "bruit sec" from the Baronne, to which the lawyer's reply, "A vos souhaits!... Vous êtes enrhumée?", illustrates again a persistent comic technique employed by Ionesco, that of contesting an absurdity not by something sensible or logical, but by another absurdity which the character who speaks cites as perfectly normal. One can see the author at work utilizing this procedure: in the foregoing quoted lines, Ionesco has added (the words are so cramped that they must have been inserted) "Il n'est pas un chien" after the query of the Baron, "Pourquoi fait-il ça?" The simple question was insufficient, since it carried only a normal reaction; the counter-assumption that Maître Cucupibi's coucou-like appearances would be logical if he were a dog redoubles the absurdity, as does the exchange relating to the Baronne's cold, which the Baron picks up with the remark, "Elle oublie toujours de fermer sa porte."

The consultation with Maître Cucupibi concerning the legalities of making the Vicomtesse her husband's "hereditary niece" constitutes the thematic center of the play, in that oppositions, paradoxes, *non-sequiturs,* paralogisms, mock-erudite references to penal codes, and the like are all combined in a devastating satire of the law's inconsistencies and complexities. The undermining of academic learning and scholastic logic so skillfully accomplished in *The Lesson* is paralleled, although far more briefly, by the assault on vagaries of the law in *La Nièce-épouse*. One is reminded, at the same time, of Molière's burlesquing of pedants and even of Racine's preoccupation with the absurdities of the law in *Les Plaideurs*. The exaggerations and irrelevancies are heightened, here with liberal doses of scatology and half-veiled eroticism; yet the implicit attack on rigid legal formalism and reliance on de-humanized verbal technicalities has the same thrust as the seventeenth-century classical social satire. While the latter depended on the inclusion of a visible "norme" or standard, in the form of a *porte-parole* or spokesman for the author's viewpoint, Ionesco's play eliminates the obvious statement of authorial opinion by opposing one ridiculous or exaggerated viewpoint to another, leaving the spectator to synthesize his own ideological reaction to the serious problem that is presented to him buried beneath layers of contradictory verbal absurdities. It would not be far-fetched to compare this procedure, in the case of Ionesco, to the well-known Brechtian "distanciation" or *Verfremdungseffekt*. Where Brecht interrupts dramatic seriousness by breaking the theatrical illusion in order to prevent empathy or self-identification in the audience, thus jolting the latter into the formation of moral attitudes towards the play's theme, Ionesco achieves distance by eliminating any possible normal standard, forcing the audience to fill in the vacuum by arriving at its own judgments.

Lawyer Cucupibi's first reaction, thus to the question of whether the Vicomtesse may be at the same time wife and niece is to opine that since "On a bien le droit d'être, à la fois, oncle et neveu, tante et nièce" (so far, *à la rigueur*, theoretically true!) as well as "père et mère" (here, the absurd extension), one must consequently have the right to be "à la fois, épouse et nièce." He then cuts short the Vicomte's delight by warning him that the law is full of all sorts of provisions which make each case unique, "selon le principe fondamental de la généralité de la loi et de la particularité des cas." The Baron raises the spectre of incest if an uncle marries his niece, adding that incest, if memory serves, "viole la loi." Cucupibi fields this objection easily: the law is only violated if the incest is accomplished against the will of at least one party. The way in which Ionesco builds suspense out of a trifle (as in the *laquelle* passage cited earlier) is again illustrated:

>*Maître Cucupibi.*   [...]   Si tous les deux sont d'accord, comme c'est
>le cas, n'est-ce pas...

>*Le vicomte.*   Certainement, nous sommes d'accord!

>*La vicomtesse.*   Nous sommes entièrement d'accord!

>*Maître Cucupibi.*   Si tous les deux sont d'accord, alors...

>*La vicomtesse.*   Alors?

>*Le vicomte.*   Alors?

>*Le baron.*   Alors?

>*Maître Cucupibi.*   Alors ils ne violent plus la loi!

>*Le vicomte.*   Ah!

>*La vicomtesse.*   Ah!   (Elle applaudit; révérences, baisers, les hommes
>s'inclinent, cérémonieusement, sauf le baron et la baronne.)

>*La baronne* (faisant entendre un bruit).   Qu'est-ce qu'il dit, le mon-
>sieur?   (Autre bruit sec.)

>*Le baron* (à la baronne).   Tu es toujours distraite.   Voilà pourquoi
>tout t'échappe...

The Baron will not accept defeat; since he himself has
studied law, he attempts to parry each new move by Maître
Cucupibi with arguments of his own. Conceding that an uncle
may marry his niece, he points out that it is only permissible
if the uncle is not already the niece's husband! Otherwise, he
falls into the offense of bigamy, condemned by the legal code.
Here, in a speech which the manuscript plainly shows to have
been subsequently touched up and made more elaborate by the
introduction of the dates of the revolution of 1789 (despair
among the aristocrats) and then of the restauration of 1815
(sighs of relief), Cucupibi cites "le cas de l'adoption du conjoint
ou adoption conjonctive, ce qui permet à un époux de faire de
sa femme, sa nièce adoptive." The Baron's protest is seized

upon to develop another pseudo-legal tangle:

> *Le baron* (avec force). C'est un abus!
>
> *Maître Cucupibi.* Oh, pas précisément!... Ça en a l'air, ça ne l'est pas.
> Ce n'est pas la même chose. C'est ce qu'on appelle on droit un
> faux abus. J'ai écrit moi-même une étude sur la doctrine qui
> tend à devenir classique...
>
> *La vicomtesse.* Ah! Ah!
>
> *Le vicomte.* Aussi classique...que l'autruche?
>
> *Maître Cucupibi.* Même davantage!...la doctrine des faux abus dans la
> législation française et en droit international!
>
> *Le baron.* Alors, si c'est un faux abus, les époux peuvent être poursui-
> vis pour faux!

Arguing, however, that magistrates habitually close their eyes to
such abuses, "surtout lorsqu'ils ont sommeil," Cucupibi sum-
marily dismisses the Baron's objection.

As the *dénoncement* begins, the various characters are
obliged to override in their speeches a barrage of outcries of
"Qu'est-çe qu'il dit?" from the Baronne. Against this strident
background, Maître Cucupibi works out his proposed solution,
for which the suggested illicit relationship between the Baron
and the Vicomtesse has served as preparation. The Baron,
Cucupibi points out, may now ask the Vicomte for his "niece's
hand," which the Vicomte may grant him as "oncle et tuteur
légal." The Baron is at first doubtful:

> *Le baron.* La main...c'est trop peu!
>
> *La baronne.* Qu'est-ce qu'il dit?
>
> *Maître Cucupibi.* Attendez. Ensuite, en tant qu'époux, ils peuvent
> très bien se séparer de corps.
>
> *Le baron.* Ça me paraît compliqué!

But when the Vicomte verifies that he will conserve all his rights with respect to his *wife,* while the Baron will possess the *niece* "empiriquement," everyone rejoices, except the Baronne, who says nothing. The humor at this point comes from a sudden outspokenness in which previously concealed relationships which had caused tensions among the characters are now made explicit in a child-like innocence of open declarations:

> *Maître Cucupibi.* Je suis heureux que vous soyez tous d'accord. Un mauvais arrangement est préférable à un bon procès.

> *La vicomtesse.* Je peux aller faire l'amour avec le babaron?

> *Le vicomte.* Mais oui, chérie, vous pouvez y aller tout en demeurant... nièce!

> *Le baron.* Je n'aurai rien à me reprocher.

> *Maître Cucupibi.* Attendez, attendez, il faut d'abord remplir les formalités.

Victor, ordered to "remplir les formalités," advises that "elles sont déjà remplies," leading to the almost predictable word-play:

> *Le vicomte.* Videz-les et remplissez-les de nouveau.

> *Le valet.* Je n'en ai pas assez, monsieur.

> *La vicomtesse.* Débrouillez-vous!

> *Le valet.* Bien, monsieur, bien, madame, j'en demanderai à notre fournisseur!

As the final scene draws to a close in a round of kisses and embraces, the "happy end" is subjected to a final mockery in which Ionesco draws together various elements from the play, with emphasis on the servant-master relationship manifest in the initial sequence:

> (Le valet veut partir. On entend un bruit sec.)

> *Le baron* (à la baronne). Oh, ma chérie, vous êtes écoeurante! Votre manque d'imagination me dégoûte!

La baronne. C'est pas moi, cette fois, c'est Maître Cucupibi!

Maître Cucupibi. C'est pas moi, je suis juriste. (Au vicomte.) C'est plutôt vous!

Le vicomte. C'est pas moi... (A la vicomtesse.) Serait-ce vous, ma nièce?

La vicomtesse. C'est pas moi, je faisais autre chose...

La baronne. Ça ne prouve rien. On peut faire plusieurs choses à la fois.

Le vicomte. Alors, qui est-ce?

Le valet. C'est moi.

Tous les autres. Pas possible!

Le valet. Oui, c'est moi. Et j'en suis fier, car, bien que simple valet, j'ai aussi ma dignité!

(Rideau.)

To sum up, *La Nièce-épouse* is an amusing scherzo in which the master Ionesco employs with practised hand many of his most characteristic techniques and develops with considerable cunning a number of implicit themes of a semi-serious nature. An attentive audience or reader may discern these beneath the farcical action and the dizzying word-play that justify in themselves the preservation of this "sketch juridique."

IONESCO AND THE FILM OF THE
TWENTIES AND THIRTIES
FROM GROUCHO TO HARPO

by Alexandre Rainof

To watch the Marx Brothers in action is to be faced, instantly, with two conflicting codes—words that do not communicate, and silence that does. Historically, this tension is understandable. The first sound film, *The Jazz Singer,* with Al Jol-
son's memorable performance, and partial dialogue, was completed in 1927; and the first full dialogue film, *Lights of New
York,* appeared in 1928. *Cocoanuts* and *Monkey Business,* the
Brothers' first two films, respectively of 1929 and 1931, reflect
these conflicting directions. Groucho, afflicted with a verbal
logorrhea which degenerates into nonsense, represents the ap-
prentice-sorcerer experimenting with his newly acquired magical
powers. Harpo, always mute on the screen, has at his disposal
the refinements of a whole generation of silent actors.

Ionesco, as he himself admits, has learned from both,
Groucho and the silent film, and has gone much further along
these lines.[1] Take, for example, Groucho's technique of "mis-
understanding" as represented by the following dialogue with
Chico (an Italian immigrant): GROUCHO - "Do you know
what an auction is?" CHICO - "Of course I know what an
auction is, I 'come' over on the Atlantic auction"; or his technique of free association, whether based on a common word
such as "long-horns, fog-horns, shoe-horns," or a common image
"long and short pansies" and "early bloomers," all flowers
blooming in the garment district. On the very same kind of foundation, Ionesco has built the whole complex structure of *The
Bald Soprano* and *The Lesson.*

This distortion of the spoken language itself, more than
any cleverness, unmasks the character's ineptness to communi-

cate. However, Ionesco, while using the same devices as Groucho, places much greater emphasis on the futility of verbal exchange for purposes of communication. Moreover, the attack on language is only a single element in a much more pervasive concern common to the cinema of the twenties and thirties and to Ionesco's theatrer: the absurdity of man's situation in the world in which he finds himself, an aggressive, threatening, mechanized, dehumanized, and anti-human world. Man is often presented as the victim of objects and machines, of having to struggle with them and almost always losing. Laurel and Hardy, for instance, are defeated in a memorable scene by a piano stubbornly rolling back down a flight of stairs, in spite of the duo's repeated efforts to bring it to the top, their bowler hats (which always end up on the wrong head, Laurel's on Hardy's, Hardy's on Laurel's), and a Hydra-like bubble-gum machine. But the substance of this type of struggle is best captured by Chaplin, another important influence on the avant-garde theatre, that is, in *Modern Times.* There we see Charlie Chaplin victimized by a conveyor belt, martyrized by a feeding machine, swallowed by the cogs (literally the teeth) of a monstrous and intricate machine, no less than a printing press, a detail which will have its importance later on in this paper.

Similarly, in Ionesco's plays, characters are pushed off stage into the sea by an invasion of chairs (*The Chairs*), cornered by eggs (*The Future is in Eggs*), buried under furniture (*The New Tenant*), submerged by a lava erupting from multiplying bowls of soup (*Anger*), surrounded by cups (*Victims of Duty*), mushrooms (*Amedée*), etc.

The technique here, as in its cinematographical counterpart, is based on repetition, proliferation, and acceleration. The car sequence in *Two Tars,* the cabin scene in *Night at the Opera,* the conveyor belt and feeding machine episodes in *Modern Times,* are only a few examples of a progression which starts at first sedately, repeats itself faster and faster while expanding, until finally it runs out of control. What is depicted in both the film and in the plays is man's subjugation, in our modern world, by machines, his loss of humanity and individuality, and his metamorphosis at the hands of this new and more horrible Circe, industry, into a robot (frequently programmed with *clichés* in Ionesco's plays). Behind these devices lies the grim statement that our "Brave New World" and the gadgets that rule it threaten to transform man himself into a gadget. In this new Hegelian master-slave relationship, one can easily guess who will be the master, and who the slave. Michael Crichton's *The Terminal Man* lends credibility to these fears.

Charlie Chaplin is unable to prevent his hands from the reflex action of tightening bolts, even though he is no longer in the factory where he has been literally attached to a conveyor belt for eight hours a day; and in Ionesco, Amedée's wife is connected to a telephone switch-board in her own apartment. Neither is better off than Benson, Crichton's character, whose brain has become a terminal for a computer. Chaplin's mechanization corresponds to the mechanical multiplication of Ionesco's new delta twins: the Bobby Watsons, the students in *The Lesson,* the eggs, chairs, rhinoceroi, geese, all of whom represent human beings transformed into mechanical parts, stripped of their individuality and humanity.

Such images are also present everywhere in Chaplin's films, from uniformed cops stampeding about with moving *esprit de corps* to Chaplin himself, a small speck, part of a long line of similar specks crawling along an immense snow-covered mountain in the opening frames of *Gold Rush.* Once more we witness the principle of the conveyor belt production applied to human beings.

As tragic and threatening as this mechanization of man may appear, in both the films of the twenties and thirties, especially in Chaplin, and in Ionesco's plays, it nonetheless has a definitely comical aspect to it.

In *Le Rire,* Bergson remarks that we laugh when we see the apt movements of a living organism replaced by rigid mechanical motion, when a set response supersedes adaptive adjustment. Mindless repetition, whether verbal or physical, provokes laughter. More explicitly, we laugh when we are confronted with "du mécanique plaqué sur du vivant," with a mechanical pattern grafted upon a living organism. Without accepting Bergson's hypothesis *au pied de la lettre,* it is clear that this is how Ionesco and Chaplin often trigger laughter. The conveyor belt and feeding machine sequences in *Modern Times* are suggestive examples of this process. In the first case, we see an industrialist who, having decided to increase production in his factory, accelerates the speed of the conveyor belts by simply moving a lever a few notches further along a graduated scale. At the receiving end, Charlie Chaplin is compelled to repeat his appointed task, tightening two bolts on mechanical devices streaming past him, faster and faster. When he cannot keep up anymore, the whole process goes out of control.

In the second instance, there is a demonstration of a feeding machine which would decrease the amount of time workers spend on lunch by valuable minutes. First we see the inventor himself, strapped to a chair in front of a revolving table. A bowl of soup is lifted to his mouth, he drinks gingerly, the bowl is returned to the table, and a mechanical arm dries his lips. The soup is followed by bits of steak pushed into the inventor's mouth by a sort of *croupier* device. He chews contentedly, and again the mechanical arm dries his lips. The process is repeated with corn on the cob skewered on a revolving spit.

When Charlie takes the inventor's place, everything goes wrong. The soup is dumped on his chest, the steak has been replaced by two metal bolts, and the corn revolves full speed, a shower of kernels flying from the victim's mouth. The mechanical arm, which has not adapted to this new set of circumstances, repeats at each stage its wiping motion, preventing Charlie from spitting the bolts and disregarding his soup-soaked shirt.

Ionesco, one should note, is as aware of Bergson's *Le Rire* as he is of Chaplin's films.[2] In his plays, these same elements of repetition, acceleration, mechanization, lack of adaptability, are present everywhere. He makes use of repetition of the same inane words, *clichés,* or sentences, as in the case of the student about to be murdered in *The Lesson* who can only whine, time and time again, "I have a tooth-ache," or the Old Man in *The Chairs* reiterating stubbornly his command, "drink your tea, Semiramis," or Jack in *Jack or Submission,* facing all situations with his statement, "I shall not eat potatoes fried in lard"; he repeats situations in the Martins and the Smiths, or in student 42 following student 41 in *The Lesson.* The repetitive action of Jack bringing baskets of eggs (*The Future is in Eggs*), or the old people, chairs (*The Chairs*) on stage, the accumulation of furniture dumped by two movers around the new tenant in the play with the same title, the mechanical proliferation of cups in *Victims of Duty,* of rhinoceroi in *Rhinoceros,* of geese in *The*

Killer, etc., are but a few instances of these stock responses to the surprising situations life creates. As Serge Doubrowsky has stated, it is not even "something mechanical grafted unto something living" anymore, that Ionesco created, but rather "something living grafted unto something mechanical."[3] Doubrowsky's point is well taken, for here Ionesco differs from his cinematographic models. In his plays, the machines are sexual; they are generative.

As important as the short-circuiting of language, or a Bergsonian approach to laughter might be for a proper understanding of Ionesco's dramatic technique, there is an even more crucial intention linking his plays to the films of the twenties and thirties. In this connection, it is Harpo, not Groucho, who becomes the prototype. The film, let us remember, which was silent for technical reasons in its incipient stages, had to develop a non-verbal language. Once extant, this "language" continued to exercise an enormous, if unacknowledged influence even after the cinema began to speak.

The *avant-garde* theater, and Ionesco perhaps more than anyone else in this group, distrusts words, and along with words, discursive logic. Words, according to Ionesco, obscure what is fundamental to man; they confuse rather than communicate. Hence his attack on language, his desire to do away with words, or use them as little as possible, and to unmask their futility whenever possible. Hence his striving towards a non-verbal form of communication. This is a matter of choice, however, rather than of necessity, which produces results similar to those of the silent film.

Ionesco's attitude towards language is not, in itself, particularly unque. The *crise du langage* and the various reactions it engenders is a dominant factor in modern literature and scholarship, from Ziolkowski to Camus, from Orwell to Wellek, from Aldous Huxley to Vance Packard and the Structuralists. The misuses of language for both commercial and political mass manipulation through mass communication have placed not only the intellectuals, but modern man, in a new situation *vis à vis* the spoken word. Never before have politics and verbal exhortations (the latter mostly one way, for dialogue is impossible with a mechanical device) been as present, as inescapable, as in the twentieth century. Orwell's essay "Politics and the English

Language" is possibly one of the most lucid and most representative texts dealing with this crisis.[4] It is probably but one particular instance of a very general *malaise,* even mistrust, that modern man has learned to feel towards the spoken word.

Being a playwright, Ionesco is less dependent on language than a poet or a novelist. Wishing to escape words, he is able on stage to communicate more directly, visually, than within the limited medium of the written page alone. It should not be surprising, therefore, that his masters could only be those he chose himself: Chaplin, the Marx Brothers, Laurel and Hardy, and so on. The literary influences he himself admits are Cocteau and the Surrealists, Antonin Artaud, and Pirandello (whom he puts on a level with Shakespeare),[5] all, it must be noted, greatly concerned with cinema, from the *Quaderni di Serafino Gubbio, Operatore,* to Artaud's more direct involvement with film as actor, and Cocteau's as director.

Branco Vuletic, in a little known article, was perhaps the first (1961) to perceive this fundamental orientation of Ionesco's theater:

> Verbal communication, and the word as the only means of artistic expression, have been transcended in the theatre by an accoustical and visual language. The essential elements of this language are: sound, motion, and the object. Theater thus tends to go beyond the limits created by linguistic differences. The language Ionesco uses...is a step towards an universal artistic language: motion tends to become ballet, sounds—music, and the object takes on pictorial and sculptural qualities. What Ionesco creates is not literature, but theater, not anti-theater, but an anti-literary theater.[6]

Ionesco himself is explicit about his concern with an universal, visual, language. In his *Entretiens avec Claude Bonnefoy,* Ionesco admits that literature is falling behind some of the technical achievements of cinema (194), an awareness already present in Pirandello's *Quaderni di Serafino Gubbio, Operatore;* and that a new theater has to assimilate these possibilities (195). He further confides "...I have tried to create a different theater, and to endow it with a poetic tone which does not exist in the spoken language, but does in the language of images" (195). Ionesco, aware that theater cannot be the same since the advent of cinema, finds himself in a situation somewhat similar to

Mallarmé's regarding music. He wants to take back from cinema what he feels rightly belongs to the theater, a sort of "reprendre au cinéma son bien."

Before the advent of cinema, aside from spoken dialogue, theater could boast of rich visual and accoustical possibilities. Cinema, however, not only has the identical possibilities, but uses for a stage the whole world, the cosmos, and even in the realm of the possible, if not of the probable, King Kong, Godzilla, and such. Theater finds itself, consequently, sandwiched between two artistic modes of expression, both readily available to a great many people, the one having developed the verbal metaphor as well as it has (and often better, as in the case of poetry), and the other having taken the visual metaphor much further than the theater has done hitherto—and, parenthetically, the accoustical metaphor as well. Ionesco is fully aware that it is not enough to escape from the Tower of Babel; one must also find the best way of dealing with the problems its erection has created.

The silent film has done precisely that. Ionesco, who has understood this, is no longer content, after *Jack or Submission,* with showing the Babelian disaster. His theater, from this point onward, seeks a solution which appears to be, from play to play, a constantly greater emphasis on visual metaphors.

Most of Ionesco's plays after *Jack or Submission* have one such metaphor at their very center: chairs in *The Chairs,* furniture in *The New Tenant,* eggs in *The Future is in Eggs,* all attacking or burying people, a body growing in geometrical progression (*Amedée*), Kafkaesque metamorphoses from humans into rhinoceroi, all examples of such highly visual devices as acceleration, repetition, and proliferation. Protagonists who fly off stage (*A Stroll in the Air*) or sink (*Victims of Duty*), and blue and golden lights which signify an iconographical return to the happiness of the Garden of Eden and the innocence of youth, (grey light, in contrast, signifies the fall, which is often presented physically on stage), these too are metaphors of a similar type.

One should not be surprised, consequently, that Ionesco is a strong advocate of a Jungian interpretation and orientation in art (his own included). For him, visual metaphors become dream transpositions on stage, manifestations of given archetypes, pro-

foundly personal and individual, *ergo* non-mechanical, and at the
same time universally graspable.

This belief in the presence of a collective unconscious
means, inasfar as Ionesco is concerned, that the path which he
has chosen, away from a verbal language and logical exposition, is
the right one, the most valid and the most universal from the
standpoint of achieving a real communication. Mircea Eliade's
influence, and the friendship Ionesco claims to have established
with him, would be, of course, particularly relevant to this orientation of Ionesco's theater in terms of both "sacred time,"
"sacred space," and a Shamanic ritual with Edenic overtones.

In this connection, it must also be noted that Chaplin himself, even though no Jungian, was aware of the universality of
his visual medium. "Talkies" appear as early as 1927, and such
films as *Cocoanuts* or *Monkey Business,* dating from 1929 and
1931, are already full-fledged examples of the so-called "dia-
logue-film." Yet Chaplin's last silent film (silent with the ex-
ception of about three minutes of song), perhaps his greatest,
Modern Times, was produced in 1936. Why Chaplin, for ten
years, avoided using verbal dialogue in his films is an intriguing
and suggestive problem. One answer might be that he felt more
at ease in a cinematographical technique he already knew well,
but it is also possible, and even probable, that he felt a non-
verbal language to be more universal than the "talkies," a position reinforced by Marshall McLuhan's statement that society is
moving away from print to visual ways of communication, from
logic and explanation to intuition.[7]

Ionesco's concern with a visual language explains the influence Chaplin and the silent film have had on his theater. However, his self-conscious attitude towards the possibilities of cinema seems somewhat at odds with his insistence on writing for
the theater rather than for cinema.[8] Nowhere does Ionesco go
beyond just stating this fact. *It could be that the impersonal
intermediary of the lens, and the heavily mechanical and sequen-
tial nature of film-making have repelled him.[9] This would be
understandable enough knowing his emphasis on the human, and
his dislike of all things mechanical. Further, cinema has priori-
ties and politics of its own, which no doubt conflict with Ionesco's. Even as politically oriented a playwright as Brecht avoided
cinema—in spite of the fact that it would have given him a much

greater audience—for these reasons.

Ionesco's choice, however, might not prevent him from using cinematographical devices on stage. A new theater, which would have partly "repris au cinéma son bien," is not far removed from a theater that has already introduced many circus elements on stage. One hopes that this might someday be the case. It is certainly a possibility knowing Ionesco's theater, and a new Ionesco to look forward to.

---

*Ionesco has broken his aversion by acting the main role in a filmed version of his novella, *La Vase*.

NOTES

1. See *Entretiens avec Claude Bonnefoy* (Belfond, 1966) as well as Martin Esslin's *Theater of the Absurd* (ch. VI).

2. *Entretiens*, pp. 59, 126.

3. Serge Doubrowsky. "Ionesco and the Comic of Absurdity." *YFS*, XXIII (Summer, 1959), 3-10.

4. George Orwell. *The Collected Essays, Journalism and Letters.* Vol. IV. Harmondsworth: Penguin, 1970.

5. *Entretiens*, p. 140.

6. Branco Vuletic. "Le Langage universel d'Eugène Ionesco," *Studia Romanica et Anglica Zagrebiensia*, No. 12 (1961), 102-103.

7. Marshall McLuhan. *Understanding Media: The Extensions of Man.* New York: Signet, 1964.

8. Ionesco, nonetheless, has two scripts for television: *Pour préparer un oeuf dur*, and *La Colère*.

9. Walter Benjamin in his essay "The Work of Art in the Age of Mechanical Reproduction" has underlined these elements, and contrasted them with the theater as early as 1936. His contrast between the stage actor and the screen actor, as well as his discussion of the "aura" of a work of art, might cast further light upon Ionesco's reticence to write for cinema. Walter Benjamin's essay is available in English in a volume of his works entitled *Illuminations* (New York: Harcourt, Brace and World, 1968).

PHILOLOGY CAN LEAD TO THE WORST

by Michel Benamou

"La philologie mène au pire", warns Marie in *The Lesson.*
And so it led Ionesco to write the dialogues of a college French
manual. Seldom entered in check-lists, the dialogues are nevertheless of a piece with his theater. How they originated, how they
function as language-learning devices and as literature, is what I
have been asked to account for. This obviously puts me in a
double bind, since if I say the dialogues are art, the Master (as in
the Zen story) will hit me, but if I say they are not art, not worth
any amount of critical attention, I shall fare no better. The way
out of a double bind is to seize the stick and hit the Master with
it: hence my title, which labels the message of this short note at
a higher level of communication. Dialogues for a language text-
book occupy in the dramatist's *oeuvre* the place of a minor
genre, half-way between grammar exercises and a vaudeville
skit. But then Ionesco is not merely a playwright. He is also
the author of journals, interviews, a novel, children's stories,
poems, drawings and screenplays. All these have to be included
in the overall view.

Enter Ionesco the philologist. At the outset, the reader
must be oriented to a double parody: of Ionesco by himself, of
ordinary textbooks by Ionesco. Self-parody points to literary
uses of the dialogues, while text-book parody has pedagogical,
almost therapeutic purposes: it is necessary to revive the "victims of duty" who succumb to the boredom of language learning.
To be enjoyed, the text-book parody in the dialogues pre-
supposes a familiarity with the lethal pabulum mouthed by our
students (from Latin *studiosus* pronounced *stooges*)[1] in the so-
called "audio-lingual" programs of the sixties. But of the twenty
pieces we published in 1969[2] the best can, I think, stand on their
own. The worst best, since, as the reviewer for the *Cahiers du
Collège de Pataphysique* put it, "*Mise en Train* is among the

best textbooks—therefore one of the worst".[3]

When I proposed to Ionesco in May 1964 that we collaborate on a series of dialogues destined to American students, I availed myself of his attempt to learn English via the *Assimil* conversation method, which helped him to discover, if little English, at least the principle of his first play, *The Bald Soprano.* He immediately suggested a plan. There would be a fishing party, and a visit from the Parkers to the Bobby Watsons, and a tribunal scene, a carnival with fights, drunks, a two-headed woman, clowns, gingerbread and police. Would humor be allowed? He was amused, he scribbled. It reminded him of the time when he taught French at a Bucharest lycée. He wanted to know what progression I would "indicate for the difficulty and the choice of words"[4], but he had yet to realize what an artistic challenge it would be to keep pace with the slow learning of grammar.

Language is the hero-villain of his miniature plays.[5] If this formulation fits the larger plays so well, it describes the dialogues even better, as they mimic and parody the discourse of teachers, pedants, doctors, logicians and swimming instructors. An element of "metadiscourse" seems plain enough in *Soprano.* It originates, I think, in the teaching of language itself, since language then becomes the object of a second language, or metalanguage. Granted, this situation is not limited to classrooms. One finds it in courtrooms, pressrooms, wherever language serves to question language. But philology is pure metalanguage. The bond between literature and pedagogy is perhaps the nexus of Ionesco's method. Involuntarily in *Assimil,* consciously in *Soprano,* the dialogues are absurd because they convey next to no information. Their information dwindles to absurdity as their redundancy increases, and redundancy is bound to increase: how else can one impart, with a minimum of new words, such immortal verities as "the ceiling is above"? Ionesco used redundancy as the literary end-result of a pedagogical process. He does so in several ways. For example the characters in dialogue four, "La soif et la faim", patiently review all the uses of the idiomatic *avoir* + noun until one of them telescopes them absurdly: "Moi, j'ai faim, j'ai chaud, j'ai froid, j'ai sommeil, j'ai vingt ans, à la fois." (*I* am hungry, hot, cold, sleepy, twenty, all at once). A language capable of such confusion must be exposed for its lack of logic, or else our lives, in which twenty years already ache as do hunger and thirst, may turn into a long tale of suffering. At the end of the dialogue, we are told it is wrong to ache all over, but it is right to need nothing. Thus the dilemma between *to be* and *to have* can never be resolved at the same level of discourse. Age is not merely an accumulation of bodily needs, even if language makes it appear so.

In his famous essay on two types of aphasia, Roman Jakobson distinguishes the ability to choose words from the ability to combine them into sentences. Aphasia results from perturbations in either function. Just as in *Soprano,* with its words gone mad, Ionesco treats the "troubles of combination" as a theme in dialogue two. Asked to make sentences out of the classroom vocabulary he has just heaped helter-skelter, a student answers: "The table is in the copybook. The teacher is in the pocket of the vest of the watch. The blackboard writes on white chalk, and the chalk erases the eraser... I open the student and the door sits down on the bench. The bell has three schools. The book has four walls. However, the dictionary has only three windows: one English and three French windows. The windows jump out of the door" etc... This is not really a dialogue, but an exercise whose purpose is to restore the leap-frogging words to their proper place. It shows that language can run away from people—and sometimes it can run people. Absurdity becomes a teaching device also in dialogue 9 where none of the small French shops sell any of the desired products. At the end, a melon warns us that it can be bought from two stores, a hatter's (for bowler-hats, or "chapeaux-melons"), and a vegetable stand. Then it adds an auto-cannibalistic comment: "Je me mange avec du sucre" (I eat myself with sugar). This ungrammatical use of the reflexive was surely suggested to Ionesco by redundancy, for the dialogue is devoted to too many pronominal "see" constructions. I kept it in because it is an instance of formal parallelism (il se mange — je me mange), a typical cause of funny errors in a foreigner's speech. Ionesco's dialogues touch the limits of language.

Once I requested of him a pronunciation exercise on the French "R". The words I had given him to practice were "la roue" / "la rue" (the wheel, the street), what is called a minimal pair in phonology. A month went by, then I flew to Paris and, at a party he was giving for a few friends, he asked one of them, the gorgeous Catherine Le Couey (a former actress of the Théâtre National Populaire), to read to us this monologue "for a Marquise of Louis XIV's time, wearing a very low-cut dress":

LE GRAND SIECLE ou LES GRANDS AIRS
(Récit)
(Pour un exercice de diction française)

Un seul personnage: *La Marquise* (elle porte une robe largement décolletée et ouverte, à taille serrée, du temps de Louis XIV)

La ruelle, près de mon lit, a une fenêtre sur la rue, par laquelle un jour je vis, horreur! mon carrosse renversé, les quatre roues en l'air, au beau milieu de la chaussée. Mon carrosse, sur ses roues, à l'endroit fut rétabli.

Le lendemain, par la Fenêtre de la ruelle près de mon lit, je vis, horreur! dans la rue, les roues en l'air de mon carrosse renversé au beau milieu de la chaussée. Mon carrosse, sur ses roues, à l'endroit fut rétabli.

Le surlendemain, par la fenêtre de la ruelle près de mon lit, je vis, horreur! dans la rue, mon carrosse renversé, les quatre roues en l'air, au beau milieu de la chaussée.

J'appelai mes gens et leur dis comment, tous les matins, par la fenêtre de la ruelle près de mon lit, j'apercevais, dans la rue, les roues en l'air de mon carrosse renversé au beau milieu de la chaussée. Mes gens répondirent qu'ils le savaient puisque c'étaient eux qui, tous les matins, rétablissaient dans la rue, sur ses roues, le carrosse renversé au beau mileu de la chaussée. «Faites donc cesser la plaisanterie», leur dis-je. «Arrêtez le plaisantin.»

Trois valets guettèrent, pendant trois nuits, de la fenêtre de la ruelle près de mon lit, le plaisantin qu'ils aperçurent juste au moment où celui-ci, à minuit, était en train, dans la rue, mon carrosse de renverser, les quatre roues en l'air, au beau milieu de la chaussée.

Par mes gens rattrapé, qui sur lui s'étaient rués, bien qu'il eût tenté de fuir, fut, de coups roué, à coups de roues, dans la rue, le rusé ruste, roulant à terre, les fers en l'air, au beau milieu de la chaussée.

(Untranslatable! But the reader, even unfamiliar with French, will recognize the "wheeling" effect of the repetitions).

A masterpiece of auditory imagination, rhythmic, serial, this tongue-twister serves many purposes besides the original intention of practicing the French "R". Its affected tone gives warning to the student that the simple past (a direct translation of the English preterite and a great temptation) simply cannot be used without ridicule in everyday French, and Ionesco's choice of a "Marquise" drives the point home. The redundancy of the text at all levels (phonetic, temporal, thematic, even numerological) makes its comic intent quite obvious. However, "Les Grands Airs" exceeded the competence of first-year college students in French. So, it became part of a concluding series of four pieces which aim to illustrate, at the second-year level, the relationships between social classes and style.

Such perfect little comedies as "Le centenaire", "Chez le docteur" and "La politesse" deserve more attention than I have space for here. "Politeness" is a complete mini-play compressing one act in twenty rejoinders. In the style of *Rhinoceros* Act One, and with equally biting satire, it moves two actions at cross-purposes. Two drivers shout insults but do no physical harm to each other, while a "gentleman" goes all the way from jostling a lady in the crowd to stepping on her toe, then gouging her eye with her cane, and finally carrying her off in his arms. The mounting sidewalk violence counterpoints the verbal duel on the roadway, a criss-cross of hehaviors ending up with the lady succumbing to the sadistic attentions of the over-polite man, while the drivers remain safe. To each social class its own form of attack. The taxi-driver threatens, but probably cannot afford the consequences of a fight. His attack aims at ridiculing the automobilist for his suspected peasant origins. On the contrary, the gentleman on the sidewalk commits symbolic rape under cover of urban protest. The police will arrest an innocent by-stander.

In *La politesse,* one is reminded that philology indeed can lead to crime. Aggressivity, pent up by French language education, is released by the automobile culture. The lesson of the dialogue lies entirely in its form, which telescopes in a chiasmus sidewalk politeness and driving violence, traditional aristocracy and the new democracy of the open road. It is this abrupt contrast, what might be called a *paratactic* form of culture connotation, which releases the information about the culture: on one side smooth words and ugly deeds, on the other no deeds but ugly words.

My editorial policy consisted in an agreement with the publisher, the excellent John Young at Macmillan, to accept as material any Ionescan art, the more fanciful the better, provided I could break it up into teachable units, generally three one-hour lessons per dialogue. The method was to teach *to* rather than *from* dialogues. For the eventual series of twenty pieces, Ionesco wrote about thirty. Four of them, judged inappropriate, are still in my possession.

In one of them, *Sophismes,* Philip asks Thomas where his wife is. She is not at home, nor could she meet him on the way. Because, says Thomas, I am not married. All the better, says Philip, I was afraid she was ill. Does it follow logically that instead of marrying a *malade imaginaire* it is better to wed a *précieuse ridicule?* No, a since ridicule is lethal. Both women must be equally incapable of existing. But they are most *sophisticated.*

When I turned down this little *clownerie,* the master sent me an irate note: "Maybe I am not Molière, he wrote, but you are not Sainte-Beuve, either". The very next day[5], however, his confidence returned, and he wrote again: if he was indeed the Molière of our century, I had to be its Sainte-Beuve, and we agreed to omit *Sophismes.*

In hindsight, I much regret not including *Chez la boulangère,* clearly one of his best short pieces. I admired it ten years ago, although I did not then realize its full impact. One of Ionesco's friends had just drowned off the coast of Africa, and had perhaps been the victim of sharks. It seems that this tragic memory invades the baker's shop in the form of a swimming instructor who prevents a customer from buying bread. Thus Thanatos may paralyze Eros, the thought of death may interrupt everyday living. But the appetite for life does not give up so easily. At least that is what is suggested by the variety of breads which the French have invented, by their funny names, and by the customer's willingness to take any of them home, even raw, to bake herself if needed. Upon this deeper structure (life against death, customer against swimming instructor), another one is overlaid, a simple polarity between commerce and conversation, which reminds us that commerce means both.

Here is a French shopkeeper who defends her right to talk to customers against her obligation to sell. In a true republic, the exchange of words is free, people are equals, equally in a hurry, but obliged to line up for their turn to speak. Speech, not food, is therefore the staple of life. With Eugene Ionesco's permission I shall quote this marvelous little comedy, dated November 1964 and until now unpublished.

CHEZ LA BOULANGÈRE

La cliente entre. Le client, accoudé au comptoir, discute avec la boulangère.

la cliente: Bonjour, madame; donnez-moi, s'il vous plaît, une baguette moulée, bien cuite.

le client (à la boulangère): Voyez-vous, madame, tout le monde devrait apprendre à nager. Un garçonnet de cinq ans peut apprendre la natation en cinq leçons. Il ne peut pas aller bien loin, certainement, il n'en sait pas encore suffisamment; par ailleurs, il n'a pas assez de force, et les enfants, comme vous avez dû vous en apercevoir vous-même, n'ont pas la force des adultes, sauf quelques rares exceptions: Hercule enfant, par exemple, qui a tué le serpent qui venait l'attaquer dnas son berceau. C'est plus tard, quand il était adulte, qu'il a perdu ses forces à cause d'Omphale. Samson aussi, parce qu'on lui a coupé les cheveux.

la boulangère: J'ai un neveu qui peut soulever un sac de farine de cent kilos. Il n'a pas cinq ans, lui, il en a vingt-cinq. Non, vingt-quatre. En plus, il sait nager comme tous les enfants de cinq ans.

le client: Même un idiot peut apprendre à nager. Au moins, il devrait savoir faire la planche pour se maintenir sur l'eau malgré la tempête.

la boulangère: Qu'il sache faire la planche ou non, il ne peut tout de même pas se maintenir sur l'eau s'il est dévoré par les requins.

le client: Ah, cela, vous savez, c'est l'imprévu! Combien d'automobilistes ont des accidents bien qu'ils sachent conduire!

la cliente: Excusez-moi, madame, puis-je avoir une baguette de pain bien cuite, ou bien un bfard, du pain de seigle, du pain bis, un pain de mie, un pain au chocolat?

la boulangère: Il y a aussi des automobilistes qui se noient. Ils entrent dans la rivière avec leur voiture, sans le faire exprès, bien entendu, une fausse manoeuvre; qui le fait exprès? Cependant, ça arrive.

le client: Bref, tout le monde devrait apprendre à nager. Je suis maître-nageur.

la cliente (à la boulangère): Deux éclairs au café, une galette, du pain d'épices, trois croissants chauds, deux chaussons aux pommes. Non, rien de tout cela. Je voudrais simplement une baguette viennoise, un petit pain au lait et des biscottes sans sel pour mon mari qui est obèse. J'aime mieux le pain frais, non, j'aime mieux le rassis.

le client: Les vieillards aussi peuvent et doivent apprendre à nager. Il y a des gens qui se réveillent trop tard. Ils veulent apprendre à nager au moment même où ils se noient.

la boulangère: Ne se rendent-ils pas compte qu'à cet instant il n'est plus temps?

la cliente: Non, donnez-moi, s'il vous plaît, un pain de campagne, pas trop cuit, saignant, presque cru. Je le ferai cuire à la maison.

le client (à la cliente): Voyons, Madame, laissez-nous finir la discussion, vous avez bien cinq minutes, faites la queue. J'étais là avant vous, depuis longtemps. On ne peut plus causer. Vous nous ennuyez avec votre pain.

la boulangère: En plus, elle ne sait pas ce qu'elle veut. Chaque fois qu'elle ouvre la bouche,—elle l'ouvre souvent—elle demande autre chose.

la cliente: Je suis pressée, madame.

le client: Moi aussi.

la boulangère: Moi aussi. Tout le monde.

la cliente: Vous n'êtes pas polie, madame, avec les clients.

la boulangère: On a bien le droit de bavarder (de faire un brin de causette), tout de même! Vous n'allez pas me l'interdire. Nous sommes en république.

la cliente: Vous n'êtes pas du tout aimable. Je vais aller acheter mon pain chez le boulanger d'en face. (Elle sort)

la boulangère: Je vais lui téléphoner pour qu'il ne lui en vende pas.

le client: Ce sera bien fait.[6]

Essentially, this refused piece is a refusal piece, like so many of the dialogues both within the plays of Ionesco's theatre and in our book. Bread is denied, as is the food at the Restaurant. Once the waiter has established, in dialogue fourteen, that restaurants are for eating and not for having one's hair cut or passing exams, once a gourmet menu has been ordered, but not from the Gothic writing for tourists out of the German Middle Ages, then only hard bread and coca cola are granted. The travel agency (dialogue sixteen) has no more seats on any train, plane or ship. The only play to be seen at the theatre is the one provided by the firemen fighting the fire which destroys it (dialogue eight). Entropy reigns everywhere: from birth, since from then on I must share a name with my parents, walk on legs (instead of four, two, which is scarcely half of four), break my legs, live in constant rain controlled by the National Weather Office, lose my parents, and stop thinking, which, since Descartes, is tantamount to death (dialogue ten). Such pessimism, in the dialogues as in the larger theatre of Ionesco, lets up only by a return to childhood (dialogue 15) or by a flight into the future:

THE FACE OF THE FUTURE

Perfumer: Good morning, young...lady. What can I do for you?

Marie-Jeanne: I'd like to buy myself a face with all the indispensable accessories.

Perfumer: When do you need it?

Marie-Jeanne: I'd like it for to-morrow.

Perfumer: It's a bit rushed. I shall do my best. Do you want a nose?

Marie-Jeanne: What shall I do with it, what good will it do?

Perfumer: You will need it to blow it.

Marie-Jeanne: I can't blow it without one? Then you must make me two noses, one with a trombone and one with a wind tunnel (un nez en trompette, un autre en colimaçon avec escalier).

Perfumer: I shall also make you some eyes.

Marie-Jeanne: Do you think I'll really need them? Are they dear?

Perfumer: Nothing's dearer. You will need two. They will be necessary for winking, that is to say, you will close one while you smile with the other, then you will open the first one, and you will go on indefinitely.

So the perfumer sells her two noses but he cannot find enough room on her face for all the kinds of mouths she will need: a kissing mouth, an eating mouth, a tooth-breaking mouth, etc. She will have to content herself with a single mouth-watering mouth. The dialogue shows how, from the initial pedagogic necessity of using as many verbs in the future tense as he could, Ionesco arrived at something close to the surrealistic mask of Roberta in *Jacques:* grammar, by imagination, assumed the face of scientific prophecy.

When the time came to choose a title for our work, I suggested *Parlez-vous Ionesco,* and he countered with *Parlons Françons par Benamon et Ionescon.* John Young was horrified. He was reassured by the final *Mise en train,* which was the heading of the first exercise in the manuscript. Some dialogues, which had appeared in *Cahier Jean-Louis Barrault* in April 1966 were performed at the Théâtre de Poche that summer.

NOTES

1. This pun can be found in the medieval poetry of *Le Roy Perce.*

2. *Mise en train* by Michel Benamou, dialogues originaux de Eugene
    Ionesco, avec la collaboration de Monique Callamand (New York:
    The Macmillan Company, 1969).

3. "Les leçons d'Ionesco", *Subsidia Pataphysica* No 11, pp. 65-84.

4. Richard Schechner, "The Bald Soprano and The Lesson" in *Ionesco,*
    edited by Rosette Lamont (Englewood Cliffs: Prentice Hall, 1973),
    p. 29.

5. Letter of June 15, 1966.

6. Here is a translation by Mrs. Edith Jonsson:

AT THE BAKER'S

A woman comes in. A man, his elbow resting upon the counter, is talking
to the baker's wife.

The woman: Good morning. Would you give me a crusty loaf of French
bread, please.

The man (to the baker's wife): As I was saying, every one should learn
swimming. A five-year old boy can learn to swim in five lessons. Of course,
he couldn't go too far, he wouldn't know yet; besides, he wouldn't be
strong enough. Children, as you must have seen for yourself, are not as
strong as adults, except for very few, such as Hercules, for instance, who, as
a child, killed the snake about to attack him in his cradle. It was only later
on, as a grown man, that he lost his strength because of Omphale. Samson
did, too, because his hair was cut.

The baker's wife: I have a nephew who can life a 200 lbs. sack of flour.

But he is not five, he is twenty-five. No, twenty-four. What's more, he can swim as well as any five-year old.

The man: Even a dumbbell can learn how to swim. At least, he ought to know how to float so as to keep above water in spite of a storm.

The baker's wife: Whether he can float or not, he cannot keep above water if he is gobbled up by sharks.

The man: Well, this, you know, is part of fate. Look how many drivers meet with accidents although they can drive.

The woman: Excuse me, please. May I have a crusty loaf of French bread, or an Italian bread. Or rye bread, graham bread, corn meal muffins, chocolate rolls?

The baker's wife: There are also drivers who get drowned. They go into the river with their car, unintentionally, of course, putting in the wrong gear. Who would do it on purpose? And yet, that's what happens.

The man: What I mean is, every one should know how to swim. I'm a swimming instructor myself.

The woman (to the baker's wife): Two dream bars, one pumpkin pie, some gingerbread cookies, three honey buns, two apple cobblers. No, none of that. I only want a lazy-daisy cake, one cinammon roll and some crackers, unsalted, for my husband, who's overweight. And a whipped cream frosting. No, a sour cream one.

The man: Old people, too, can and should know how to swim. Some people shape up too late. They want to learn swimming right when they're drowning.

The baker's wife: Don't they realize it's too late then?

The woman: No. Please give me a wheat germ loaf, underdone, rare, almost raw. I shall bake it at home.

The man (to the woman): Now, lady, you let us finish our conversation. Can't you wait five minutes? Get back in line. I was here long before you. We can't even talk. You're making a nuisance of yourself, with those loaves.

The baker's wife: What's more, she doesn't even know her own mind.

Every time she opens her mouth, and she opens it quite a bit, she's asking for something else.

The woman: I'm in a hurry.

The man: So am I.

The baker's wife: So am I. Every one is.

The woman: You're not very polite with your customers.

The baker's wife: Every one is allowed to talk (to tittle-tattle) without any one else interfering, I expect! This is a democracy.

The woman: You have the most unpleasant manners. I'm going to buy my bread at the baker's across the street. (Exit)

The baker's wife: I'll call him up on the phone, so he won't sell her any.

The man: That will teach her right.

E. I.

THE FRAGMENTS OF EUGENE IONESCO

by Irving Malin

When we think of Ionesco, we offer clichés about the "theater of the absurd," black comedy, and existentialism, but we can understand his plays more thoroughly if we approach them as obsessive (or personal) documents. By analyzing his journal, I hope to isolate his favorite themes and images—the ones which haunt him. Although I do not relate the journal to his plays, I believe that my explication can suggest new directions for future critics.

Fragments of a Journal is a valuable starting point for the close reading of Ionesco's plays, but it can stand alone as an impressive work of art. Perhaps the best way to enter it is by means of the title. We are informed that we are given fragments, rather than polished and closed form. There is an implied contrast between the broken and the complete—a contrast which we shall see reverberates throughout the entire work (and world). The irony is double—a journal is, by its very nature, selective and incomplete because no writer can detail his *entire* life; he must "fragment" it. The title is, then, redundant—it implies *fragments of fragments*.

When we read the journal itself, we notice that it begins with "scattered images of childhood." No dates are given; we do not know the specific age of the narrator as he writes (or the "character" he writes about). These images exist out of time; they are apparently eternal.

The first entry deepens mysterious contrasts. "I have never been to Beauchamps. There's no road to take you there." We are given a "foreign" place seemingly between worlds which is, nevertheless, named. How can the narrator (or is it the child?) know that Beauchamps is a "tiny village, lost in the meadows" if

he has not been there? Only through rumor or imaginative construction can he describe the unseen village. Already Ionesco
suggests that he must fuse scattered images (or rumors) in order
to certify his life. *He* must create Beauchamps, childhood, and
adult journals.

We expect the first entry to be long and well-rounded. It
surprises us; it ends abruptly and enigmatically. There is a space.
Then we read the second entry: "From the top of the hill I can
see the Mill, its old roof hidden in the mist." Ionesco does not
relate the first and second entries in any logical, progressive, or
plotted way. He simply throws them at us. He compels *us to*
fuse them. This is not to imply that he is merely lazy. He wants
us to join him—to grope in the dark as he does—and, in effect, to
become his collaborators. Of course, he helps us. We realize,
letting our free associations (which are really "determined")
accumulate, that the second entry is a reflection of the first
because it presents the hidden, misty Mill as another Beauchamps. *Both places exist in shadows—the shadows of consciousness.* In a strange way they mirror childhood itself, which
is so far (and will continue to be) highly secretive. The entries
are bound symbolically and emotionally; we are compelled to
read them in a circular way, referring one back to the other.
The entire book is structured in this "artless" way.

Entries rush past. The narrator is sent back to Paris (after
summer in the countryside); he stares at merry-go-rounds,
ladies in fine dresses. But he returns to the Mill because it is
the perfect place for dreaming. Now there is a slower pace as he
broods about his first awareness of time. (The countryside and
childhood are, as we have seen, "eternal")

One entry is of particular interest. He tells us that as a
child he believed that "everything was in the present." Things,
events, and people seemed limitless. At twelve he realized that
things *would end.* The revelation shook him so much that he
tries to rediscover a present. He hopes to capture childhood because he wants "a world that is for ever, young for ever, that is
Paradise." Adulthood is linked to speed, Hell, "progress"—it is
the Fall.

The ironies are not smoothed over. The narrator understands that he has been destroyed by time. No matter how much

he surrenders himself to his "scattered images of childhood," he cannot master them. Nor can he marry them: "I have just recalled that village in the light of a summer Sunday. It is still a blessed place, as it used to be; a tiny village; but I am no longer there." There is a break; "eternity" is fragmented.

We are given an italicized passage. It is more dreamlike than the previous images of childhood, but it shares their pre-occupations. Deterioration; war; holes; the barbaric Establishment; mirrors—such themes and symbols do not startle us because they grow out of the earlier entries. They are bound to the past; they are our old friends. The narrator, nevertheless, wants to be sure that we understand the connections. He sermonizes, informing us that although he is shaped by various incidents from childhood—it is striking that he refrains from completely describing his parents!—he is also a representative man: "I am all the others in their essential humanity..." He believes that he "exists"—such existence is more painful than joyous—only when he orders images and communes with others by means of his art. His plays—and this journal—are therapeutic not clinically but metaphysically: *they affirm his existence.*

But the doubts persist. The narrator wants to go beyond art—to share fully "common distress." He cannot break through; personal images (and words) block him. He is trapped in his existence. He yearns for transcendence—call it revelation, eternity, or plenitude. He cannot find it. He dreams in circle, dreaming of the "absolute dream," but it flees from him and on waking, he remembers "nothing about the dream within a dream, the dream of absolute truth, the dream that explained everything."

The narrator is strangely tired. Although he seeks the absolute truth—he continually refers to voyages; we need only cite the first entry in this journal—he refuses to leave the ground. His weariness obsesses and imprisons him. He fears movement (while he desires it). He suggests that "we cannot take a single step beyond our own impotence; outside those walls I feel sick and giddy." He writes now out of boredom or indifference; he is too weary to change his routine.

Thus we are prepared for the next series of entries grouped under "The Crisis of Language." We move from personal crisis (weariness, the inability to fuse "scattered images of childhood") to "universal" crisis. Such movement is appropriate because the narrator is aware of the personal, unconscious sources of his humanistic plays.

The tensions between childhood and adulthood, quest and weariness, are reinforced by the separation between thought and life. Words or thoughts are detached; they are not alive. Unable to express "living thought"—to unite the polarities—we fall back upon "Clichés, automatic expressions." The narrator hates such surrender; he hopes to endure, or, better yet, to resist them.

He is fascinated by dreams because they are revelatory; they use fresh images. He gives us a dream-entry filled with claustrophobic symbols (dark house, mysterious walls), hoping to purify the abstract statements he has just made about life and language. But as he realizes, he cannot certify to us his interpretation of the various dream-elements. We are, after all, ourselves; we are locked in private reveries. He goes on writing; he offers more entries; he keeps beginning. "I keep beginning again. I keep taking a fresh notebook."

It is grimly amusing to discover that the following entries are *not new*. They echo previous images and ideas. They are as dark as the house he has just mentioned—they are, indeed, his claustrophobic *structure* (like his body). One entry emphasizes the resemblance. "I open my eyes in the darkness. But this darkness is like an unfamiliar brightness, a negative light. And this black brightness brings me, with a certainty beyond question, 'the revelation of disaster, of catastrophe, of failure irremediable and absolute.' There is nothing left." He is wrong. Something is left—the hopes to recreate childhood as a miraculous world. (We have seen that such hope is fleeting.)

The section on "the crisis of language" ends with repeated references to "light like no other," darkness, density. The narrator stresses images because he wants to move beyond words into some miraculous realm (like childhood). He informs us that silence is the answer. He is, however, fooling himself (as he himself knows); he cannot share his feeling about crisis without *employing words*. He is "verbose" as he seeks wonderful silence.

There is a blank space at the end of the section. If the narrator were true to his dreams, he would not write any more. He would not deface the page. But he does; he continues to be inconsistent, ambivalent, and "circular." He now offers us excerpts from a journal—notes for his play *Exit the King*. Perhaps he wants us to realize that the dialogue in it arises out of his personal problems. The play, like the dream, thrives in the relationship of conscious and unconscious motives.

The Queen asks: "How could you get so rooted in this world?" She demands that the unnamed other (who is probably the King) destroy his longings to hold fast; she urges the death-wish upon him. Only by dying can be triumph over weariness and indifference. But the King holds fast. He cannot give up so easily. He pleads in desperation: "Help me to die." The two royal personages are, obviously, symbols of the narrator's ambivalent attitudes; they incarnate his death-and-life forces.

It is no wonder that the narrator inserts passages from his own life between passages from *Exit the King*. He hopes to die easily—to die as a child. He wants to break the "deplorable habit" of living. We now realize that his journal begins with "scattered images of childhood" because he wants to get out of his adult routine, out of his weary consciousness.

The play passages continue. The executioner commands the King to let go gracefully—"to flutter down gently..." His advice is not heeded. The King tries to delay his death; he struggles and runs away. He cannot untie the knot. It is interesting that we are not given the end of the King (or the play). The last line we read is: "We are made for joy." (The Second Queen speaks this one.) Presumably there is a "happy" conclusion.

But the narrator frustrates us (as he himself is frustrated by life). He asserts that he will continue to write books; he has never done anything else. He leaves us with "deplorable habits," not joy.

"Knocks" is the title of the next italicized passage. It is highly suggestive—it promises entrance into a new life (after the exit from this one). But we see that it really means the blows or obstacles that hurt us: *"I felt the first knock. It bent me."* There is not any apparent pattern to the knocks; they are haphazardly arranged. The narrator, like the King, cannot die gracefully because he cannot shape the knocks. He is powerless. He must passively wait for the "correct" knock. The waiting—that is the greatest obstacle of all! He *"stops his watch"* at the end of the passage. He is suspended between knocks (between life and death, here and there, adulthood and childhood etc.). He dangles.

After this dream-passage there is a space. *We are suspended; we are not given any direction indicated by a title.* We are plunged into dark fragments which begin with "According to Freud..." The narrator is not especially fond of Freudianism; he writes that "Psychoanalysis passes no judgment on our judgment." He wants to move past simplistic psychoanalysis. He is, as we have seen, eager to die. It is easy to interpret his desire as sick, but we must also affirm his metaphysical longing—a longing which is beyond childhood traumas or deprivations.

What is compelling, then, in these fragments is the conflict between "illness" and "health." The narrator eleborates his dreams, refusing to consider them as merely infantile—he believes that they are articles of belief: "one is only conscious, only lueid in dreams." He will not reduce them to clear-out symbols. He will not destroy their lucidity.

One of his dreams is especially revealing. He exists in a plastic case in the middle of space. He sits in it like a child; in front of him is another child who looks like his twin. He offers some convenient explanations; he is helped throughout these pages by Z. (who affirms the archetypal nature of dreams). But this does not matter in the long run. The packing-case may be the tomb (or the womb or the natural country of childhood); the double may be the "other" the narrator fears and loves (the audience or the parent). The point is that the meanings (of the dream and life) *ultimately resist classification.* They are beyond Freudian terms.

Such dreams persist (with their recurring rooms, voyages, and mirrors). They are short and long, comical and sad. They merge with waking states of consciousness. The narrator says: "I am alive. It's warm in this room. The light is shining. I take up a book. When I'm too frightened I take shelter in the moment: a precarious nest." He is presumably awake; yet he is concerned again with the claustrophobic room (or wall in several entries); with the brightness around him; with art—including

his own—as a "precarious" shelter against anxiety. The reverber-
ations are profound. He refuses consciously to detach himself
from his dreams. He claims, indeed, that *he is a dream.* (In a
way he resembles the narrator of Kafka's diaries who also does
not separate himself from his dreams—the source of his art). We
can say that he wants to fuse fragments of his life, ironically
recognizing all the while that this is an impossible task.

The narrator does not know how to play the game. Should
he be serious? Should he laugh? What rules should govern his
actions? These questions are endless. In perhaps the longest
paragraph of this section of dark fragments, he assumes various
roles and attempts different answers. But circular "reasoning"
persists: "I seem to be going round in a circle. Perhaps I'm not
going round in a circle. Perhaps there is no circle." Finally his
movement stops; he is paralyzed. Or so he thinks. His final
horror is that he is not sure *where* he is (or *how* he moves). He
repeats the word "seems": "It seems to me, too, it seems that
someone, some sort of supreme consciousness must be laughing
heartily at us."

It is a relief to turn from these tortured, circular thoughts to
the next italicized passage. The title is *"The Fiery Coconut
Palm."* Immediately we confront a powerful image, and we forget the cruel abstractions which have plagued him. We *see without thinking.*

The passage is, as we would expect, one of revelation and
deliverance at first. The narrator rushes to *"the land of olive
trees,"* a *"homeland"* which is far removed from the noise and
abrupt change he defines as *"factitious metamorphoses."* He
emphasizes vivid color and movement. He is amazed by *"living
fireworks."* He says: *"we are at last what we are."* He is also
calm and sleepy. (Perhaps he associates the new land with the
drowsy womb.) He buries himself in *"Sunday velvet,"* dying
gracefully as the King refused to do.

Later the narrator wakes. (Notice the dream-within-the-
dream effect; it parallels the many duplications throughout the
entire journal.) Suddenly he perceives cosmic *"merrymaking,"*
the Universe *"blossoming"*: *"In the midst of flames rises and
spreads out the coconut palm."* It rules over all.

There is still irony. The narrator tries to tell the others—he is always a stranger—about his vision of universal meaning. But they shun him. They are not interested in such *"a commonplace affair."* He is left alone. This is his final revelation!

Yet he goes on. His "deplorable habits" continue. Unable to talk to the others in the dream passage, he nevertheless persists in writing because it is only "through another's writing, that's to say his confession, it's only by immersing oneself in his universe, in his innermost depths, that communion can be achieved." How noble! How illogical! How can be immerse himself in *another* universe if he cannot get out of his *own*? How can he commune with others in such a one-sided way? The narrator is not even aware of these questions—let alone their answers—because of his driving need to flee from stasis. Earlier he condemned "the crisis of language." Now he worships words.

And yet doubts strike at his new-found faith. He broods about self-pity, self-disgust, self-hatred; he surrenders to more impotence and paralysis. His entries repeat themselves; they bore him and us. Only when he develops the metaphors for passivity does he gain strength and write freshly: "I should like to spread my whole life in a bright bare room in a nursing-home." (The home resembles the light he has mentioned several times). Elsewhere he uses the metaphor of "knots." (Does he pun on this word?) Although the narrator does not "progress," he is able to experience moments of illumination (caused by his metaphorical constructions?) and accept sudden "lightheartedness and joy." He regards the joy as "a gift from heaven." It is senseless, inexplicable, and supernatural. He even compares it to "grace." We can surmise that he is a frustrated religionist. Unable to believe in self, words, and others except at rare times, he secretly longs for *divine help* but refuses to call it by its right name. Instead he uses words like "cleanness." He secretly desires conversion.

The narrator cannot hold on to these hopes—they come and go of *their own will.* He is left with death (really another form of longing for escape or transcendence) and he obsessively charts its dominion. "People die of hunger. They die of thirst. They die of boredom. They die of laughing." The ritualistic inventory does not confront him because he does not know where *he* belongs—how *he* will die.

The mixture of painful (or, better yet, mortality) and light-hearted joy is wonderfully rendered in the narrator's account of his marriage. He describes the meeting of his mother and his wife. They paly a "sacred game" in which they assume new positions: "My mother entrusted me to my wife, who assumed responsibility for me and who subsequently became my sole relative..." It is, of course, tempting to call the narrator "infantile"—he does, after all, call his wife his mother—but such name-calling disregards the "sacred game." "Wife," "mother," "child"—these are only words and cannot contain the mixed roles any one person can play. *It is the game which is important, not the words to describe the game.* And this game helps the narrator (and the others) to get out of themselves.

"My mother died three months after my marriage." But he does not suffer. He is someone else—"the mystery that has been accomplished is too great." (He *does* suffer as we can tell from all the references to the "lost mother" in the journal). He lives in a new world; it is, he believes, a "permanent datum."

Now the journal speeds along. Within six pages there are three different entries: "An Old Dream," "Last Night's Dream," and an untitled, italicized passage. These entries are, expectedly, powerful—they present dramatic images of death. The first dream centers about the narrator as patient surrounded by a ring of doctors. He is informed that he will soon die. The second dream involves his grandmother's "ragged" appearance and the burning of an old house. In the third entry he realizes that everybody has disappeared. Thus the narrator drowns in images of emptiness, destruction, and temporality; these are commented upon—"Do I really want to be saved?"—but they are not caught. They elude careful, final explanation.

It is little wonder that the narrator tells us at the beginning of his next series of entries that he has not written for almost a year. We are not told about the events of the missing year. Time is viewed only in relation to mental turmoil; it is present only when he thinks or writes. What irony! He wants to get out of time but resents such transcendence (when it occurs) as the lack of creative progress. He is ambivalent or, to use his word, "mistrustful." He knows darkly that he is true to his muse (or himself?) only when he *concentrates* upon his spiritual crises: "I have always been at the foot of the wall, I have always been in front of a locked door. There is no keys."

The narrator suffers greatly. Waiting for some miracle, he cannot master the images which plauge him. His condition worsens to the point of break-down. He enters a nursing-home; his claustrophobia finds a real place. He understands that he is merely another patient (no pun intended). He experiences "boundless night."

The narrator passes his "dark night of the soul." He finds "salvation" in his art—for the time being. His "conversion" enables him to affirm that he, like any artist, has "ideas *in his head* which are potentialities, living seeds which shoot up and blossom in their own way, according to their own nature..." He will be his own mother nourishing the seeds and, metaphorically speaking, creating a countryside of the mind—a countryside we have seen at the beginning of the journal. The circle is complete, especially when he has the courage to interpret the natural elements in his private manner. Earth as decomposition; water as decomposition—by recognizing the "contrary," special quality of objects, he asserts his freedom.

The journal rushes toward "the end" (another "beginning"). Dreams flood the narrator; he informs us in one entry that he "can find the answers in dreams." But his "dream of absolute truth," which he had had before, eludes him. Consequently, he settles for "relativistic" dreams (and images), hoping to find the ultimate clue to his circular existence.

There are several strong dreams. One presents the fall of children from a window; it is an educational experience (echoing the narrator's descent into adulthood, city life, and confusion). In this dream he protests against such dangerous exercises. Unfortunately, he encounters their instructor—perhaps the latter is the super-ego or the father who stands between him and his cozy mother?—and he is rendered powerless. He cannot be "the catcher in the rye."

In a related dream, which occurs a few pages later, the narrator is also weak: "I dream that I have only one molar left in my top jaw and that it has grown loose; in fact I pick it out with my fingers..." Again he hopes to fix things, improve upon natural laws, and become free of impediments. But the tooth-obstacle will not yield to him. *He wants to be rid of it at the same time as he needs it.* His ambivalence is concretely rendered.

We should stop here. The narrator understands (in another entry) that criticism, including his own, tends "to repudiate and destroy a work. If you reduce a work to its psychological content, it becomes merely the stuff of psychology..." His dreams are beyond simplistic psychology—the tooth and the fall evade our grasp and remain mysterious totems of life-learning.

We are left finally with the narrator as "this particular eddy," moving in a river of many eddies. Every eddy has its own reality, its own symbolic structure. We cannot chart his eddy—although we have tried to do so at length—because we have our own. Eddy within eddy; dream within dream; mirror within mirror; fragments within fragments! The journal is, then, a reflective work of "reflections." It presents one man's life, but it is also a "unique pattern" which contains his attempt to *organize himself through language.* He has the last words—for the time being: "I am so very true that I cannot escape from myself. I organize myself." We do not know whether *these last words will help him to live freshly.* But our doubt is the subject of another fragmented journal!

IONESCO'S LATER PLAYS:
EXPERIMENTS IN DRAMATIC FORM

by Germaine Brée

Découvertes (Discoveries), one of Ionesco's more recent essays, came out in 1969 in the semi-de-luxe series entitled "The paths of creation" published by Skira. The over-all title of the series is self-explanatory. Writers—Aragon, Butor, Prévert—and critics—Barthes, Caillois, Starobinski, Picon—approach the topic from various, personal angles. Ionesco's contribution is disarming, partly because it is unpretentious and obviously genuine and partly because it is vividly illustrated by Ionesco himself.

A dozen brightly colored plates, full page or spread over a double page, and a few small marginal sketches, cherry-trees or childishly simplified figures—accompany the text. Dominant is the figure of "the king," plastic in shape and diversely colored, a humorous, appealing and something disturbing projection of his creator's self-image in various situations and moods. Then there is the eye, detached and immobile, contemplating with obvious stupefaction brightly colored shapes moving across the page; or sometimes carried along in their flow. There are, besides a couple of picture stories done in a child-like—but vigorous—idiom: a walk in the country for example, one of Ionesco's familiar methaphors for happiness.

A double of Ionesco is present in these illustrations, a self-projection, whether as king, eye, or participating figure, a visual record of the manner in which Ionesco perceives himself in what he calls his "encounters with the world." That these illustrations are closely connected with both Ionesco's personal and his stage world it is easy to see at a glance; they are proof of how visual, spatial, and idiosyncratic are the forms of expression that come naturally to him. The self-images of *Découvertes*, the verbal images Ionesco uses to describe his "paths" to creation, are re-

lated to his sense of the stage. Ionesco perceives himself as
situated in space; and it is in spatial terms that he defines a range
of intense emotions through which he responds to the world.
Let me give just one example, linked to the initial perception of
the self as "eye."[1]   In *Découvertes* Ionesco describes the child
in the pram as enthralled spectator to the flow of shapes and
colors flowing past him in the light. These are analogous to the
brightly colored shapes moving across the page of the book and
they recall the "apparitions," Ionesco describes in *Notes...*
"fruits of the void, flowers of nothingness...movements, configurations, colors" that float before his eyes at those moments of
exhilaration when he happens to "love the world" and in it
"discovers beauty."[2]   But a gigantic unknown object moves
across the space—the shadow of a tree sensed by the child as a
personal menace and deliberate aggression, causing an inner
shrinkage of his world, and terror. The incident is revealing
and fundamental and its patterning of a shrinking space as the
shape of fear is a constant in Ionesco's stage world. The "I-eye"
watches a world that deploys its changing colors and configurations harmlessly "like a carpet," harmlessly and boundlessly.
"The seasons seemed to spread out in space. The world was a
decorative background, with its colors now dark and now bright
with its flowers and grass appearing, then disappearing, coming
towards us, moving away from us, unfolding before our eyes,
while we ourselves stayed in the same place, watching time pass,
ourselves being out of time..."[3] The image denotes a contemplative state of non-involvement and delight, which one might call
aesthetic. Disturbance comes when the "monstrous shadow"
invades the space of both contemplator and contemplated, veil-
ing the light. The darkening is a threat, an aggression, a terrifying
"apparition," accompanied by the contraction of the spectacle,
the shrinkage of the boundless space. Fear as we have seen is a
contraction of free space and the disruption of the spectacle.
It is a premonition of the "fall" which Ionesco describes again
in spatial terms: "Then all of a sudden there came a kind of
terrible reversal; it was as though a centrifugal force had projected me out of my immutability into the midst of things that
go and come back and go away for good... At sixteen it was all
over. I was in time, in flight, in finiteness."[4] The monstrous
shadow then is death.   Ionesco's perception of himself, as he
describes it in these very early schemas, contains one highly
dramatic element: his sense of discomfort in a closed or con-
tracting space. For him the "room" or "house" will never be the

habitual intimate self-contained space in which the self is at home in a protective shell. It cuts the "I-eye" out of its rightful realm. Nothing in Ionesco's language refers us to a "place within," and the hastily improvised refuges in which Ionesco withdraws are always flimsy and temporary: "I settle down in the moment, I surround myself with the walls of the moment. I shelter under the roof of the moment..." but the moment passes.[5]

Subjective, emotionally charged, and spatially organized, Ionesco's world is not introverted. And when Ionesco speaks of his stage-world as an "architecture" he certainly refers to something other than the merely verbal patternings of the plays themselves. The stage, after all, is the locus of a spectacle and it is closely akin too to the limiting, self-defensive, temporary room, thereby to the two basic though antithetical images Ionesco has of his relation to the outer world, his "encounters with the world." It is not surprising then that when in *Découvertes* he goes back to his childhood, what he refers to first of all are his perceptions of that world. In their freshness they seem singularly absent from the greater number of his plays, at least until the sixties. The child Ionesco moves in the vast space of a countryside that furnishes the elements of a privileged spatial imagery, a language of the emotions, quite simple in its elements: delight is a "fête," a spectacle of "changing perspectives" where sky, color, fruits, fields deploy ever fascinating configurations under the play of light; boredom is a dreary sky over a vast grey endless steppe; mystery is a threshold, when, stepping through a breach in the ramparts the boy saw a field of corn, golden in the sun, the emblem of a world "beyond the gates." Fear is the giant shadow of a tree thrown across the sunlit path. The visual and spatial elements are strong, and the emotions intense. But not the conflicts. In fact conflicts are singularly absent from these images. One could readily surmise what Ionesco suggests that it is as a protest against the absence of that world that he created its obverse: the enclosed Ionesco stage. It is a form of exorcism.

Ionesco's essays *Notes and Counter-notes, Fragments of a Journal* and *Découvertes* show the simplicity of the metaphors that underly Ionesco's stage worlds, and how closely connected they are to his own modes of perception. Abstraction is not his forte. He is temporally adverse to theoretical reasoning as

his polemical exchanges—with Kenneth Tynan for example—
have shown. His violent dislike for ideologically "committed"
writers among his contemporaries is visceral; his reactions to
Brecht, Sartre and even Camus are notorious. Even in debate,
his language, sometimes confusedly, tends to become visual and
spatialized: "Les Sartrismes nous engluent, nous figent dans les
cachots et fers de cet engagement." (Sartrisms glue us, gell us
into the prison cells and irons of commitment.) It matters little
to Ionesco that the spatial metaphor of the prison cell and the
solidity of the irons are incompatible with the borrowed Sartrean
image of engulfment in a viscous substance like glue. What matters is the sense of fear and physical discomfort the words convey. On the whole, Ionesco is not sensitive to the full implications of the words he sets on the page but rather to their cumula-
tive value as signs rather than expressions of his feeling. Thence
a certain poverty and haphazardness in the linguistic texture of
his plays, particularly striking if one compares it to the rich
tonalities of a Beckett text. What compensates for the lack of
resonance is the mobility of the verbal patternings—so often and
so extensively analyzed—that give his theater its baroque flavor.
Here again the language develops on a single plane, flatly.

The only work Ionesco recognizes as having influenced his
approach to art is Croce's *Aesthetic.* He often seems to be merely echoing the *Aesthetic,* to which he refers specifically in
Découvertes, but here again in a rather haphazarad way. Art, as
he conceives it, is "intuitive knowledge," "lyrical intuition," the
objectification of subjective perceptions. An autonomous free
activity, it transmits a concrete individual "vision," born of
emotion that freely shapes a "whole" imaginary situation. One
can readily identify Croce's language: "aesthetic intuition";
art as an "individual expressive fact"; "expression" as "free inspiration."[6] Ionesco has vehemently reiterated, too, Croce's
contention that "the search for the end of art is ridiculous"
and his injunction to "leave the artist is peace." In a rather
broad sense one might say that Ionesco's theater as a whole is
a long and vehement injunction to the society of men to leave
him in peace. But beyond this, there is nothing systematic about
his ideas. Hence his frustration when his concept of art as "the
expressive elaboration of impressions," to use Croce's words, is
challenged. This aesthetic would hardly in itself, however, account for the stage-world he has set up, although as we have seen,
it does correspond to his natural inclination. What remains un-

explained is the connection of those impressions to the forms of drama he has elaborated.

It may come as a surprise that Ionesco considers "wonder" as the most fundamental of those emotions that opened up his way toward creation. In *Découvertes* he designates wonder as the "deepest reaction" of his consciousness. He describes it as the physical state, of elation or euphoria in the presence of light which he considers the fundamental experience of his childhood. "It is in order to speak of that light, to speak of that wonder, of a light, a sky, a wonder stronger than anguish, dominating anguish, that I turned to literature" (60). Wonder or, as Ionesco also notes "stupefaction" in the presence of the everyday spectacle of the world is connected to an immediacy of apprehension that can inform—as Gide would say—both the absurdist's and the mystic's illumination. Ionesco, in a recent interview, seemed to designate the first when he spoke of the "negative illuminating" of his childhood concerning death and annihilation.[7]   Their obsessive role in the shaping of his theatrical idiom has been abundantly discussed.   But no one, to my knowledge, before Ionesco himself has stressed the "positive" illuminations which appears in *Découvertes* as dominant in his work.   This is certainly paradoxical.

The assertion, it is true, has come late.   Ionesco himself had heretofore stressed rather his state of "conflict with the universe" as the only "capital" faction in his psychic make-up. The more affirmative statement seems to coincide with a recent cast of mind and to have accompanied Ionesco's desire, as playwright, to transcend certain limitations in his work.

Since the sixties, notably, Ionesco has become an ever more active participant and in fact protagonist in his own plays. Whereas the Béranger of *Rhinoceros* is hardly more than a state of mind, King Bérenger I in *Exit the King*,[8] Herbert Bérénger, the "stroller in the air" and Jean, the central character in *Hunger and Thirst* are far more obvious projections of the author. And in the last two plays he has included not only himself, but the family trio, himself, his wife and daughter. Ionesco has recently carried this development into film. He appears as actor, for the first time, in a film entitled *La Vase (Slime)*; and as sole actor portraying his own disintegration and absorption into the slime of a river-bed.

In the three plays, all produced in the sixties, Ionesco does seem to me to have conceived his stage-space and sets in a new fashion although in some aspects it is anticipated in the early *Chairs* and *The Killer.* Herbert Bérenger may well be very close to his creator when he declares "literary activity is no longer a game, can no longer be a game for me. It should be a passage toward something else" and adds that he seeks "inner renewal." One might suspect of course that Ionesco is mocking some "serious" theory of art; but in the light of *Découvertes* it does not seem so: he speaks in quiet earnestness. With all due caution passing from the ambiguous stage experience of Herbert Bérenger to the autobiographical *Découvertes* one notes that Ionesco, speaking of the "light" and "wonder" that flooded his childhood, also speaks of himself as moving at present, along "an upward slope": "Perhaps even today, after tens of years, it is still that light which nourishes me, which keeps me alive, which has proved stronger than my bouts of distress and my depressions, has guided me through abysses and allowed me to find the path, if not to the top at least to the upward slope" (61).

In spite of the simplicity of its language, *Découvertes* presents rather startling assertions. Several times Ionesco refers to what he calls "the Manifestation," capitalizing the word, relating it to those moments of wonder that are flooded by light: "We do not know the essence of things or of the Manifestation, but we can use things or compose with them" (28). "Thought expresses itself in or through language, language being the reflection of the universal Manifestation which expresses the pre-existent thought of God" (44). "In the immobility of the recaptured plenitude of awareness, I mean of an awareness in which I recover myself, it is the essential event only that I recover, the primordial event, the Manifestation, like a luminous veil through which I glimpse the shadow of what is manifested. In the immobility of my attentive gaze, it is not time that flows past, it is the Manifestation which unfolds as in a space outside time, without time" (83). And again, after describing moments of depression, Ionesco returns to his image: "There will be, there are new dawns, the fête. Yes all can change, suddenly. I can recover childhood.[9] And the world can be made to fit me. Tomorrow, tomorrow there will perhaps be a different universal Manifestation, another Creation and I shall be dazzled by it once again, absorbed in contemplation, vainly trying to orient myself in it... Tomorrow, a completely new world, more astonishing than ever, with another or other suns, in another sky" (126). The illumination of the world from some unknown source unfolding before the immobile contemplative "I-eye" situated somewhere within it now as spectator sends us back to the child in the pram, to the child-spectator of the puppet-show, to God's thought immanent in his creation.

Most individuals inclined, to contemplation have experienced comparable moments of stillness and harmony; but not perhaps with the same intensity of "illumination." Clearly Ionesco here has borrowed the esoteric language of the initiates to transmit what he sees as a recurrent quasi-physical and essential relationship with the world, lost and found and lost again, but nonetheless always there "beyond the gates." I am not suggesting that Ionesco ever immersed himself in Sufism for instance or other forms of oriental cults. But the vocabulary is indicative: path, light, immobility, plenitude, vision, veil, timelessness, strangeness, Manifestation. Whatever the origin of the vocabulary the experience it relates seems genuine enough and seems to be connected with Ionesco's renewal of his dramatic idiom in the sixties. His attempt to express the transcendent on the stage does not seem to have proved satisfactory to Ionesco himself: "I have never been able to say this adequately," he notes of those moments of recovery, "What I say is never true enough, the words are not right enough, I have not yet found the appropriate language for these thoughts, feelings, emotions, for the unsayable truth that I keep trying to express which is stronger than all anxiety" (75). Somewhat self-consciously, Ionesco seems here to be combatting the negative image of himself as the destructive playwright of the absurd. But Jean, the protagonist of *Hunger and Thirst*, when urged to give an account of his extensive travels, proves as inarticulate as his creator. "Illumination" is not easy to translate into words. There seems to be a further admission of defeat in *Découvertes*. Ionesco will, he says, henceforward "write no more dramas" remaining content to "construct small make-believe worlds" just to amuse himself. It is a fact of course that of those three plays of the sixties so intimately connected with his own tête-à-tête with himself, the only one to enjoy success was *Exit the King* (1962). French audiences and critics reacted coldly to the spectacular fantasy of *A Stroll in the Air* (1963), while the most ambitious of all Ionesco's plays to date, *Hunger and Thirst* (1966), was an unmitigated failure.

The year 1972 opened with a production of Macbett,[10] the first major Ionesco play since that failure. It could hardly be described as a success. Ionesco's description of the play suggested that he was trying for something beyond parody, but yet more removed from his own universe. While still struggling with the theme of death, though in a more detached frame of mind, Ionesco proposed to dramatize the "problem of power, ambition and nefarious action." Reversing a current cliché, as he so likes to do, Ionesco proposed as a solution to man's inhumanity to man, a society governed by a computer, carefully programmed by a few sages whose distributive justice—social and economic— would be free from men's propensity to exploit and enslave other men. From that standpoint what better remedy than the "dehumanization" of the computer? The play, whatever its merits or demerits, seems closer in type to *Rhinoceros* than to the three more subjective and introspective plays of the sixties. A phase perhaps in Ionesco's development is over.

I propose to examine briefly the three plays of the sixties from the point of view of and in relation to the essays of the same period. The articles collected in *Notes...* (1962) go back to the fifties. Consequently, I shall refer primarily as I have already done to *Fragments of a Journal* (1967) and *Découvertes* which with the three plays comprise the bulk of Ionesco's work between the popular *Rhinoceros* and the dubious *Macbett*.

The first and most striking feature of the three plays is the manner in which Ionesco makes use of the stage space. In the stage direction to *Stroller in the air*, Ionesco refers to "primitive" painting which he distinguishes from the "surrealistic." He was pointing to the use medieval artists make of the flat space of the picture to suggest other dimensions of the story depicted. In his three plays, he clearly wanted to give the sense of different spheres of consciousness co-existing within the same space. The basic action in the three plays is that of "passage." The departure, journey, or "stroll" are fundamental metaphors in all three and, in fact, constitute the action. In *Exit the King* the king must pass from his rapidly disintegrating habitat into a limitless space. In *Stroller in the air*, the "anti-world" impinges upon Herbert Bérenger's given world, and a visible bridge entices him into the vast reaches of that world. In *Hunger and Thirst* each episode takes place in its own compartment, each connected to the other by Jean's long journeying. At the end, beyond the walls and bars that hold him prisoner, Jean sees, as in a medieval painting, the idyllic garden with his wife and child, out of reach but co-existent and self-contained within its own space. Obviously Ionesco was attempting to overcome the spatial limitations of the stage. Ionesco has always used the stage, like the expressionists, as a metaphor to objectify an inner ambience. But in no sense did his stage suggest the presence of a quasi-metaphysical dimension in the character's existence; this is surely what the new "architecture" of the three plays of the sixties conveys. Ionesco seems to have wanted to project his doubles onto a cosmic plane, "a space outside time," suggestive of a destiny beyond. The new dimensions are awesome and inhuman, it is the "universal landscape" to which he alludes in *Découvertes.* Herbert Bérenger leaps light-heartedly into the world beyond, but he returns a sobered man bearing tales of devastation and a terrifying void. As to Jean, he measured his own solitude in the rarefied atomosphere and "pure light" of a terrace suspended in the void of the "kingdom of light". The "grand route" and the circle are recurrent images, but the journey to the center of the circumference remains inconclusive. The necessary passage can be made only in solitude. King Béranger's palace, like his kingdom, crumbles and decays; Jean runs away from the disintegrating basement apartment into which he has just moved with his wife and child and in *A Stroll in the Air* as the play starts, a bomb destroys Bérenger's pleasant English house. What matters in a writer's work, says Ionesco, are the questions he asks and he defines his work as an "architecture of question"—disposed as it were in three layers—"What is all this here?' "Who am I?' "Why am I here, surrounded by all that?' For Ionesco the metaphor of the voyage is linked to the metaphysical why: it is "only by travelling from one why to the next as far as the why that is unanswerable; that man attains the level of the creative principle." (*Fragments...* 26) Thus the theme of the solitary journey seems intentionally connected with the attempt of the playwright to transcend the former limits of his stage. And yet the "architecture of questions" is not quite clear. For *Exit the King* seems rather a statement on how to die than on "Why do I die?" and Bérenger's adventures bear more on confrontation with the unanswerable than on the questioning of it. In these plays Ionesco attempted to situate his protagonist beyond the way and in relation to the unanswerable: death, the immense spaces of the "anti-world," the solitary heights of Jean's journey towards the light. If it is not always very clear on stage in what terms he is asking the why, it seems certain that it is not in rational terms. The three plays attempt to create moods, hence situations, in which the rational underpinning of everyday life is no longer operative; the structure of the plays is thereby affected. This "leaving behind" of the world of the real and ordinary has always been characteristic of Ionesco's stage. But not until the sixties did he attempt to do more, through the interplay of setting and the distortion of language, than use the stage in parodic fasion, somewhat like one of the Surrealists' autodestructive machines.

It might be surmised that it was in part the growing success of Brecht in France, from 1954, when the Berliner ensemble took Paris by storm, into the sixties, that moved Ionesco both to the kind of self-analysis evident in the essays and to a deeper concern with the structure of his own stage-world. In this perspective *Rhinoceros* might well be considered as a transitional play, a ferocious attack upon the Brechtian ideological stage. *Exit the King, A Stroll in the Air, Hunger and Thirst* use and reverse Brechtian patterns: the insatiable appetite of Jean recalls the craving for food or drink of many Brechtian characters from Schweik's friend Baloun on; as does King Bérenger's obligation to consent to his own death. Above all, it is Jean's confrontation with and his imprisonment by the burlesque and sinister monastic order which provide a bitter comment on Brecht's call to the individual to accept social discipline in the interests of a higher cause. Ionesco seems furthermore to have confronted somewhat the same problems as a playwright: how to connect the inner world of feeling to outer reality so as to establish it concretely on stage. His problem, however, was the obverse of Brecht's since the French dramatist's theater has consistently been founded on feeling, on a visceral distrust of all formalized social compartments. His own sensibility then is the only ground he trusted for the foundation of his stage world. The shift from the negative and gleeful parodic destruction of everyday reality to the sense of the play as communication to the audience of the positive feeling for existence that justified the destruction of illusory reflections posed the question of a new theatrical language. How could a playwright project concretely on the stage the inarticulated and ambivalent perceptions which he describes in *Découvertes?* The statement could only be metaphoric and individual—thence the open use of the autobiographical "double" as protagonist.

In a quite different way from Brecht's, Ionesco turned to a narrative form of drama, transferring feeling into fantasy. Whereas in his first plays he manipulated language itself to estrange the spectator while ruthlessly gearing him to the destructive mechanisms of the play, in these later plays the fantasy could come alive only through the emotional power of the character's situation as revealed in his language. The main difficulty for Ionesco seems clearly to lie in the initial metaphor that establishes the character's world, the stage world of the play. He had to turn his former stage world inside out and obtain the identification of his public with the protagonist—himself—rather than bring about a shared estrangement. Bérenger in *Rhinoceros* is a typical example of this turnabout, although it is already adumbrated in *The Killer.* But in both of these plays the protagonist's posture is refusal. And, it may be inferred, useless refusal. He is destroyed along with the situation with which he enters into conflict.

There is no doubt at all that the Crocean conception of the intuited form seems to apply to Ionesco. He has amply documented the wholly emotional quasi-physiological origin of the basic, and complex, metaphors that put so personal a stamp upon his plays. His dilemma is that the strongest of these psychic moods or "climates" coincide with a loss of the sense of reality. The sense of reality for Ionesco coincides with immobility, with himself as "eye" and center to the world: "The earth and the stars moved around me who stood still at the center of everything. The earth and its fields and its snow and rain all moved around me." (*Fragments...* 22) This creates a positive view of the world as spectacle, and is hardly dramatic. What is dramatic is a loss of the equilibrium. Ionesco has repeatedly described the two forms of disequilibrium that plague him: one is elation, that sense of "taking off" physically from an imponderable world, which furnished the end metaphor of *How to get rid of it,* (Amédée's exit in a balloon) and the whole movement of *A Stroll in the Air;* the other, the sense of slow suffocation and dissolution in slowly rising mud, Ionesco's metaphor for routine and habit.[11] This is the more predominant of his stage building blocks.

For Ionesco, the room, peculiarly well suited for transferral to the stage-set, is no symbol of refuge; it is charged with a sinister metaphoric meaning. The house sinks "into the ground like a basement, with damp walls and slits for windows...always on the point of sinking in...of being flooded, of falling to pieces..." The earth on which it rests is not a refuge either: "For me, earth is not a foster mother, it means mud...decomposition...death which terrifies me...tombs." But the dangerous and disquieting element is water: "Water for me does not mean abundance, nor calm, nor purity; it generally appears to me as dirty, anguish." The primarily concrete terms in which Ionesco's fears and obsessions beset him are clearly symbolic. "When I dream of the inside of a house, it is always sinking down into the damp earth." And the house can be a transparent subterfuge to ward off the reality of time: "I settle down in the moment, I surround myself with the walls of the moment, I shelter under the roof of the moment."[12]

The "good-evil" duality in this dramatic system is ambivalent both physically and conceptually. The stage world itself is a temporary structure set up in a spatialized, boundless continuity, within which outer and inner spaces operate, interpenetrate, exclude one another or coincide. These are the spheres out of which Ionesco has sought to fashion his plays, not out of events or ideas: "What I want to concretize," he stated, "is the expression of origins. Not what comes to pass, but what does not come to pass or does not pass." (89) The spatialization of mood and the synthesis into a single image are characteristic: the rising mud is both fear and time; the act of levitation is ecstasy and freedom to view a world "deployed" outside time. But it shuts Ionesco out of the world. "I could not hear nor see anything that took place. They no longer heard me from the world which had become for me a forbidden space...a closed world...wrinkled as it were, fissured, metallic, infinitely hostile...in a light without light." (*Découvertes,* 104).

If the intimate, the familiar, the customary become potentially dangerous and disastrous, so does the alluring unknown, new and untried. A double movement animates Ionesco's perception of himself in regard to reality and it fashions the spatial images through which he projects himself. His stage world is in fact a physical extension of that perception, an attempted exorcism of inner danger via the stage. Only occasionally does Ionesco "become again the spectator of the whole spectacle." And, if he started to write plays, it was, in order to "surround himself with a world, to speak from out of that world, from that stage-world to the world." (Découvertes 91).

The personal concerns of Ionesco are clearly stated through the metaphors that shaped the stage-world of the three later plays: the disintegrating palace and kingdom are correlatives for the decay of a body, and of the whole system of relations of which it is the center; Bérenger's "Stroll in the air" leads him, via the magic bridge into hostile cold spaces where he is "shut out" from human warmth. Jean's escape from the mud-invaded family basement lifts him to the exalted but solitary peaks, thence into a prison for those who hunger and thirst for certainty, an illusory refuge whose symbolism I shall explore later. Ionesco has taken pains to emphasize the personal and emotive source of the play: "I had written the work so that I might learn to die. It was to be a lesson, a sort of physical exercise, a gradual progress, stage by stage towards the ineluctable end, which I tried to make accessible to other people" (*Fragments...* 88), he says of *Exit the King.* When discovering *A Stroll in the Air,* he notes that it was born of a long-time dream of an English holiday and his biographical allusions to *Hunger and Thirst* are innumerable: "I have travelled in search of an intact world over which time would have no power. The food I hunger for, the drink for which I thirst are not an infant's food or drink. Knowledge is what I hunger and thirst for. If I really knew what I hunger and thirst for I should feel easier... The man who gives everything becomes like someone dying of hunger and thirst, lying on the grond, pale, gasping, begging for a glass of water. It is going to be an endless business feeding him. The man who has given everything takes everything back. He is insatiable." (*Fragments* 11, 60, 89) In this context, the pseudomonastery of the play, with its suave brainwashing techniques and ruthless apparatus of coercion and constraint, is Ionesco's symbolisation of totalitarian attempts to control and exploit that inner craving, itself expressed in the vision of the garden just out of reach—the garden enclosing the loved wife and child, removed from the trivialities of everyday living.

These three plays unquestionably reveal an aspect of Ionesco which has heretofore remained elusive, but they are also a key to his limitations. They develop through initial metaphors that cannot evolve dramatically; it seems plausible to surmise that the cinema would prove a more satisfactory medium. The most successful of these plays is *Exit the King,* where the situ-

ation, the stage metaphor and the personal emotion at its source
are particularly well integrated. But the difficulty with which
Ionesco must contend is nonetheless obvious. Once the image
of the disintegrating world has been posed in terms of the physical environment of the king, only through reports can its step-
by-step progress be registered in the play until it actually reaches
the body of the king. In other words, the metaphor can only
be reiterated and diversified, not greatly extended. A baroque
verbal inventiveness alone reflects the struggle between the
king's failing hold on life and the final relinquishment of life
in death. The baroque and rather lugubriously comic visions
of the king's real decrepitude visible in the physical space a-
round him function a surface diversions rather than as expressions of a growing inner awareness. Much in the same way
the fantasy world of *Stroller in the Air* is presented visually
rather than dramatically; it is episodic in structure. Although,
in my eyes at least, the fairy-tale quality is real and both theme
and techniques valid and innovative, the actual stage display
overshadows the personal communication Ionesco intended:
levitation in space, like physical disintegration, does not harbour
many dramatic possibilities. In other words, since in these plays
the essential theme is visually expressed, language is in fact
accessory. This is disconcerting for the audience at a loss to relate the visual to the commentary it elicits. What Ionesco seems
to have tried to do is paradoxical. An "inventive or creative"
language, he notes in *Découvertes,* is the attempt to "seize, state,
integrate and communicate something incommunicable to still
uncommunicated"; and in order to make his statement the
writer must "disarticulate" language, make it transparent so that
the world can appear "through it in its original strangeness."
But in fact, as he "organizes his phantasms"—to use his terms—
on stage in *A Stroll in the Air,* the actual language through which
the "world," Ionesco's world, appears is largely hieroglyphic.
The central theme is the physical "take off" of Bérenger into the
spaces beyond, his disappearance and return and his unwelcome
attempt to communicate the emptiness and void he has en-
countered. The idea is simple and the stage metaphor through
which it is enacted is simple too, an adaptation to the stage of
circus acrobatics. But the ambience within which Bérenger's
exploit takes place is intricate, involving criss-cross patterns of
situation and mood, in pure Ionesco style, developing one out
of the other through the interplay of language. One may fully
enjoy the "fête" as Ionesco calls it of changing perspectives,

as language effectively disrupts rigid patterns of behavior to display mood—a mood of delight in things, and harmony with them.
It is possible too to follow the development of the situation as
Bérenger's elation turns into vision, and the "anti-world" begins
to invade the real. But from there on any creative use of language is lost as the significance of the situation is polarized in the
concrete image of Bérenger's acrobatics in space. The stage
image, is not strong enough or rich enough to give the play a
continuing impetus, and it weakens what appears to be Ionesco's
intent: to communicate his own sense of a man's immense curi-
osity for and confrontation with the unknowable. *Hunger and
Thirst* seems to have been Ionesco's attempt at a total objective
statement of the contradictory inner experience born of his
"encounters with the world." He seems to have sensed the limitations put upon the development of the play by the metaphoric
extension of mood to a physical outer stage space. *Hunger and
Thirst* seems to evidence his desire to move out of the one-act
single situation pattern prevalent in his theater. It certainly
suggests a cyclical pattern: in the first act Jean's sense of the
familiar world of wife and child as intolerable routine and
limitation is symbolized in the disintegrating basement of the
stage set and the conflict between his love for his wife and his
revolt ends with his disappearance; the emergence of Jean on the
high mountain summit outside a museum in pure and dazzling
light is the locus of the second act, a dead end where Jean's expected rendez-vous with "her" does not take place. In the third
act Jean, worn out and starved, arrives at the ambiguous inn-
monastery where he is held. Through the bars he glimpses
his goal, the ideal garden in which the wife and child he left
fourteen years before dwell in harmony. The metaphor of the
voyage links the three main scenes. But again they themselves
are static. And the drama seems to reside in their immutability,
and one might infer, in their co-existence. It would of course be
necessary to study in greater detail the play of language within
each unit so established, but this would go well beyond the limits
of this paper.

What I have attempted to establish is that the three plays
in question constitute an earnest and deliberate effort on the part
of Ionesco to communicate, via the stage, a view of life as pro-
visional, sincere, problematic, yet positive. It is an attempt to
transcend the closed world of the individual ego. If the dramatist
did not fully succeed, I have suggested that it is largely because

his initial awareness of existence is essentially contemplative and passive, embodied in the spatial metaphors by which his characters are bounded and which elicits their reactions. The drama in the three plays of the sixties arises from the central character's obligation in *Exit the King* or, in the other two plays, his impulse to "pass beyond," a passage only realized in death.

Ionesco has been reproached for his foray into metaphysics. Yet, in terms of the playwright himself it corresponded to a need; and though as a result, these plays except for *Exit the King* have been less successful than the earlier ones, they are undoubtedly far more interesting as a key to the man's sensibility, and perhaps to his limitations. For Ionesco a play is essentially a "projection of the self into that substance which is the world... that is to say a pattern, a shape, an architecture." (*Fragments*, 129) It would be idle to attempt to differentiate between the three words as applied to his work. But all three point to an overall static design rather than to any dynamics within the structure. In the last analysis one is tempted to conclude that, in a very real sense, Ionesco's language was used in his first plays as a form of collage, a sonorous outer substance. The last plays are attempts at regaining conscious control of one's emotions; they present mature forms of structuring that seem uneasily poised between the episodic fable, personal and didactic, and the lyrical quest with its episodes of departure, alienation, return and reconciliation. But in neither case is the basic "pattern", "shape", or "architecture" dramatic, except insofar as it is a spectacle wherein Ionesco as playwright re-establishes himself as "eye" confronting, first through the malleable stuff of language, then through his mythical doubles, his disturbing "encounters" with the world.

NOTES

1. "I was eyes, wide open in stupefaction and incomprehension." *Découvertes* (Geneva: Editions Albert Skira, 1969), p. 28.

2. *Notes et Contre-notes,* Gallimard. Collection "Idées" 1962 (295-96). I shall refer to the volume as *Notes...* "Apparitions" and disappearances whether of people and things have been a constant, sometimes refreshing, sometimes tiresome feature of Ionesco's stagecraft. They are obviously connected with his perception of reality as gratuitous spectacle and transferred to his stage via the mediation of puppet show techniques; the puppet show in itself, as Ionesco has often said, was one of the most memorable "apparitions" in his childhood world.

3. *Fragments of a Journal* (New York: Grove Press, 1969), p. 11.

4. *Ibid.*

5. *Ibid.,* p. 147.

6. Croce's clear-cut distinction of the intuitive-aesthetic and logical-demonstrative, his attack upon "historical intellectualism," his insistence upon the "non-logical, non-historical character of the aesthetic fact" are all echoed in Ionesco's essays. One might summarize Ionesco's fundamental point of view by quoting Croce as follows: "The aesthetic fact is altogether completed in the expressive elaboration of impressions. When we have achieved the word within us, conceived definitely and vividly a figure or statue, or found a musical motive, expression is born and is complete; there is no need for anything else" (*Aesthetic* translated by Douglas Ainslee [New York, The Noonday Press, 1960]. p. 50).

7. *Le Figaro littéraire,* January 7, 1972.

8. He identifies himself as King, not only in his illustrations but in

Fragments of a Journal: "I am the principal figure, the center of the cosmos (that developed over the years)" p. 109.

9.   Ionesco specifically connects the Manifestation with childhood, with a world from which "the shadows disappear" and in which "wonder" enlarges his eyes once more as the world opens up again.

10. "Never have I written with so much pleasure on a theme or themes that are rather sinister," said Ionesco of *Macbett.* "In spite of all that is going on around me I was seized as I progressed, in spite of Pakistan, Ireland, India, Africa, Asia, America, Europe, by a happiness I don't understand myself." *Op. cit.*

11. He links it with his childhood terror at the flooding of his house by the rising water of the Seine.

12. *Fragments of a Journal,* pp. 117, 134, 147.

IONESCO'S CLASSICAL ABSURDITY

by Roy Arthur Swanson

Eugène Ionesco says he was astonished (*tout étonné*) to hear his audience laugh during a performance of *The Bald Soprano*.[1] He claims to have thought that he had produced the "tragedy of language."[2] He seems not to have thought of the play as a true comedy. Whether or not his displeasure as expressed in "My Critics and I" is real, he appears seriously enough to believe that a tragic character is real, one who does not change but breaks, and that comic characters do no exist as people.[3] He appreciates Aeschylus, Sophocles, and Shakespeare (especially *Hamlet, Othello,* and *Julius Caesar*), and confesses to have been bored by Molière.[4] Aeschylus and Sophocles wrote true tragedies. By "true" we may understand "integral" or "unmixed." Molière produced comic characters, but his predisposition was to mix the tragic with the comic. Shakespeare wrote tragedies which included substantial elements of comedy—for example, the humor of character (the comic Rosencrantz, Guildenstern, and Polonius) and situation (the encounter of Cinna, the poet, with the Roman citizens). Ionesco and his kindred absurdists write tragedies at which audiences laugh; that is to say, they write genuine tragicomedy.

Tragicomedy is best defined as a drama which *blends* tragic and comic elements; as a blend, tragicomedy is a compound, not an admixture, of these elements. Among handbook compilers, M. H. Abrams has joined Dan S. Norton and Peters Rushton in calling *The Merchant of Venice* a tragicomedy because it presents a severely serious situation which ends happily.[5] But the same is true of Aeschylus' *Eumenides* or Sophocles' *Philoctetes.* In *The Merchant of Venice,* and in the *Eumenides* or the *Philoctetes,* tragic and pleasant elements are coextensive; they are not blended: they can be distinguished as separate constituents. In a play in which the threat of disaster is happily averted at the

last, the threat and the aversion of the threat are separate constituents. In what is properly called tragicomedy, the threat and
the aversion of the threat would be one and the same thing, a
unity which is, in fact, intimated in the peripeteia of Greek
tragedy. But in peripeteia the unity is always ironically incomplete; there is always something of which the agonist is unaware;
so far as the audience is concerned, it is no unity at all because
the audience is aware of all the constituent circumstances. In
Beckett's *Endgame,* by way of comparison, Hamm lives under
the threat of Clov's departure, and Clov's threat is indistinguish-
able from the aversion of this threat. He cannot do other than
threaten to leave, nor can he do other than remain. His leaving
would be a disaster for Hamm. His very remaining is his threat
to leave, and his threat to leave is his stasis. The last scene in
Endgame is a tableau of this stasis. In *The Merchant of Venice*
tragedy surrenders to comedy; in *Endgame* tragedy is comedy.

There are at least three different definitions of tragicomedy:
(1) a drama which *blends* tragic and comic elements, (2) a drama
which *includes* tragic and comic elements, and (3) a drama in
which tragedy is averted. Marvin T. Herrick concludes his long
study of tragicomedy with an example of the second definition.[6]
Both the second and third definitions can obtain either to plays
which are properly called tragedies or to plays which are properly
called comedies. The first definition obtains exclusively to what
must be called true tragicomedy—for example, a play like *Waiting
for Godot,* which is properly identified by Beckett in his English
translation of *En attendant Godot* as a tragicomedy in two acts.
In *Waiting for Godot* the tragic elements and the comic elements
are one and the same, an identity which is featured in many
scenes from the comedies of Charlie Chaplin. Vladimir and
Estragon desire the arrival of Godot. The desire is unrelievedly
frustrated. The frustration is comic; it evokes laughter from the
audience. In tragedy the nature of the desire would change in
consequence of its patent failure of fulfillment. In comedy the
desire would be satisfied in some degree, if not fully. In tragicomedy the unchanged desire and its reiterated frustration present an absurdity which, when seen as such, becomes humorous
indeed. The theatre of the absurd makes tragicomedy conform
to its proper denotation and definition, that is, to definition 1.

This is the definition toward which Johann Elias Schlegel
tends in *Gedanken zur Aufnahme des dänischen Theaters* (1747):

as Karl S. Guthke summarizes, "What [J. E. Schlegel] talks about is no longer a succession or juxtaposition of the emotions a-roused by the comic and the tragic but an indissoluble fusion of the two in such a way that they do not weaken each other, but rather throw light upon each other and, thereby, even intensify each other."[7]   What is wrong in Guthke's summary is the idea that two genres *in fusion* can continue to affect *each other:* genres in indissoluble fusion are made *one,* and there is no *other;* the error is due to J. E. Schlegel's inconclusiveness, but it is ag-gravated by Guthke's failure to challenge the inexact terminol-ogy. Guthke notes that Johann Adolf Schlegel (1751) and Les-sing, "less than a generation later," concur in the idea "that it was not beyond human aesthetic sensibilities to view one and the same object in diametrically opposed moods at one and the same time."[8]   Here, again, the cognizance is actually not of one genre created from the blending of two, but of two genres in undissolved mixture; and J. A. Schlegel's image of viewing "an event on stage with one weeping and one laughing eye"[9] is ap-propriate to such an admixture. Tragicomedy, though, should bring a viewer's *two* laughing eyes to a tragic event on stage. Ionesco may have been astonished to *hear* laughter, but we ought not to surmise that he expected to hear *weeping* (or, for that matter, both laughing and weeping). Ionesco's Father Robert, in *Jack, or the Submission,* says that the word "heart" softens him in one eye and makes him cry in the other two. Father Jacques' raction is "it's the truth!" A little later Father Jacques says that truth has "only" two sides (*deux faces*), "but it's the third side that is the most important." The third side is the mid-dle or mean by which the *deux faces* are integrated—the tragic and comic *faces,* for example, of *picassien* freakishness; Ionesco notes that *Roberte était monstrueuse, cepedant belle,* "Roberte was monstrous, yet at the same time beautiful": she had three *visages,* like a Far Eastern female deity, with "four eyes, three noses, three mouths" and with nine fingers on one hand. "Only when both directions in the heightening of effect are integrated," says Guthke in his own right, "can we speak of the complex and yet simple phenomenon of the tragicomic."[10]   He blunts this excellent point about integration, however, by adding that, in tragicomedy, "the comic and the tragic are identical and *mutual* conditions of *each other*" (*my emphasis*) and by bringing the one-laughing-and-one-weeping-eye to the first two acts of Albee's *Who's Afraid of Virginia Woolf?*[11]   Yet Guthke, with apparent reluctance, makes the precisely valid critical observation when he writes, "Paradoxically [...], one can speak only of that Ionescan 'comic' which, as an intuitive perception of the absurd and unendurable, is the same as the Ionescan 'tragic'."[12]

In Ionesco's *The Walker on Air* (or, *A Stroll in the Air: Le Piéton de l'air*) a bomb destroys the home and lives of the principals, who are then transported into the anti-world. John Bull, the classical Coryphaeus, then asks the Small Boy what he wants to be. The Small Boy says he wants to be a bombardier. The passage is humorous, not in spite of its tragic coloring, but because of it. Ionesco's anti-world, like Nabokov's Anti-Terra, is the real world of human desires and motives, the world in which laughter at tragedy is no longer repressed. It is the world viewed by the Marquis de Sade with his inversion (not perversion) of erotic values; the "inversion" is actually a reversion—a conscious reversion to primitive sensibility with no loss of sophisticated cruelty. Ionesco calls for a landscape ambiance which is dreamlike, as though produced by an *artiste primitif*. It is the Freudian world of the Unconscious exposed to and apprehended by the Conscious. When John Bull shoots and "kills" the two children, the tragedy is akin to that of the Euripidean Medea's slaughter of her two children; but in the anti-world, the real world, which Marthe wants not to accept as the real world ("Ce n'est pas vrai [...].") , the tragedy is humorous. The judge in the Tribunal which condemns Mme. Bérenger is terrifying in stature but comic in aspect (with, possibly, a large doll's head atop his red robe). The audience can laugh here at tragic terror. The Ionescan comic and the Ionescan tragic are identical. Ionesco is concerned, though, that his audience attend, not simply to humor, but to the humor of tragedy. This attention should be born and nurtured through an appreciation of Ionesco's classical antecedents in, specifically, Greek tragedy.

From Greek tragedy one learns how to adjust to the absurdity of human life defeated by its universal environment. The adjustment is a serious matter and it produces dignity. From Greek comedy one learns how to laugh at certain indignities. From the theatre of the absurd one learns that laughter at the indignities imposed upon men by the absurdity of human life completes the adjustment to this absurdity. Ionesco's New Tenant, for example, maintains a dignity beneath the barrage of the caretaker's self-serving chatter and beneath the immense heaps of furniture which all but buries him as it moved into his new quarters. Absurdly, the indignities to which he is sub-jected are made up of two factors by means of which men pur-sue dignity, oral expression and material acquisition. Ionesco's audience laughs at the tragic affront to human dignity which is effected by factors of the human quest for dignity.

Adjustment, to *l'homme absurde*, is a matter of balance, an achievement of equilibrium. A man achieves equilibrium when he understands that he cannot have what he wants. This under-standing does not eliminate his wanting; instead, it puts his desire in its proper perspective. He continues to want and to strive for what he wants, but he no longer presumes that his wants are attainable. Why struggle to fulfill desires which cannot be ful-filled? Why attempt to bring the Sisyphean rock to rest atop the hill? Why fight like a Hector against an Achilles who is bound to win? Why exert oneself in an endeavor to realize unrealizable ideals? Why, finally, live if one must die? One cannot cease to desire, given his rejection of suicide; consequently one cannot really give up the struggle to fulfill his desire. One cannot defeat death, but one is alive to the degree that he attempts to defeat death; and he is adjusted in proportion to his awareness that his attempts are ultimately futile; moreover, he completes and sus-tains his adjustment in his ability to laugh at the ultimate futility of his efforts. Murray Krieger wisely characterizes the vision of tragedy as a confrontation with nothingness.[13] Tragicomedy provides the same thing with a sense of humor. When Bérenger, the Walker on Air, reports his apocalyptic view of the physical, psychological and moral universe, he reveals that beyond all modes of existence there is nothing: "Rien. Après, il n'y a plus rien, plus rien que les abîmes illimités...que les abîmes"; and the play concludes with Marthe's wistfully Candidean thoughts of gardens—of a restoration of some kine of balance.

Every Greek tragedy—or, at least, each of the extant Aes-chylean and Sophoclean tragedies—is imbued with balance. In each, a protagonist who presumes to be more than he is or to know more than he does is forced to shed his presumption and to suffer its effects. His "flaw" is his presumption, a natural symptom of human imperfection. His "fall" is his awakening, his moment of awareness. In his presumption he is off balance. In his awareness he has suffered a painful resumption of balance. Equilibrium results from his acceptance of resumed balance after his painful exclusion from the presumption of imbalance. To put this another way: when a man wants what he cannot have, he becomes unbalanced in presuming that he *has* or *can get* what he wants; he regains his balance in the terrible realization that he can only strive vainly for what he wants. This realization is expressed by Camus in his notion of becoming and remaining aware of the absurd.

Sophocles' Oedipus wans to escape his fate: patricide and maternal incest. He becomes unbalanced when he assumes that he has escaped his fate. He "falls" as he learns that he has already suffered his fate. He recovers from his fall and fully resumes his balance when he accepts the truth of what he has learned. He retains his awareness of this truth for the rest of his life. The balance that he achieves is reflected in the construction of both *Oedipus Tyrannus* and *Oedipus at Colonus.* At the beginning of *Oedipus Tyrannus,* the young king is at the height of his good fortune: he is an attractive and beloved sovereign; he has a beautiful queen; he has great wealth; he is physically sound. There are only two clues to the fact that all this material prosperity and happy perfection are no more than semblances. The first clue is the name "oedipus" itself: "swollen foot" is a reminder of imperfection. The second clue is the mysterious plague that is decimating Thebes. At the play's end, when the name "oedipus" is fully explicated and the cause of the plague is known, the young king is an ugly and detested sovereign; he has no queen; he is dispossessed of his wealth; and he is physically mutilated. Viewing the play as a whole, we see a balance of extremes in its beginning and ending.

A similar balance of extremes is worked out in the *Oedipus at Colonus.* At the beginning of the play Oedipus is in a state of degradation. With each episode his spiritual stature increases. At the end of the play he is exalted as a charismatic patriarch. Bérenger, as the patriarch in *The Walker on Air* (= *A Stroll in the Air*), is a walker on earth in the first half of the play, and he graduates to air-walking in the second. In a sense, there is a balance of extremes in the earth-air differential; but Bérenger equates machineless flight with swimming, walking, sitting and standing. In his own person he nullifies the extremism of air-walking. More significantly, he remains a source of wisdom throughout the play, whether he is expatiating upon life for the Journalist in the opening scenes or is doing so for his family and the others in his presence in the closing scenes, not to mention his edifying remarks on the nature of the anti-world in mid-play. His intellectual stature is constant. This kind of balance is that of a single mean, instead of that of two extremes; but it is balance.

Greek tragedies, exemplified by the Oedipus plays, effect balance by presenting a movement from one extreme to another. Absurd drama effects balance by presenting a changeless mean. Ionesco's *The Bald Soprano* opens and closes with the same dialogue.[14] There is, as in other of Ionesco's plays, a classical beginning-middle-end, or tripartite, structure; but all three parts of the structure exhibit the same tragedy of language—its invalid service as a means of communication, or, more profoundly, its destruction of that communication which it is presumed to serve. The first eight scenes, centering on the Smiths and Martins, are balanced by the last two (or three, if we take the repetition of scene 1 as "scene 12"); and in between are the three scenes which center on the Fire-captain. In each of the three parts language fails in the same way—that is, it fails to establish communication—although it is directed in different channels: conversations, reminiscences, exposition (e.g., "*MARY, entering:* I am the maid."), greetings, deduction (the Martins' discovery that they are married), reaction to stimuli (the clock's striking and the doorbell's ringing), fables, puns, verse, epigrams, proverbs, alliteration, homoioteleuton, assonance, vowels, consonants, shouting, repetition, emphasis, and the general juxtaposition of two different languages (French and English). The beginning, middle and end are the same, in that there is no progrssion: language gets nowhere. The situation is epitomized by Mary's laughter-tears-smile sequence ("*MARY, éclate de rire. Puis elle pleure. Elle sourit.*"), in which laughter and weeping become a single action; Mary's smiling after her laughter and tears is, in effect, a smiling *at* them, and the three-part action is an epitome of tragicomedy. Likewise, the comedy of Mrs. Smith's telling her husband that their two-year-old daughter is named Peggy (or the Martins' discovery that they share the same bed and the parentage of the two-year girl, Alice) is tragic in its implications; and the absurd implications themselves evoke laughter.

The Lesson opens and closes with the arrival of a female Student whom the Professor, in his attempt to elucidate philology, will stab to death. The weapon may be either real or imagined. If it is an imaginary knife, we may understand that it is the word "knife" which causes the death of the girl. At first the student tends to intimidate the professor; as the scene develops, the professor rises to intimidate the student. The professor tries to teach the girl the differences between addition and substraction; he belies his instruction by proving the two processes to be the same when he, by *subtracting* her from the living, *adds* her to the corpses of her predecessors. The girl can memorize but cannot reason; the professor can reason but only from erroneous premisses. The channel of language in *The Lesson* is instruction; and, as a means of communication, it fails as severely as the many channels in *The Bald Soprano* do. Language enables neither the student to learn nor the professor to teach. The professor cannot learn that he is unable to teach. He knows the tragedy of language: "Of themselves, words, filled with meaning and weighted down by their import, fall and always sink and die in the end." He does not know that he is part of this tragedy and that he is as much a victim of words as words are of themselves. His absurd efforts to offset the tragedy of language evoke laughter. He remains ignorant of the fact that he is attempting to extricate himself from this tragedy. Ignorance, manifest in both the student and the professor, is, in *The Lesson*, a changeless mean.

Beckett's tragicomedy, *Waiting for Godot,* illustrates the same kind of changeless mean. Oedipean imperfection, for example, is represented in *Godot* by Estragon's visibly swelling foot in Act One, and in Act Two by his injuring his foot as he kicks Lucky. That is, Estragon's foot pains him in both acts. Oedipus has to be reminded of his once-injured foot; Estragon is constantly aware of his injured foot. The tragic agonist comes into an awareness of the absurd; the tragicomic agonist sustains an awareness of the absurd. Oedipus' foot is a symbol of his tragedy; it does not evoke laughter. Estragon's foot, equally a symbol of his tragedy, does evoke laughter.

In all respects, Ionesco's *Walker* (= *Stroll*) and Beckett's *Godot* realize that tragicomic ideal which Eugene M. Waith assigns to the invention of Fletcher: "not a mechanical combination of the attributes of tragedy and comedy but a subtle fusion in which each loses its identity."[15] I fail to see that the subtle fusion is evinced in any of the Beaumont-and-Fletcher plays. These regularly correspond to either definition 2 or definition 3

above. Fletcher himself is explicit in the matter: "A tragie-
comedie is not so called in respect of mirth and killing, but in respect it wants deaths, which is inough to make it no tragedie, yet
brings some neere it, which is inough to make it no comedie:
which must be a representation of familiar people with such
kinds of trouble as no life be questiond, so that a God is as law-
ful in this as in a tragedie, and meane people as in a comedie."
Yet, from this statement, which forms part of Fletcher's summary of *pastoral* tragicomedy, Waith infers Fletcher's advocacy
of the subtle fusion.[16] The Beaumont-and-Fletcher plays are,
in the main, amalgams of four generic constituents—tragedy,
comedy, satyr-play, and pastoral drama.

Waith cites Guarini to better purpose.[17] *Il pastor fido e il
Compendio della poesia tragicomica* explicitly asserts the difference between tragicomedy and tragedy or comedy and insists
that tragicomedy is a genre independent of tragedy and comedy.
But Guarini, in defending his pastoral tragicomedy *cum satyro*,
invokes classical tragicomedies (Euripides' *Cyclops* and Plautus'
Amphitryo) which again correspond to definitions 2 or 3 above.
He notes that his classical models include varying degrees of both
tragic and comic elements: the *Cyclops* has a preponderance of
tragic elements, and the *Amphitryo* is manifestly more comic
than tragic. He explains the difference between tragedy and
tragicomedy as consisting in their aims: the end of tragedy is
catharsis; the end of tragicomedy is the tempering of terror by
laughter. The constituents, terror and laughter, nonetheless remain separate in Guarini's theory and, so far as I can determine,
in his practice. For all his subtlety of analysis, Guarini is essentially in accord with Tirso de Molina, who in *Cigarrales de Toledo*
defends tragicomedy as an ingenious mixture of tragedy and
comedy, producing from both genres a delightful third type of
drama which participates in the nature of each, that reflects both
the variation and constancy of Natural species.

Tirso anticipates Dr. Johnson, whose strictures against the
infelicitous confusion of tragic with comic elements are qualified
by his recognition of the tragicomedian's special role: "It ought
to be the first endeavor of a writer to distinguish nature from
custom, or that which is established because it is right from that
which is right only because it is established; that he may either
violate essential principles by a desire of novelty, nor debar himself from the attainment of beauties within his view by a needless

fear of breaking rules which no literary dictator had authority to enact."[18]   Johnson defends Shakespeare's "mingled drama" by an "appeal open from criticism and nature."[19]   In other words, Shakespeare combined tragedy and comedy neither needlessly nor to any good purpose.

According to Dr. Johnson, "Shakespeare has united the powers of exciting laughter and sorrow not only in one mind, but in one composition. Almost all his plays are divided between serious and ludicrous characters, and, in the successive evolutions of the design, sometimes produce seriousness and sorrow, and sometimes levity and laughter."[20]   The telling phrase here is "divided between." Johnson does not claim for Shakespeare the subtle fusion of tragic and comic elements; he claims only a consistency of composition whose diverse ingredients are in accord with Nature. Compare this claim with Ionesco's belief that the comic is "une autre face du tragique" (*Les Nouvelles littéraires*, 1960).

Granting for the moment that many Renaissance and eighteenth-century dramatists elevated tragicomedy to a higher pinnacle than those occupied by tragedy and comedy; granting also the fact that pastoral tragicomedians like Fletcher and Guarini conceived tragicomedy as an ideal blend or fusion of tragedy and comedy; we are still at a loss to discover that ideal blend in any dramatic work prior to those of the theatre of the absurd, just as we are unable to concede the superiority of *The Faithful Shepherdess* and *Il Pastor fido* to Greek tragedy.

In *The Pattern of Tragicomedy in Beaumont and Fletcher* Waith reproduces the title page of the 1616 Ben Jonson folio. He comments: "From Tragicomedy's lofty position on the title page we may legitimately conclude that for some critics in 1616 this hybrid was the highest achievement of the drama. We see also that a definite relationship is assumed between Tragicomedy and certain other allegorical figures. This clothing, a combination of what Tragedy and Comedy wear, shows—what Fletcher implies—that the nature of tragicomedy is a blend of the natures of these two; at the same time the figure of Tragicomedy has an expression, a stance, a gesture all her own" (pp. 46-7). Waith disregards the fact that the Satyr and Pastor occupy positions that are also loftier than those of Tragedy and Comedy. I think it unlikely that we are here to conclude that satyr and pastoral plays were considered by some critics in 1616 to be higher achievements of drama than tragedy and comedy. Tragicomedy's clothing, moreover, is easily separated into tragic garb and comic garb; for example, Tragicomedy sports the crown, cape and sceptre of Tragedy and the tunic and footlets of Comedy. The constituents of Tragicomedy's apparel are easily distinguishable; the individual garments are not blended or subtly fused into something new.

This "something new" involves that which is hilariously sad or excrutiatingly funny, like the compulsive love-game between Jean and Marie in Ionesco's *Hunger and Thirst.* The absurdist comedian, Norman Frederick Simpson, has expressed his opinion that life is "excruciatingly funny."[21] In tragicomedy (definition 1) we are saddened by what regales us and amused by what depresses us In these ambivalences we achieve balance. The human comedy and the human tragedy are reconciled and suffer, not coextension, but confluence. Either kind of ambivalence is an absurd attitude; and, as Camus says, "If an absurd attitude is to be sustained, it must retain an awareness of its gratuitousness."[22]

Classical Greek tragedy anticipates the ambivalence produced by the theatre of the absurd. By means of excitement a Greek tragedy evokes calm. By means of horror it establishes serenity. The theatre of the absurd merely substitutes humor for calm and serenity. The Aeschylean Prometheus' cataclysmic descent to Tartarus and the Ionesco planet-explosion, with which the film scenario *Anger* concludes, are virtually identical comments on the failure of human intelligence; we are sobered by the first and regaled by the second, yet in each case we are granted the experience of balance through ambivalence.

The Greek tragedian, then, stabilizes awareness of the absurd by such structural balance as we have observed in *Oedipus Tyrannus* and *Oedipus at Colonus.* Aeschylus' *Oresteia* illustrates this balance equally well.

The *Oresteia* begins in darkness. There is a pinpoint of light as the watchman sees the torchlight in the distance. The trilogy ends in a flood of light as the Eumenides leave the sunlit upper world and carry torches into the darkness of the lower world itself. In the *Agamemnon* the bloodletting of the Trojan War is succeeded by the bloodletting of Agamemnon and Cassandra under the murder-knives of Clytemnestra and Aegisthus. In the *Choephoroe* the murderers are slain by Orestes. All of the blood revenges accomplished in the Trojan War and as a result of the curse on Atreus' house have been informed by ulterior motives of selfishness or ambition. Orestes alone has nothing to gain by his act of bloodletting. To slay his mother is to win no more than exile and the torments of remorse. His execution of Clytemnestra is an act exclusively in the interest of justice: the execution of one's mother requires the most uncompromising impartiality. He serves justice and accepts the personal consequences of his service—that is, disgrace and the horrors of conscience—and he is vindicated. In the *Eumenides* the bloodletting has come to an end. The movement from darkness to light is paralleled by the movement from injustice (indiscriminate bloodletting, in the name of justice but primarily or incidentally for personal gain) to justice (Orestes' trial).

These parallel movements, which effect a balance of extremes, are enhanced by supporting images; for example, the images of animals and nets. Animal imagery abounds in the *Agamemnon,* in which play the savagery of blood shed is animalistic; this imagery diminishes in the last two plays as light and justice succeed darkness and injustice. And, to be sure, the bestial Erinyes are tentatively domesticated. The net of injustice in which Agamemnon, like prey, is entangled and slain, comes to be disentangled by Electra and Orestes, who are compared by Aeschylus to corks upon a net, and is spread out in the sunlight after the execution of Clytemnestra and Aegisthus.

The focus of the trilogy is Orestes' act in the interest of justice. On one side of this act there is darkness, savagery, entanglement, and injustice. These negative elements are balanced, on the other side of Orestes' act, by light, docility, disentanglement, and justice. The effect of the trilogy as a whole is not of progression but of balance. When we center our attention upon the umbilicus of the trilogy, we are presented, not with the succession of darkness by light, but with the tense equipoise of light and darkness. In the human world the most that can be done in the interest of justice, or in the quest for justice, is to balance the good and the bad. This balance is implicit in Orestes' act, which is good because it avenges a wrong and bad because it is matricide. The absurd paradox is the commission of evil in the interest of good: the means are not justified by the end; it is the reverse: the means justify (make just) the end. In the same mode, Clytemnestra (evil) gives birth to Orestes (good); good is a product, not a justification, of evil.

We take note that in *Rhinoceros* Ionesco reverses the Oresteian pattern of animal imagery; he develops a proliferation of rhinoceroses. The reversal of pattern is not an essential change in dramatic structure; it is no more than a variation in usage. The play opens with one rhinoceros in a world of humans and ends, after Daisy's exit, with one human (Bérenger) in a world of rhinoceroses. The tragic balance between the worlds of non-conformity and conformity is achieved in classical Greek dramatic fashion but with humorous instead of grave effect. There is no definite movement from non-conformity to conformity; what we get is a rhinoceros-hided exposure of stultifying conformity as a changeless mean.

Leonard C. Pronko offers a deft comment on Ionesco's classical balance: "While *Amédée* begins with a feeling of oppression, heaviness, and opacity, and ends with the euphoria that is described metaphorically by Amédée's escape into the night sky, *The Killer* begins with an evocation of the radiant city in which all men seem destined to be happy, and ends in darkness, silence, death. The décor of the first act is suggested by lights, brightness, clarity; it seems a spring day. The last act shows us twilight, dusk, the nightfall of man's life."[23] We may add that one changeless mean, namely, the ignorance of reality and unreality, is common to both plays.

Of the thirty-one extant Greek tragedies those that begin happily end unhappily, and those that begin unhappily end happily.[24] In each the effect is that of balance, not of progression; and the movement in each is regularly toward a restoration or resumption of balance. The Greek audience would attend, not merely to the conclusion of the tragedy, but to the total work; it would leave the theatre with a perception of beginning, middle and end; the middle, so perceived, would emphasize or define the balance of beginning with end. One of the functions of the choral stasima was certainly to contribute to the audience's experience of stasis. John Bull gives humorous depth to this function in (= *A Stroll in the Air*). Greek tragedy presents the paradoxes of human life, those ridiculously unreasonable or incongruous factors which inform human life. A tragic hero comes into an awareness of these factors, and his audience is made to experience and sustain this awareness. Absurdity is bearable so long as its incompatible factors are recognized as such and are held in balance. Donald Watson, in the "Retrospect" to his translation of *Amédée, The New Tenant,* [and] *Victims of Duty* (New York: Grove Press, 1958), speaks of the "dynamic tension" of Ionesco's world: "a world in which the familiar and the unfamiliar, the logical and the illogical coexist but never correspond." Tension is the life of balance in Greek tragedy and Ionescan drama.

As an absurdist, Ionesco, like Beckett, establishes precisely that kind of balance which is manifest in Greek tragedy. The absurdist's balance is achieved by frustrating the actions and desires of characters, or by immobilizing characters and events, or by running actions and events in snake-swallowing-tail cycles. To the stasis of balance the absurdist playwright adds the element of humor as *une autre face du tragique.*

Ionesco's *Unhired Killer* (or, *The Killer: Tueur sans gages*) and Pinter's *The Dumb Waiter* are like the *Oresteia* in their presentation of the inevitability of killing. Aeschylus underscores the absurdity of killing as a necessary means of combatting killing. The denominator common to the act of injustice (the killing of Agamemnon and Cassandra) and the act of justice (the killing of Clytemnestra and Aegisthus) is the killing of a man and a woman. The difference between the two acts of killing lies only in their respective motives. In the Ionesco and Pinter plays the element of differentiation (motive) has been removed: killing, despite its inevitability, can be assigned no meaning whatsoever. In Greek tragedy the possibility of assigning meaning to actions and events is realized. In absurdist theatre the possibility exists but is not realized. In both forms of drama it is clear that meaning is arbitrary and gratuitous in view of the facts that it *can be assigned* and is therefore not absolute.

Greek tragedy regularly establishes a context of assigned meanings: *hubris* is destructive; killing indiscriminately or with ulterior motives is unjust; *aretê* is ennobling; etc. Humor is inappropriate to such a context. Absurdist theatre disestablishes contextual meaning, and actions and events become merely ridiculous; they become humorously tragic. They become so tragic that they are funny, like those in Stanley Kubrick's *Dr. Strangelove* (as compared, say, to the American filming of *On the Beach* or the Russian filming of *War and Peace*). They become tragicomic. In Ionesco's radiant city, Bérenger's ineptitude is comic (Chaplinesque, Kafkaesque, etc.); it is also tragic—not now-comic-and-now-tragic, but indissolubly comic *and* tragic. The antics of Pinter's Ben and Gus, as they strive to fill the orders from above, are tragicomic.

The theatre of the absurd is the theatre of humorous tragedy. It is drama in which the absurdity of human life, long ago recognized by the Geek tragedians, is seen for what it is and occasions laughter. Le Roi Jones' play, *The Toilet,* and Michael McClure's play, *The Beard,* are not absurdist: the tragedy which they touch upon is upheld by shock, violence, and sensation, but not by humor. Albee, Beckett, Grass, Ionesco, Pinter, and Simpson rarely fail to evoke the humor of tragedy. They and playwrights like them have given us the genre of absurd drama. If Jones, McClure, et al., have any historical antecedents, those antecedents must be Seneca, Hrosvitha, Kyd, and the Shakespeare of *Titus Andronicus.* The antecedents of the absurdists are Aeschylus and Sophocles.

Ionesco's *The King is Dying* (or, *Exit the King: Le Roi se meurt*), for example, is a Sophoclean as Anouilh's *Antigone.* Anouilh has written a "black play" which serves as a tragedy that defines tragedy: "[...] the conqueror, already conquered, alone in the midst of his silence [...]. Tragedy is honest. It is calm and certain [...]. There is tranquillity in tragedy [...]. Guilt is a matter of assigning roles! One person kills, another is killed, according to the role in which he is cast. Above all, tragedy is restful because it assures us that there is no longer any hope, foul hope."[25] Anouilh's *Antigone* is Sophoclean because it *expresses* the nature of Sophoclean drama. Ionesco's *King* is Sophoclean because it *reflects* the nature of Sophoclean drama. Anouilh's *Antigone* is not absurdist, as the *King* is: the *Antigone* is quite without tragic humor. The tragedy of Anouilh's Creon is not humorous; that of Bérenger I is very humorous.

The state ruled by Bérenger I and the state of his being are synthesized as the state of ignorance in a skillfully constructed pun on "l'État, c'est moi." Bérenger I takes note of his ignorance by saying that he is like a schoolboy who takes an examination without having done his homework, like a *comédien* (actor) who does not know his part on opening night, like a speaker who is led to the platform without knowing the first word of his speech or the character of his audience: "I do not know these people. I don't want to know them. I have nothing to say to them. What a state I'm in!" The guard announces that the king has made a reference to his state; and Marguerite comments, "Dans quelle ignorance."[26] Bérenger I then rushes to the window to cry out to the people, to the world, that he is going to die, that he must die; but no one pays attention.

The Bérenger of *Unhired Killer* (= *The Killer*) and the Bérenger of *Rhinoceros* are both aware of their own ignorance and are both frustratingly confronted with ignorance of ignorance. No one in the radiant city is ready or willing to stare death, the irrational killer, in the face. Bérenger alone, in the concluding scene, converses with the implacable killer. He faces the nothingness of death and recognizes the absurdity of life. In *Rhinoceros* Bérenger again stands alone. He is as ignorant of the force represented by the rhinoceros-disease as his *Killer* counterpart is of the force represented by the irrational killer. At the same time, each Bérenger is as aware of, respectively, the killer and the disease as he is ignorant of the forces inherent in them. At the conclusion of *Rhinoceros* it is Bérenger's awareness of his personal ignorance which prevents his becoming a rhinoceros, even though he could be disposed to become one.

A historical model for the Bérenger of *Unhired Killer* (= *The Killer* [1959]) might be Alphonse Marie Bérenger (1785-1866), the great lawyer who made a career of advocating reforms in criminal law and seeking the institution of criminal rehabilitation. A fitting model for the Bérenger of *Rhinoceros* (1960) could be Bérenger de Tours, a non-conformist theologian (c. 1000-1088), whose concerted attacks on the doctrine of transsubstantiation won him the condemnation of the high church, to which he managed never completely to capitualte. The Bérenger of *The King is Dying* (= *Exit the King* [1962]) may call to mind Bérenger I, king of Italy (898-924) and emperor of the West (915-924), who was assassinated at Verona. But the literary model for all of these Bérengers and for the Bérenger of *The Walker on Air* (= *A Stroll in the Air* [1963]) is best identified as the Sophoclean Oedipus, who learned that he did not know, intensified his awareness of his not knowing, and then became the patriarchal teacher of those who did not know that they did not know. This is the movement of Sophocles' Theban cycle, with its extremes of *hubris* and *aretê;* and it is the movement of Ionesco's Bérenger cycle, with its changeless mean of ignorance.

In his use of animals as effective symbols of ignorance, Ionesco is, again, like Aeschylus, whose Oresteian world of darkness (ignorance) is infused with the animal imagery we have noted. Ionesco equates the killer with people's indifferent ignorance of the killer by having Bérenger call him monkey, tiger, mule, hyaena, and cur. The rhinoceros, likewise, represents both ignorant conformity and the state of being unaware of ignorant conformity. There is, incidentally, a striking parallel to animalism-as-ignorance in Matthew Arnold's citation of Joseph Joubert: "Ignorance, which in matters of morals extenuates the crime, is itself, in intellectual matters, a crime of the first order." He goes on to refer, figuratively, to "our implacable enemies, the *Church and State Review* or the *Record*,—the High Church rhinoceros and the Evangelical hyaena."[27]   William Inge's motion-picture scenario, *All Fall Down,* outlines the fatal effects of noncommunication that is symptomatic of ignorance; the disease and its cause are united in the central figure, a willfully indifferent rake named Berry-Berry (cf. beri-beri, and seeds or fruit of destruction) and nicknamed "the old rhinoceros."

The imagery of ignorance in *The King is Dying* (= *Exit the King*) is Sophoclean again. Ignorance is manifest in the death-counsel given the king by his two wives and his doctor. Bérenger I appears initially as a headstrong, youthful Oedipus. The very first physical indication of his moribund condition is the pain in his legs. Like Beckett's Oedipal Estragon, he has foot pains; and he limps. When the Tiresian doctor tells him that he is to die, he behaves at first with the same impatience and outrage that Sophocles' Oedipus directs to Tiresias. Gradually Bérenger I accepts the fact of his death, but not without rebellion and an increased love of live. As he stares death in the face and resists death by living as fully as he can, he achieves a superiority to his two wives and his doctor, each of whom tries vainly to inject scientific or philosophical meaning into the king's death. But science and philosophy are ultimately no more than disguises of the facts that life is life, that death is death, and that every living man is mortal. The king sees through the disguises and, like Oedipus disappearing among rocks,[28] he fades away in a mist.

The doctor is a surgeon and a bacteriologist; but he is also an astrologist and an executioner: science cancels itself out in its inevitable service to quackery and death. Marguerite and Marie, the two queens, serve death in their respective attempts to reconcile death with life. Juliette, the maid and nurse, serves death by failing to see the sublimity of life in even the most menial tasks. Bérenger I alone refuses to serve death. The others, who think they uphold the spirit of man by their various interpretations of literal life, are no better than the guard, who takes everything literally. Juliette says that life is not pretty ("La vie n'est pas belle"), and the king answers, "It is life" ("Elle est la vie").

Sophocles' Oedipus and Ionesco's Bérenger are both, to use a worn-out but accurate phrase, everyman figures. Both are toppled from presumption to a painful awareness of the essential unhappiness and absurdity of human life. Both are conquered by the mystery of death after tenacious resistance to death and futile struggles to solve its mystery, which tenacious resistance and futile struggles are not obscured by ignorance of death's irresistibility or by the futility of struggle.[29]

The Bérenger cycle holds up life as death's joke. Ionesco's antidote to the fear of death is laughter at its joke. Black comedy makes jokes about death, but it does not show that life is death's joke; moreover, its true character, like that of sick comedy, is unabashed tastelessness. The "theatre of cruelty," whose chief practitioners are Antonin Artaud and Jean Genet, exposes the sickness of conventional morality; it does not present everyman caught up in the ridiculously humorous struggle of life against death. Death's joke on everyman is a prime subject of Ionescan theatre, which sets the tragicomic pace of the theatre of the absurd.

My singling out tragicomedy as the distinctive characteristic of the theatre of the absurd has involved an acceptance of (1) the concept of the tragicomic and (2) the existence of the theatre of the absurd. I have noted three varieties of the concept of tragicomedy and have related the first of these to the theatre of the absurd. My agrument has been that Ionesco's absurdist plays, like those by Beckett, Adamov, Pinter, et al., present a view of human life that coincides with the view presented in classical Greek tragedy and that the theatre of the absurd is itself the recreation of Greek tragedy in a comic milieu.

The idea of a "theatre of the absurd" has been investigated by two distinguished critics: Martin Esslin, whose argument for its existence I find conducive to an understanding of Ionescan drama as tragicomedy (definition 1), and Lionel Abel, to whom the phrase in quotation marks is a *flatus vocis.*

Esslin's *The Theatre of the Absurd* is "an attempt to define the convention that has come to be called the Theatre of the Absurd; [...] to show that this trend, sometimes decried as a search for novelty at all cost, combines a number of very ancient and highly respectable traditional modes of literature and theatre; and [...] to explain its significance as an expression—and one of the most representative ones—of the present situation of Western man."[30]   In my opinion, Esslin succeeds in his attempt; but where he discovers elements common to this theatre and a host of other modes I prefer to recognize this theatre as a re-creation of Greek tragedy, which, devoid of assigned values and meanings, stands as the real creation of tragicomedy.

Esslin's "definition" of absurdist theatre, is, I believe, too broad and indiscriminate.   Although I consider his book far more valuable and informative than Lionel Abel's *Metatheatre,* I agree with Abel in this section of his criticism: "Esslin maintains that there is a particular spiritual crisis, and that a certain kind of dramatic art has been produced in order to express it; but he cannot maintain, then, that forms of theatre like those being produced now long antedated the crisis. Yet in a chapter entitled 'The Tradition of the Absurd,' Esslin ranges through past history for prototypes of the new kinds of plays now being written. The mimes of the Middle Ages, the court jesters, the clowns of Shakespeare, the harlequinades which entered into the British music hall and American vaudeville, the Commedia dell'Arte, the nonsense verse of Lear and Lewis Carroll are all called on to account for the character of specifically modern works, which character, in turn, is supposed to be due to a special contemporary predicament."[31]   But Abel, smarting from Esslin's negative reaction to his "Samuel Beckett and James Joyce in *Endgame*"[32] prefaces the passage just quoted with claims that "there was not and that there is no such thing now" as a theatre of the absurd.

"Metatheatre" is Abel's term for plays written by authors who are inclined to write tragedy but find it unadaptable to their subject and expression or untenable by their talents. A-mong such authors he includes Shakespeare (except for *Macbeth*), Calderon, Schiller, Genet, Beckett, and Brecht. The "basic postulates" of "metatheatre" are "(1) the world is a stage and (2) lie is a dream." Presumably "metatheatre" exposes and intensifies the theatricality and unreality of life. I believe that this exposition and intensification are characteristic of Ionesco's plays, most especially of *The Walker on Air* (= *A Stroll in the Air*) and *The King is Dying* (= *Exit the King*), and that this theatricality informs absurdist drama.[33]

Abel is as indisposed to admit the existence of tragicomedy as he is to admit either the existence of the theatre of the absurd or the existence of modern tragedy. He objects to "tragicomedy" as a "self-contradictory" term which implies "two different kinds of plays, amalgamated no one knows just how. If it said: by the 'genius' of the playwright—is that not asking the playwright to do the critic's task?" Hardly. The critic's task is to recognize such amalgamation where it appears—as, for example, in Ionescan drama—and to recognize a playwright's genius; he is then in a position to speculate as intelligently as he can upon how the genius accomplishes a given task and to introduce his readers to the excitement and importance of this speculation.

In order to define his viewpoint, Abel is obliged to eliminate "tragedy" as a term generally applicable to Shakespearean, Spanish, and post-Shakespearean drama, to eliminate "tragicomedy" as a valid critical designation, and to eliminate "the theatre of the absurd" as a term indicative of a particular trend in modern drama. It is wiser, I think, to be more conservative and to concede the existence of Shakespearean and Spanish tragedy, however different from Greek tragedy they may be; to investigate the concept of tragicomedy; and to continue the attempt to define the theatre of the absurd. Abel arbitrarily coins the term "metatheatre" in an effort to pass his opinions off as discoveries. Esslin, with more critical acuity, notes how writers like Ionesco make use of the term "absurd" and proceeds to relate the concept of the term to the theatre in question.[34]

The concept of "the absurd," as descriptive of the human condition, is the undeniable occasion for much thought and speculation on the part of twentieth-century philosophers, existentialists, novelists, and dramatists. Camus qualifies his ideas of the absurd with references to Greek thought and Greek tragedy, especially to the Sophoclean Oedipus. Ionesco—with Beckett, Pinter, and others—effectively, if not deliberately, re-creates the mode of Greek tragedy and makes it an object of humor. The re-created mode, so translated, is a realization of the tragicomic ideal abortively attributed by Eugene M. Waith to the seventeenth-century John Fletcher.

I cannot read Chekhov's *Peasants* without laughing at the tragedy of Chikildyeyev. I am amused, not by a man's death, but by the ridiculous joke that death makes of life. This episode, like Ionesco's *The Chairs,* is a *farce tragique.* I cannot read Gogol's *Dead Souls* without reacting to the humor of its tragedy as Adamov does in his adaptation of that "poem" to the absurdist stage. Edward Albee's George and Martha make a hilarious game of their tragedy, not by deluding themselves, but by refusing to delude themselves into taking the game, whose rules they refuse to break, as anything but a game. Peter Nichols' Bri and Sheila see the humor of Joe Egg (doing nothing; zero; meaninglessness) and manage thereby to live with it. Bri tells Freddie: "Living with Sheila, you get to welcome death. With life burgeoning in every cranny."[35] The vegetable daughter of Bri and Sheila is called "Joe," a boy's name, and is, as a vegetable, neither male nor female, and, as a human, neither alive nor dead. A day in the life of Joe Egg is, as the original title (restored to the 1972 film version) of the play states, a day in the death of Joe Egg. Ionesco's *The Future is in Eggs* portrays the hatching of meaningless existences (human lives) which are reducible to vegetable and mineral matter; eggs are hatched by Roberte as bankers, cooks, existentialists, chemists, etc., and are destined for omelettes in a confusion of identities. The meaninglessness of preserving the Caucasian race by hatching eggs to replace the dead is the tragedy of life itself. The humor of the tragedy is implicit in Beckett's poem, *Whoroscope,* in which Descartes contemplates eggs. Ionesco presents this tragedy as a farce. In *The Future is in Eggs, Who's Afraid of Virginia Woolf?,* and *Joe Egg* the tragedy of non-identity and meaninglessness is given humorous orientation. The same is true of Adamov's *Professor Taranne.* Oedipus in the modern world is still trying to find out who he is; he is still finding out that he is nothing but what he decided to say he is, that what he says he is has no metaphysical or transcendental meaning, and that all his actions are ultimately senseless and useless; but now he sees the joke (the "Joe Egg") of it. If the future is in eggs, there is nothing to look forward to except eggs.

David I. Grossvogel, in *Four Playwrights and a Postscript* (Ithaca: Cornell University Press, 1962), says, "In the theater, tragedy is absurd." True. But we ought to add that in Greek tragedy the absurd is *exposed* and in the theatre of the absurd it is *exposed to laughter.* Ionesco specifically calls our attention to classical Greek tragedy in his preoccupation with what we may call the theatre of the absurd; yet Grossvogel says that Ionesco "dismisses" classical tragedy, "terming it 'distinguished natural-ism'." Ionesco may also be cited as "dismissing" absurdism: "It has been said that I've been a writer of the absurd; the word is one of those that gain currency, that is in vogue now but later will not be. In any case, it is now vague enough no longer to mean anything and facilely to define everything. If, after some time, I have not been forgotten, there will be another word in currency, another accepted word, to define me and others without actually defining us."[36] Against dismissals of this kind we have to measure other of Ionesco's statements. "I have labeled my comedies 'anti-plays'," he says, " 'comic,' and my dreams 'pseudo-drama,' or 'tragic farces,' for, it seems to me, the comic is tragic and human tragedy is ridiculous. Nothing can be taken in complete seriousness or in complete levity by the modern critical mind. I have tried, in *Victims of Duty,* to blend the comic with the tragic; in *The Chairs,* the tragic with the comic, or, if you will, to pit the comic against the tragic so as to combine them in a new theatrical synthesis. But it is not a real synthesis because these two elements do not merge, they coexist in permanent opposition, they stand in contrast each to the other, each criticizing and denying the other; and in this way, thanks to this opposition, they manage to produce a dynamic balance, a tension."[37] This was written in 1958. Two years earlier he had said in an interview, "I recognized, after all, that I wanted to produce, not anti-theatre, but theatre. I hope I have rediscovered intuitively, in myself, the permanent mental make-up of the theatre. I am, after all, for classicism; that is the *avant-garde.*"[38] If Ionesco opts for classicism and dynamic balance (*équilibre*) and if, as I have noted at the beginning of this essay, he appreciates Aeschylus and Sophocles, then his "dismissal" of classical tragedy is nominal at best.

If he strives for a blend of comedy and tragedy and brings about a union of them in sustained tension, if he sees the comic as tragic and the human tragedy (*la tragédie de l'homme*) as ridiculous (*dérisoire*), then he is engaged in tragicomedy (definition 1), however tentative or apparent he may claim his synthesis to be. If the tragic amuses and the comic bemuses, as it seems to me they certainly do in the later plays (*Killer, Rhinoceros, King,* and *Walker* [= *Stroll*]), then the tension is the synthesis.

Ionesco's disclaimer of absurdism is of a piece with Heidegger's and Camus' disclaimers of existentialism. What history of modern existentialism would be complete without attention to Heidegger and Camus? What study of the theatre of the absurd would exclude Ionesco? The problem centers on a justifiable abhorrence of labels. Ionesco obviously dislikes even those labels (classicism, anti-, etc.) which he himself now and then attaches to himself and his work; labels and classifications are inhibitive to artistic endeavor. Unlike art, criticism is regularly in as much need of classifications and lables as science is. In *Findings,* Ionesco objects to the critic as *un homme de science* and reminds us that, even though literature itself may entail scientific methods, critical work is immediately dependent upon the work criticized.[39] As an artist—or, to use his word, a *créateur*—Ionesco is not alone in his aversion to criticism which tends to manipulate art instead of studying it. Criticism does go astray when, instead of defining its own classifications and labels as generic concepts, it uses these to define or pigeonhole the artist and his work. (It is with this in mind that I have attempted in this essay to clarify certain generic terms—tragicomedy, classical balance, absurdity, to be exact—and to identify classical absurdity as a recognizable element in Ionesco's drama. It is not my intent to pigeonhole Ionesco as *a* classical absurdist. I wish to suggest, however, that with what may be called classical absurdity Ionesco is among the most successful of those dramatists who, intentionally or not, have created true tragicomedy.)

Martin Esslin is far from satisfied with the application of his phrase, "the Theatre of the Absurd," as a definitive classification: "for what I intended as a generic concept, a working hypothesis for the understanding of a large number of extremely varied and elusive phenomena, has assumed for many people, including some drama critics, a reality as concrete and specific as a branded product of the detergent industry."[40] Esslin is no less appalled than Ionesco at the dramatist's being asked, "Do you agree with Martin Esslin that you belong to the school of the Theatre of the Absurd?" It seems to be the fate of effective generic terms that they come to be construed as specific or as definitive of schools or that they are misapplied in any number of ways. An ineffective term like "metatheatre" is in little danger of misapplication; e.g., Myron Matlaw's *Modern World Drama. An Encyclopedia* (New York: Dutton, 1972) includes an article on "Absurd, Theatre of the" but no mention of "metatheatre": it does, however, include a brief article on Abel as a playwright, while John Russell Taylor's *The Penguin Dictionary of Theatre* (see note 34) takes no notice of Abel at all.

Lèo Gilson Ribeiro, an unpretentious and searching critic, treats Ionesco—along with Kafka, Büchner, and Brecht (!)—as a chronicler of the absurd. He draws a parallel between Kafka's *Metamorphosis* and Ionesco's *Rhinoceros* as illustrative of an absurdity which is discernible in the classical Roman philosopher-poet Lucretius.[41]

Esslin, too, is focusing his attention upon chronicles of the absurd and not upon a school of the absurd, especially not upon a school established either by the dramatists he studies or by himself. The introduction to *The Theatre of the Absurd* includes pointed mention of Ionesco's sympathetic criticism of Kafka's absurdism in "The City Coat of Arms." Perhaps too pointed: "In an essay on Kafka, Ionesco defined his understanding of the term as follows: 'Absurd is that which is devoid of purpose... Cut off from his religious, metaphysical, and transcendental roots, man is lost; all his actions become senseless, absurd, useless'."[42] The "essay" is only a brief comment *en guise de post-face* (as it is called in *Notes and Counter-notes*); and the passage is only indirectly a definition of the term—without lacunae, it reads: *Est absurde ce qui n'a pas de but: et ce but final ne peut se trouver qu'au-delà de l'histoire humaine, c'est-à-dire lui donner sa signification. Qu'on le veuille ou non, ceci révèle le caractère profondément religieux de tout Kafka; coupé de ses racines religieuses ou métaphysiques, l'homme est perdu, toute sa démarche devient insensée, inutile, étouffante.* A less Procrustean translation is as follows: "That which has no goal is absurd:

and this final goal can be found only beyond history; it is that which must guide human history, that is, give it meaning. Whether one likes ir or not, this reveals the profoundly religious character in all of Kafka; man, cut off from his religious or metaphysical roots, is lost and all of his movement becomes senseless, vain and stultifying."[43]

Camus makes similar observations about Kafka and objects to the Kierkegaardian religious tone of *The Trial* and *The Castle*.[44] Both Ionesco and Camus present the religiously and metaphysically deracinated man who must adjust to the incontrovertibly non-existent "final goal." Ionescan adjustment amounts to a demystification of history which will restore to history, as demystified literature restores to literature, the "purity of its archetypes" and myths.[45] Demystification is tantamount to classicism: "[...] I am for classicism: that is the *avant-garde*. Discovery of forgotten archetypes which are immutable but are expressed in new ways: every true creator is classical... The *petit-bourgeois* is one who has forgotten the archetype in his preoccupation with the stereotype. The archetype is ageless."[46] Given Ionesco's appreciation of Aeschylus and Sophocles and given his attention to archetypes, we can conclude that by "classicism" he does not mean simply French classicism.

He recounts in *Findings* that he had once said, "If God exists, literature has no meaning; if God does not exist, the making of literature has no meaning," but that he has since come to believe that "God and literature can coexist; or even that the absence-of-God and literature can coexist." "But then," he adds, "what's the good of that? The precariousness of the universe is unacceptable."[47] These are the reflections of an absurdist, whether or not he calls himself one—an absurdist who has opted for classicism.

The detective (*le policier*) in *Victims of Duty* tells Nicolas d'Eu that he is faithful to Aristotelian logic and to his duty. "I do not believe in the absurd," he says; "everything is coherent, everything is subject to comprehension." The dective is a *petit-bourgeois* enmeshed in the stereotype. But so is Choubert, the interior of whose home is designated as *petit-bourgeois*. It is Choubert, not Ionesco, who "dismisses" classicism as "elegant detective drama, quite like naturalism" (*'théâtre policier distingué. Comme tout naturalisme'*): This is Grossvogel's mis-

leading "distinguished naturalism"). If any of the characters in
Victims of Duty speak for Ionesco, it is the "poet" Nicolas
d'Eu, whose name anagrammatically suggests "Ionesco" and
who, replying to the detective's statement that people ought to
write, says "No use. We have Ionesco and Ionesco, that's
enough."

Nicolas sees the contemporary theatre as enmeshed in stereotyped forms and in need of a psychology of antagonisms. He
conceives of an oneirical theatre in which the characters lose
their form in the formlessness of becoming and each personage is
less himself than someone else. According to Nicolas d'Eu [gène
Ionesco], the tragic is becoming comic and the comic is tragic.
Significantly, after Nicolas kills the detective he becomes less
himself than the detective as he assumes the detective's duty.
At the beginning of the play Choubert is momentarily less himself than an anticipation of Nicolas when he (Choubert) reminds Madeleine that "suggestions abruptly take on the appearance of rules, of strict laws." The play appeared at least eight
years before Martin Esslin's *The Theatre of the Absurd,* the
suggestions in which, to Esslin's displeasure, came to take on
the appearance of rules.

Choubert's vision of a magic city is dissolved in darkness.
Bérenger I's sensation that *his* existence is *all* existence transports neither him nor existence to a "final goal." Bérenger the
Walker's vision of all existence serves mainly to disclose that
there is nothing beyond existence. In these moments of Ionescan drama we are reminded of the coexistence of absence-of-
God and literature and of the unacceptable precariousness of an
absurd world.

Ionesco is explicit about his classicism but resists being
classified as an absurdist despite the obvious absurdist elements
in his theatre (and in the ruminations of *Findings*). Esslin calls
attention to the obvious absurdist elements in Ionescan theatre,
but writes, directly, next to nothing about Ionesco's classicism.
Indirectly, Esslin does provide an admirable *précis* of Ionesco's
classicism in his summary of the aesthetic "rule" of form-equals-
content (the emphases are Esslin's): "An examination of any of
the really successful works of the Theatre of the Absurd will
confirm this rule: the symmetry of Acts I and II of *Waiting for
Godot,* the rigid ritual structure of *The Blacks,* the movement

from repose to paroxysm and back to repose in *The Bald Soprano,* the inexorable accumulation of empty chairs in *The Chairs,* the strophic form of the duologues in *The Dumb Waiter,* are cases in point. Each play of this type has to find its *own,* rigidly formal pattern, which must inevitably arise from and express the *basic conception* of the play. Much of the tension and suspense in this kind of drama lies in the gradual unfolding of its formal pattern. Hence its formal pattern must embody the very essence of the action. And so, in the Theatre of the Absurd, form and content not only match, they are inseparable from each other."[48]

We have noted that Ionesco prefaces his declaration for classicism with his preference of "theatre" to "anti-theatre." This should not be taken as a rejection of the anti-play element in his first dramatic work. *The Bald Soprano* is an *anti-pièce* because its material, language, works against its own aims; the anti-play remains "theatre," however, (essentially classical theatre) because, in its form-content identity, it exposes the humorous tragedy of language.

Ionesco dislikes Brecht because he is "didactic and ideological," because he is elementary (*primaire*) instead of primitive, simplistic instead of simple, and because he is "himself the reflection, the illustration of an ideology." He admires Beckett because he is "essentially tragic."[49] His affinity with Beckett is nicely illustrated by Tom Bishop's report that Ionesco reacted to Beckett's being awarded the Nobel Prize by saying, "We really deserved it."[50] Beckett is tragic because, in his work, "it is the whole human condition which comes into play, not man in this or that society, nor man seen through and made over by a particular ideology which both simplifies and curtails his historical and metaphysical reality, the authentic reality within which man is integrated";[51] and Ionesco associates Beckett's *Endgame,* "a dramatic work which is called *avant-garde,*" with the lamentations of Job and with *the tragedies of Sophocles* and Shakespeare.[52]

Ionesco's insistence now upon the tragic character and now upon the comic character of his plays appears to be his method of opposing their being designated exclusively as one or the other of the stereotyped forms: "I have read the American reviews of [*Rhinoceros*] and have noted the consensus that the play was funny [*drôle*]. Well now, it is not funny; although it is a farce, it is chiefly tragedy";[53] "Ah! Molière! he is, to be sure, a master for us all—despite his realism... But when the old writers employ a mixture of the comic with the tragic their characters, in the end, do not come out as funny: the tragic gets the upper hand. In what I do, it is the contrary: they begin as comic, are tragic for a moment, and end in the comic or the tragicomic."[54]

The comic, Ionesco thinks, is "another aspect of the tragic," *une autre face du tragique,*[55] as I have pointed out above. This opinion corresponds with that of Plato's Socrates at the end of the *Symposium.* Ionesco, moreover, is something of a Socratic gadfly of the theatre: "One of the great New York critics complains that, after I have destroyed one orthodoxy without putting anything in its place, I leave him and the audience in the void. This is exactly what I meant to do. It is from this void that a free man must pull himself, alone, by his own strength and not by that of others."[56] Ionesco's free man, like the tragic (and absurd) hero, looks at nothingness without pretending that it is something, without deceiving himself into thinking that something is there.

Ionesco's free man, as tragicomic hero, *does* something—he rebels—in the face of nothingness; and laughter furthers his efforts and fulfills his action. Humor provides us with the only means we can have "of detaching ourselves from—but only after having recognized, assimilated and surmounted—our comico-tragic human condition, our existential *malaise*"; "logic is revealed in the illogicality of the absurd, of which one has gained awareness; laughter is unique in respecting no tabu and in precluding the establishment of new anti-tabu tabus; the comic is unique in giving us the strength to endure the tragedy of existence."[57] Amédée is absurd, not because poisonous mushrooms grow in the hero's living room and a fifteen-year-old corpse expands in geometrical progression, taking up all the space in the living quarters, but because Amédée is unable to do anything about the situation. Amédée Buccinioni, a *petit-bourgeois* playwright who has written only two lines in fifteen years,[58] manages to recognize the human condition for what it is, an absurd amalgam of vegetable existence and human death—of which "Joe Egg" is another version. He assimilates it to the weight of frustrating procrastination under which he fails effectively to work or struggle. He rises above it (literally, in the play) by *trying* at last to do something about it. Then, like Oedipus or Bérenger I, he vanishes.

Classicism, absurdism, and tragicomedy are at one in Ionescan drama. I have attempted to elaborate on Ionesco's classicism and tragicomedy and to relate these to what I believe Martin Esslin has rightly and astutely identified as the theatre of the absurd. Lionel Abel concedes that Ionesco "fits Esslin's formula"; specifically, he states that "only Ionesco" does so. Aside from the fact that Esslin concocts no "formula," Abel's remarks here have merit; and they would have been the more meritorious for having hit upon the affinity between Ionesco and Beckett. But it is true that in Esslin's study of the theatre of the absurd, Ionesco emerges as the exemplar; and of the individual dramatists considered in Esslin's book, Ionesco receives the most attention.

Ionesco, the absurdist playwright, is like Pär Lagerkvist, the cubist playwright, in that he discovers classicism, with its constants of balance, tension, primitivism, and archetypality, to be the vehicle and not the fellow-traveler of certain modes or genres. Lagerkvist's classicism incorporates cubism and tragedy; Ionesco's incorporates absurdism and tragicomedy. The two dramatists share an aversion to being classified by critics. In each case the aversion is qualified: Lagerkvist upholds classicism and virtually defines it as cubism; Ionesco is willing to be identified as a classicist. But Ionesco is not willing to be labeled as a dramatist limited to any one of the modes which contribute to his classicism—for example, to, comedy, tragedy, or absurdism. With proper qualification of the critical terms that bear application to Ionescan drama, it is feasible to conclude that Ionesco, well attuned to the absurdity exposed in Aeschylean and Sophoclean tragedy, has transmuted this exposure into true tragicomedy and has become the classic dramatist of the theatre of the absurd.

NOTES

1. To maintain the uniformity of translated Ionescan titles in this book
    I shall, throughout this essay, either use the titles of the Grove Press
    translations or supply the Grove Press titles in company with those
    title-translations for which my preference is particularly strong. I
    prefer to translate *La Cantatrice chauve* as *The Bald Cantatrice* but
    I shall use the Grove Press title instead. I strongly prefer *Unhired
    Killer* to Grove Press' *The Killer* for *Tueur sans gages; The King is
    Dying* to *Exit the King* for *Le Roi se meurt;* and *The Walker on Air*
    to *A Stroll in the Air* for *Le Piéton de l'air.* All translations from
    Ionesco's works are, in this essay, my own, except where otherwise
    noted, and are based on the Gallimard edition (Paris, 1954 [vol. I],
    1958 [vol. II], 1966 [vols. III, IV]) of Ionesco's *Théâtre* and on
    editions of other works as cited individually in the notes.

2. *Notes et contre-notes* (Paris: Gallimard, 1962), p. 65.

3. *Ibid.,* p. 160.

4. *Ibid.,* p. 7.

5. *A Glossary of Literary Terms* (New York: Holt, Rinehart and Win-
    ston, 1941; rev. 1961), *s.v.* "Tragedy."

6. "Tragicomedy, as the name implies, is a mixed drama utilizing both
    tragic and comic qualities." *Tragicomedy, Its Origin and Develop-
    ment in Italy, France, and England* (Urbana, Illinois: University of
    Illinois Press), p. 313 of the 1962 reprint.

7. *Modern Tragicomedy, An Investigation into the Nature of the Genre*
    (New York: Random House, 1966), p. 41.

8. *Op. cit.,* p. 43.

9. *Op. cit.,* p. 44.

10. *Op. cit.*, p. 59.

11. *Ibid.*

12. *Op. cit.*, p. 127.

13. *The Tragic Vision: Variations on a Theme in Literary Interpretation* (New York: Holt, Rinehart and Winston, 1960), pp. 14-16.

14. This mirror-repetition device is used by Jean Cocteau in *Orphée* (1926), in which scene 8B is an instant repetition of scene 8A; but the device here contributes to mirror imagery and does not constitute a changeless mean. The symmetrical scenes in Strindberg's *Till Damaskus I* (1900) are clearly kindred to Ionesco's dramaturgy, but not as manifestations of tragicomedy.

15. *The Pattern of Tragicomedy in Beaumont and Fletcher* (New Haven: Yale University Press, 1952), p. 44.

16. *Ibid.*

17. *Op. cit.*, pp. 46-9.

18. *Rambler*, no. 156.

19. *Preface to Shakespeare.*

20. *Ibid.*

21. Quoted in *London Daily Mail* (25 Feb. 1960), as noted by Martin Esslin in *The Theatre of the Absurd* (New York: Doubleday—Anchor Books ed., 1961), pp. 219, 329; rev. ed. 1969, p. 260.

22. "Une attitude absurde pour demeurer telle doit rester consciente de sa gratuité." *Le mythe de Sisyphe* (Paris: Gallimard, 1942: ed. augmentée), p. 137.

23. *Eugène Ionesco* (New York and London: Columbia University Press, 1965), p. 25.

24. *Oedipus Tyrannus* begins happily, with Oedipus at the height of his powers, and ends unhappily. *Oedipus at Colonus* and the *Oresteia* begin unhappily and end happily. It may be argued that *Oedipus at*

Colonus ends unhappily because Oedipus dies; but the play ends with Oedipus' elevation to grandeur and worshipful respect. He is, moreover, old and tired and ready to welcome a release from the responsibilities of life, although he shirks no responsibilities and is unremitting in his struggle against existential *malaise.* He constantly seeks out rocks and stones, the symbols of death in this play, and rests upon them; and at the end he disappears among the rocks.

25. The chorus in *Antigone* (1942), in *Nouvelles pièces noires* (Paris: Les Éditions de la Table Ronde, 1961), p. 161.

26. Marguerite's words parody the King's "dans quel état" and may be translated as "What ignorance [he's in]." The word-play connotes the following: the King and the state are in a state of ignorance; if the King *is* the state, he is ignorance personified. Ironically, unlike the professor in *The Lesson,* the King *knows* that he is futilely trying to extricate himself from the tragedy with which he is identified.

27. *Essays in Criticism, First Series,* I. *Re* Joubert and his *Pensées,* cf. Choubert in *Victims of Duty.*

28. See note 24 above.

29. Richard N. Coe is rewardingly informative on the theme of death in Ionesco's theatre; see *Eugène Ionesco* (1961; 2nd ed., rev., New York: Grove Press, 1968), esp. pp. 63-71 (First Evergreen Black Cat Edition, 1971).

30. *Op. cit.,* p. xii (rev. ed., p. xiv).

31. *Metatheatre* (New York: Hill and Wang, 1963), p. 142. "The Theatre and the 'Absurd'," pp. 140-6 of *Metatheatre,* appeared originally as a review of Esslin's book in *Partisan Review* (Summer 1962), pp. 454-9.

32. In Esslin, *op. cit.,* pp. 32-3 (rev. ed., pp. 46-7).

33. It may be unfair to adduce *Walker* (= *Stroll*) and *King,* which appeared almost concurrently with Abel's work, but they would hardly have caused him to change his mind about the existence of a theatre of the absurd. In any case, Abel actually does little more than observe that the playwrights, exclusive of Racine, from Shakespeare's time through recent times—the playwrights, that is, upon whom he focuses

his attention—do not honor the principles of Greek tragedy. For example: "Shakespeare and Calderon did not write tragedies; at least, they did not write good tragedies. (Shakespeare wrote one great one, *Macbeth;* Calderon, not even one.) What these playwrights did create was a new type of drama, one with very different assumptions from those of Greek tragedy, and with very different effects. Often they produced this characteristic and new form while intent on writing tragedy" (p. 77). Students of the drama are far more likely to acknowledge the existence of a theatre of the absurd than they are to agree with Lionel Abel that (1) Shakespeare did not write tragedies, (2) Shakespeare did not write good tragedies, and (3) Shakespeare wrote one great tragedy. Abel betrays a puzzling ignorance of Greek tragedy itself when he insists that the protagonists of Greek tragedy lack self-consciousness: "Now the Western playwright is unable to believe in the reality of a character who is lacking in self-consciousness. Lack of self-consciousness is as characteristic of Antigone, Oedipus, and Orestes, as self-consciousness is characteristic of Hamlet, that towering figure of Western metatheatre" (*ibid.*). If Aeschylus' Io, Agamemnon, and Orestes, if Sophocles' Oedipus, Antigone, Electra, Odysseus, and Neoptolemus—not to mention Euripides' Hecuba, Admetus, Agave, and Medea—have no consciousness of self, then "self-consciousness" needs a radically new definition.

34. Arnold P. Hinchliffe, in *The Absurd* (London: Methuen, 1969), accredits Esslin with the invention of the term "the Theatre of the Absurd" and with the contribution of the term to critical idiom. "No apology," he says, "is needed for following in Martin Esslin's footsteps" (p. vii). By comparison, "metatheatre" has failed as a catchword, and Abel's footsteps have left little imprint. Hinchliffe cites John Russell Taylor's concise article on the Theatre of the Absurd in *The Penguin Dictionary of Theatre* (1966), which states that "the central theme of the writers in the Theatre of the Absurd, most notably Samuel Beckett, Eugène Ionesco, Arthur Adamov, Jean Genet, and Harold Pinter," is "a state of metaphysical anguish" produced by humanity's plight of "purposelessness in an existence out of harmony with its surroundings." He also cites Kenneth Tynan's "very reasonable disquiet" with Esslin's plethora of "forebears of the Absurd," a complaint which is substantially the same as Lionel Abel's defensible objections to Esslin's "The Tradition of the Absurd" (see note 31 above).

35. *Joe Egg* (New York: Grove Press, 1967), p. 61.

36.   *Notes*, p. 194.

37.   *Ibid.*, p. 14.

38.   *Ibid.*, p. 110.

39.   *Découvertes* (Geneva: Albert Skira, 1969); see pp. 7-16.

40.   "The Theatre of the Absurd Reconsidered." *Reflections—Essays on Modern Theatre* (New York: Doubleday, 1969), p. 182.

41.   *Cronistas do absurdo* (Rio de Janeiro: J. Alvaro, 1964), p. 146.

42.   P. xix (rev. ed., p. 5).

43.   *Notes*, pp. 231-2. Ionesco's "postscript" appeared originally as "Dans les armes de la ville" in 1957 (*Cahiers Madeleine Renaud—Jean-Louis Barrault*).

44.   "L'Espoir et l'absurde dans l'oeuvre de Franz Kafka" (1942), *op. cit.*, note 22 above, pp. 167-85.

45.   *Découvertes*, pp. 115-16.

46.   *Notes*, p. 110.

47.   *Découvertes*, pp. 120-21.

48.   Art. cit., note 40 above, p. 190.

49.   *Notes*, pp. 113-4.

50.   "Ionesco on Olympus." *Saturday Review* (16 May 1970), p. 91. I am indebted to Melvin J. Friedman for calling this article to my notice. Bishop, incidentally, adjudges *The Bald Soprano* a play with a "tragicomic image of life" (p. 22). He writes that it is "hilariously funny yet anguishing"; it would be better to read "because" for "yet."

51.   *Notes*, p. 114.

52.   *Ibid.*, p. 40.

53. *Ibid.*, p. 185.

54. *Ibid.*, pp. 99-100.

55. See *Notes*, p. 99.

56. *Ibid.*, p. 188.

57. *Ibid.*, pp. 122-3.

58. *Cf.* Camus' *petit-bourgeois* "novelist," Joseph Grand (in *La Peste* [1947]), who cannot get beyond the first sentence in the novel he is writing. Also, like Camus' Jean-Baptiste Clamence (in *La Chute* [1956]), Ionesco's Amédée admits to having remained inactive in the presence of a woman drowning. *Amédée ou comment s'en débarrasser* appeared in 1954. The possibility of mutual borrowings is perhaps not worth considering, but it is intriguing that the two writers have constructed identical incidents of absurdity.

DESIGNATION AND GESTURE IN *THE CHAIRS*

by Robert Champigny

Regarding the ties between signifier and signified, I find it useful to distinguish between a poetic mode (what is signified as a quality of what signifies) and prosaic modes. These prosaic modes divide into gestural and designative. The designative mode subdivides into analytic and narrative. In these preliminaries, I shall stress the distinction between designative and gestural modes of meaning: this is the one which matters for my analysis of *The Chairs*.

To the extent that it is designative, discourse names and describes individual events, states of affairs, processes; it defines non-temporal essences, concepts; and it may also formulate generalized processes, possible events. Thus: "Nietzsche wrote during the second part of the nineteenth century; he died in 1900"; "Nietzsche is a philosopher; a philosopher is a man; all men are mortal; hence Nietzsche is mortal." The designative mode basically disposes and composes what is signified in spatio-temporal order (narration) or according to the logic of classes (analysis).

The gestural mode is used to mime (perform, not designate) attitudes, functions, roles. "It hurts," said in a plaintive voice, helps perform the attitude of the sufferer. To this extent, the utterance does not designate the concept of suffering, nor does it designate an event of pain (though it may also do this). Interjections, passwords, greetings, insults emphasize the gestural mode: "Good morning!" and "You pig!" are not, respectively, a meteorological and a zoological statement. Dramatic dialectic is the basic kind of coherence which helps compose verbal and non-verbal gestures into roles and interplays between roles, the various grestures and roles acting as stimuli and responses.[1]

From a pragmatic standpoint, I find it useful to distinguish between engaged (cognitive, utilitarian) and disengaged applications of the modes of meaning. The disengaged application could be divided between merely playful and, more narrowly, more formally, esthetic. It is to be noted that the poetic mode would belong only to the disengaged side of the ledger. This would be an echo, in my terminology, of the traditional distinction between prose (utilitarian) and poetry (esthetic). But this dichotomy is insufficient. Thus, according to reader and moment, the same narrative may be interpreted as history or fiction. Or you come upon two persons quarrelling bitterly and then you change your interpretation: they are rehearsing a scene in a play.

Designative discourse, in its engaged aspect, is taken to refer, correctly or incorrectly, to something which takes place in our historical and practical world. In its disengaged aspect, it designates something in the closed field of a game or work of art: related to our practical incarnation, what it says is not considered as either true or false. Compare what is narrated in the news, in a joke, in a children's game, in a work of fiction. In its engaged aspect, the gestural mode is used to act directly on historical persons (the speaker himself in any case) and also on historical things. The term of magic is commonly reserved for the influence of verbal and non-verbal gestures on the behavior of inanimate entities. But it could be applied to the whole range, and in particular to interhuman relations. As we pray to god, man or nature, as we beseech, request and threaten, try to coax and intimidate, encourage, depress, impress, each other and in any case ourselves, individually and in groups, we act as sorcerers.

As it is composed and interpreted, a piece of speaking or writing may emphasize one semantic mode or another. But the modes are not exclusive: after all, they draw their tools from roughly the same lexicon and syntax. If you order someone to get out, the gestural mode dominates, but the designative mode is also at work: to have practical influence, your words must refer to a historical and geographical situation. The attempt to influence carries an attempt to refer: the departure of a certain person from a certain place is intended, in both senses. Conversely, designation may be construed as the performance of an attitude which is implicitly expected to have a magic effect. Applying a causal law, even retrospectively, is to give an order to nature, and also to human beings, in any case to oneself: you order yourself to believe what you are saying. Prediction and prescription imply each other. And retrodiction involves prediction: if something has happend, it will have happened.

It is also to be noted that, whatever else we do, we cannot help incarnating ourselves historically and practically. I read a novel, I watch the performance of a drama at a historical moment in a geographical place. The experiential data are interpreted in two perspectives: as the historical performance of a drama and as a (performed) dramatic world. To the extent that the performance is successful in my eyes, I see both the actor and the character; but I do not confuse them. The pseudonaive upholders of the theory of art as illusion make me wonder why they do not jump on stage to restrain Othello and save Desdemona. Do they equate, in this case, esthetic intentionality with sadistic voyeurism?

However, if esthetic and practical perspectives can be clearly distinguished in theory, the possibility of mixture and confusion should also be recognized. The fact that we, humans, cannot switch entirely to a playful, or esthetic, intentionality favors the confusion. Besides, it may be tempting to adopt a perspective which posits its entities as neither fictional nor historical, and yet somehow both: such confused perspectives and contradictory entities I call mythical. Performing social functions is properly to be judged from a utilitarian and ethical standpoint, which does not prevent us, if we are lucky, from enjoying playing them as dramatic roles. But we may also attempt to identify the actors and agents we are with the roles we perform, so as to escape practical fear and ethical concern.[2] Legend is the confusion between history and fiction: we try to turn ourselves into legendary figures. And since the roles we perform, however obscurely, are consecrated, we try to confuse them with essences: the Mother, the Lover, the Professor, the Revolutionary, for instance. We pretend that our all too human city is platonically divine, that culture can absorb and redeem nature. A legendary figure should suffer only like a fictional character; and an idol is self-justified.

Narrative fiction emphasizes designation (of a non-cognitive type). Drama emphasizes gesture, verbal and non-verbal. As noted, gesture involves designation. This does not mean, however, that developing gestural meaning requires a parallel development of designative meaning. In my eyes, the main technical and semantic interest in *The Chairs,* as in some other plays of the fifties, lies in the way designative meaning, while not disappearing, is ruined and gestural meaning correlatively brought into relief. I shall examine first the negative aspect of this strategy which tends to sharpen the apprehension of the theatrical as such.

Fabulation is a traditional element where designation is much in evidence. By *fabulation,* I mean talk about what is not to be performed on stage: events before the dramatic action begins (the past of the characters, their relationships), outside events (reports of deaths), events after the end of what is to be performed (announcements of marriages; Joad's prophecy in Racine's *Athalie*). The general means of preventing designation from taking the upper hand in such instances is to motivate the report as purposeful speech within the dramatic dialectic of stimulus and response: Sophocles' *Oedipus* would provide a classical example. Apart from this, dramatists can contrive, if they wish, to lighten the designative load in various ways.

Fabulation may be eliminated: see, for instance, Tardieu's *Les Amants du métro* (*The Lovers in the Subway*). Or it may be made contradictory. By this I do not mean contradictions which are eventually resolved, errors or lies which come to be recognized as such. I mean contradictions which not only the characters, but also the spectators, are unable to resolve. Pirandello would provide illustrations, also quite a few plays in the fifties. Adamov's *Professor Taranne,* in particular, could be set in significant opposition to *Oedipus Rex.* In *Professor Taranne,* the designative load appears quite heavy if taken in suitable segments. But these segments contradict one another: fabulation cancels itself.

Stark unresolved contradictions can also be found in *The Chairs:* the two protagonists have a son and they have no chil-

dren; the weather is foul and nice; the old woman does not know
the colonel and has known him for a long time; the old man has
let his mother die alone and his parents have died in his arms;
one of the blank characters is a doctor; no, he is a photo-engrav-
er.   In this instance, however, the latter title appears to be accepted, which would resolve the contradiction.   More generally,
violent contradiction does not predominate in *The Chairs*.   It
is a limiting case which takes its place in a scale of various devices: less formal inconsistency, lack of distinction between
recollection and fancy, designation turning into puns and dog-
gerel.   Rather than being set in systematic opposition, the theses
collapse into fast-changing and recurring themes which, here and
there, tend to be absorbed by mock-poetry.   Fabulation is neutralized through dissolution.

     Take the spatial and temporal setting.   The old man wants
to watch the boats outside in the sun.   The old woman objects
that it is night.   The old man agrees; so the contradiction is resolved.   But he adds that it is six "in the afternoon."   "In the
evening" would be more normal.   In any case, this would mean
that the action takes place in a season when days are shorter than
nights.   But the old man goes on to say that in the old days it
was not like this: it was still daylight at nine, at ten, at midnight.   At first we might think that he is confusing the seasons;
but the addition of "midnight" turns possible error into fancy.
Besides, the old woman does not object this time: she says
that it is quite true and that he has a wonderful memory.   A
little later, the old man embarks upon a story: walking into a
village; the name of the village was Paris, he thinks.   The old
woman objects that Paris never existed.   The old man retorts
that it did exist once, that it was the city of light (not a village)
and that it flickered out four hundred thousand years ago.
Rather than with contradictions, we are dealing with playful
applications of the name "Paris."   This kind of spirit reacts
upon our original temporal assumption: that it is night outside
rather than day.   As far as I am concerned, it even contamin-
ates the spatial assumption: that there are water and boats outside.   True, this assumption is confirmed by mentions of water
sounds.   But these are only stage-directions: non-verbal indications are the actual fabulation in this case.   And I see no reason
why these noises, whatever device may be used to produce
them, should be interpreted in a spirit different from that of
the verbal fabulation.   The water sounds play the theme of

mutability and recurrence, thus serving as a background to the mutability and recurrence of the themes with which the protagonists play.

Consider also the pieces of information we are given about the protagonists. The old man says he is *a maréchal des logis* (sergeant) since he is a *concierge*. Thus, the military title serves only to introduce the theme of social titles, made ludicrous through the fanciful adjunct of "in chief": the old man could have been President in chief, King in chief, Orator in chief, Marshall in chief, Sailor in chief. As a *maréchal des logis,* the old man is said to have quarrelled with every marshall (in the military sense). Shall we assume at least that he is a *concierge,* in the sense of janitor, caretaker? But in the rest of the play he is always referred to as a *maréchal des logis* and even once as a *maréchal.* Besides, the job of *concierge* hardly agrees with the decor, which does not look like a porter's habitat, and with the kind of gathering which is to take place there. *Concierge* too is part of a theme: in its other sense, that of idly curious and boring gossip-monger, this word helps set the tone of the message theme.

The thesis, or hypothesis, that there is a message is not flatly contradicted: the orator's ineptitude is no proof that there is no message; the laughter at the end is no proof that a message will not be bequeathed to posterity and that the protagonists will not have a street named after them, as they prophesy. Here again, the effect of what is said regarding the message is to turn thesis into farcical theme. See in particular the caricatural evocation of literary history conceived as secular hagiography. The orator is enjoined to be a literary *concierge:* a pious biographer, he will make trivial and disgusting details appear touching and portentous.[3]

How old are the protagonists? They have been married for seventy-five years. As a matter of fact, the way they talk might be ascribed to a second childhood. Their longevity, at least that of the old man, is quite remarkable: according to him, he did not marry before the age of forty. Still more remarkable: he was in love with one of the guests one hundred years ago. Add to this that the old woman has to juggle with chairs like a furniture mover in his prime.[4]

They are fond of reminiscing. But their memories appear invented to illustrate themes: the sensitive child, the ungrateful son, the devoted son. One story "progresses" through puns. Another turns to uncouth free verse with a sprinkling of rhymes.

Consider also the orator and the other guests. A character arrives who is recognized by the protagonists as the orator who had been announced. He acts as if he were deaf and mute. He might be an imposter, or he might pretend to be unable to speak. The guests who have been announced remain invisible. Yet the protagonists and the orator act as if they were present. Furthermore, the bell rings and at the end laughter is heard which may be interpreted as coming from the guests. Even before the episode of the party, the way the guests are listed shows that it would be irrelevant to consider what is said about them in a thetic perspective. The list pays more attention to rhyme than reason. It drifts to "pen-holders" and "chromosomes"; and it includes a mild inconsistency: all the guests are supposed to be "scholars" or "landlords," even though "proletarians" are mentioned.

In the last paragraph, I have encroached upon the topic of inner designation: information about what took place, will take place or is taking place on stage. *The Chairs* is remarkable for its use of simultaneous inner designation. Normally, self-indication takes care of this aspect: the characters posit themselves through being seen and heard. But, in *The Chairs,* we are dealing with blank characters: the guests are designated by the protagonists, the orator, some lighting effects (for the emperor's entrance), and by the chairs, which are, to borrow a definition from Magdelon in Molière's *Précieuses ridicules,* "the commodities of conversation." Thus, inner designation, in *The Chairs,* is equivalent to outer designation (fabulation) and it is treated in the same spirit: the style discourages an interpretation of the blank characters as hallucination.

Only the first guests and, at the end, the emperor are individualized. The rest is an indistinct crowd. The protagonists then address no one in particular. Their conversation reduces to rudimentary snatches. At one point, the old woman switches to the part of an usherette and ice-cream vendor. Besides, individual descriptions are subverted with the help of devices already noted in the fabulation. A lady has changed and has not changed. Her hair is white, brown, blue. Her husband brings a gift which might be a flower, a cradle, a pear-tree, a raven, or a picture.

∽

From the standpoint of historical spectators and actors, the world of the play (not the performance) is fictional: we take the designative aspect not as false, but as neither true nor false. Traditionally treated, fabulation lays down the rules of the game, whereas, from the standpoint of the characters, it offers statements for belief. In *The Chairs*, the subversion of designative meaning likens the protagonists' perspective and the spectators' interpretation: rules on the one hand, statements on the other, are turned into themes.

On the whole, this conversion likens the perspective of the protagonists to that of the spectators and actors, instead of the other way round (which would be the way of illusion). Like rules of games, like axioms, themes are to be taken as neither true nor false. The true-or-false question becomes idle from the standpoint of the characters themselves: it would be irrelevant to ask whether the protagonists are really old in their own eyes, whether they consider their stories as lies or not, whether the guests are for them really present or really absent.

Designation is neutralized as theme. "Theme" is a neutral term: you can extract themes from any kind of discourse.[5] What matters is that, on the positive side, these themes are absorbed by roles, projected by gestures, verbal or not. The protagonists play the roles of old people. They are like children playing adults. They are characters caricaturing children playing adults, old people, or even children.

It is the instability of the themes which sets them apart from normal fabulation: it prevents the rules from setting. Compare this fluid mutiplicity with the hierarchical duality of the classical play-within-the-play device. The rules of the enveloped play and of enveloping play are kept distinct and the art of the playwright consists generally in establishing some relation between the two sets of rules: contrast, homology, symbol, dialectic relation as in *Hamlet*. In *The Chairs*, we have instead a multiplicity of playlets set on one level, some of them as fugitive as gleams on breaking waves. The protagonists play the games of excuses, remorse, sickness, erotic postures, the game of the message-which-will-save-mankind, the game of literary quotations and other clichés, the game of family relationships (husband and wife, mother and son), the game of converting adult talk into puns and singsong, the private game of imitating the month of February, among others.

At times, the application of this strategy cannot avoid a certain amount of facility, superfluity, cheapness.[6] On the whole, however, several factors prevent *The Chairs* from dis-integrating into minute, unrelated pieces. The various devices and roles can be grouped into a few overlapping sets. There is a common caricatural approach and burlesque tone. The pro-tagonists always communicate smoothly; their verbal and non-verbal gestures are in unison, like those of well-trained dancers.[7] They may contradict each other: they have a son; they are childless. But this designative contradiction is not a dramatic discrepancy, any more than a blue and a yellow constitute a pictorial inconsistency. And, even though there is no clear and simple hierarchy of roles, there is at least one main theme which keeps the swarm of atoms oriented in one direction: the mes-sage-and-lecture theme.

Thus, it could be said that *The Chairs* transfers to the realm of gestures the basic way in which we compose events into a sequence: there are fugitive events (or gestures), but there are also the ties of recurrence and permanence (in *The Chairs* a guiding goal). It could even be said that the development pays homage to the classical distribution between exposition, main action and dénouement. The zig-zagging of roles in the exposi-tion, however erratic, remains oriented toward the episode of the guests and sets the perspective in which to interpret it. With the intervention of the blank characters, the device of the dotted line takes precedence. Culminating in a passage where the pro-tagonists' speech reduces to snatches, the device shows how far one can push the dramatic counterpart of the geometric defini-tion of a line through discontinuous points.

I must confess, however, that I am uneasy about the final part. No doubt, the entrance of the orator is a powerful *coup de*

théâtre; and the change of visible characters may also be welcome. A spectator without previous acquaintance with the play
is likely to expect the guests to be visible: they are not. He is
then likely to expect the orator to be invisible: he is not. *Coups
de théâtre* are not to be despised. However, what matters for an
esthetic appreciation is what becomes of the effect of surprise
or shock when the play is watched again or when a novel, a detective novel for instance, is read for the second or third time.
The effect is not simply obliterated; but it is transformed. For
we are in a position to appreciate the effect within the whole.

According to the stage-directions, the orator is "real."
But, "while the invisible characters must have as much reality
as possible, the orator should look unreal." The orator is visible
like the protagonists; vocally, he is almost as deficient as the
blank characters. The stage-director is enjoined to stress him
as a link and equalizing factor between the two sides. This conception of the orator would fit into my interpretation of the
play: the "unreality" of the orator would incite the spectator
not to take too seriously, for instance, the fact that the protagonists appear as old people.

But a play is not a novel. The task of the director is quite
different from a little juggling with the words "real" and "unreal." Whatever he may do, I am afraid that the human appearance of the orator will tend to emphasize, instead of playing
down, the difference between full-fledged and blank characters.
Thus, the spectator may be tempted not to take ironically the
passage where the old woman touches the orator's arm, as if to
"make sure that he exists," and where the protagonists exclaim
that he does exist, "in flesh and blood," that "it is not a dream."
They might then be viewed as sorcerers astonished at the extent
of their success. Instead of social sorcerers, as we all are, creating
purely social beings, they would be the recipients of a supernatural power.

I wonder whether a puppet, or a human actor made up and
acting as a puppet, would not be the best means of implementing
what is required of the orator's part, according to the stage-
directions and to my own interpretation of the play as a whole.[8]
The advantages of visibility would be kept: *coup de théâtre,*
variation in the situation on stage; ability to move, write, "talk"
(for instance, like a record going awry, repeating, perhaps, what

the old man has already said). And there would be added advantages in having a non-human character, with or without a human actor. The passage about "flesh and blood" existence could not be taken seriously. One would also eliminate the relevance of questions as to who or what the orator "really" is (thus: an accomplice? an imposter? an inept disciple? a ghost? a trick of the devil?). Finally, the device could effectively link, not oppose, the human protagonists and the blank characters. The two sides could even be made to converge by giving the puppet, or puppet-actor, a wooden appearance like the chairs and the features of the old man. The play could thus end on the image of the old man immobilized in the commanding gesture of a statue, which would be a proper way of disclosing the message dramatically: it would be performed.

No doubt, this kind of staging would soften the effect produced by the ineptitude of a character announced as an orator: less would be expected of a puppet than of a human character. But, in my opinion, this softening would also contribute to the homogeneity of the play and to the distinctness of its significance. The ineptitude of a human orator might well be construed as stressing a lack of interhuman communication.[9] In order to link this feature with the protagonists' feats of dramatic communication, we would have to adopt a success-and-failure schema for the play as a whole: the protagonists would succeed in their own yes; but the orator would fail to deliver the message. The trouble with this interpretation is that it hardly goes with the farcical demeanor of the protagonists, the way the fabulation has been neutralized and the stage-directions regarding the orator: it involves our taking seriously the message as a philosophy, the old man as a philosopher, the orator as an expounder and commentator. If the orator were recognized as a puppet finally immobilized in the gesture of a statue, the success-and-failure schema could more easily be absorbed by the opposition between gestural and designative meanings. For, according to my line of thought, the orator's inability to expound a message is to be interpreted simply as one more example of the neutralization of designative meaning. The kind of staging I am suggesting would stress the counterpart: the message would be performed as the dramatic gesture of a statue.

There would still be the matter of the fictional audience's reaction to be decided upon. For this reaction also bears on the gestural meaning of the message: its performance is effective or ineffective. The stage-directions suggest laughter. The message would thus fail as gesture if we assume that the protagonists did not want this kind of reaction. In this case, a mixed reaction would be preferable. But the main thing to note is that the way the protagonists have treated their guests and the message theme discourages the assumption that they intended one kind of re-action rather than another. A puppet-like orator, instead of a human character, should be a further deterrent.

It should also dissuade the historical spectators from con-fusing their perspective with that of the fictional audience, hence their interpretation of the message theme with the in-visible characters' reaction to the orator's performance. The metadramatic significance of the message theme should not de-pend on whether the orator's performance appears as an inef-fectual social gesture or not. It should rather be, according to my interpretation, that a message exists socially as gesture and that its designative content is, to this extent, irrelevant.

∽

To conclude, I turn to a topic upon which I have begun to encroach: the significance of *The Chairs*. Understood esthetical-ly, language makes no direct reference to facts in our world; and the gestures in a play do not involve historical persons directly in their dialectic. But a play represents dramatic art in general; and it represents the theatrical aspect of our lives. Esthetic disengagement allows this theatrical aspect better to be isolated from other aspects and thus to afford a more distinct under-standing. Plays should give us tools of comprehension, if not of knowledge. They provide these tools, not through concepts, but through stylized fictional illustrations. A play can thus function as a critique. The enjoyment of a play in itself and the consideration of its significance (its critical exemplariness) be-long to different perspectives. But there is some correlation be-tween the quality of the enjoyment and the quality of the significance.

A play like *The Chairs* has a strong reflexive aspect. By this I mean that it invites us to reflect upon what is essential to theatrical art and dramatic comprehension. The neutralization of designative meaning sets off the gestural. Like some other plays, *The Chairs* shows that the subversion of designative logic need not impair gestural logic and understanding, and that a character may have a full dramatic existence without firm, coherent fabulation: outside their roles on stage, the protagonists are blank. To be a character is to be a set of gestures.

But *The Chairs* is more original, though not unique, in its use of blank characters on stage. In their case, the self-designation normally provided by actors is eliminated. Yet these characters do enjoy a rudimentary dramatic existence. For they are circumscribed by the protagonists' play and the frozen gesture of the chairs. The discontinuity is not fatal to the dramatic dialectic of stimuli and responses. This incites us to reflect that, even in a normal situation, the job of dramatic comprehension, like any other kind, is to provide bridges over the discontinuity of the given. Even in the case of a normally enacted character, the only things which constitute the dramatic data are the gestural input and output. A character may describe inner phenomena (feelings, desires). But designations of this sort function as tactical methods: dramatically there can be gestures of pain, but no feeling of pain. The ideal of behaviorism was to consider us as dramatic characters and nothing else.

Concerning the resonances of *The Chairs,* that is to say, its significance beyond the field of dramatic art, I have already noted an analogy between the protagonists and children playing adults. And, as adults, we can still play the roles of adults. We may enjoy playing them, in full awareness that we are actors, not the characters we play; and we may enjoy watching others do the same. But the selection of roles in *The Chairs,* their instability, and the one, are invitations to look beyond.

Instead of enjoying role-playing for its own sake, we may adopt a practical perspective: the role takes its place among other means which, in the last analysis, receive their meaning from an ethical, rather than esthetic, end. This perspective does not appear in *The Chairs.* As a matter of fact, to the extent that we are dealing with pure theatre, purely gestural meaning, it cannot appear, except as something beyond, on the horizon. When a practical action has failed, it may assume the air of a "mere gesture."

There remains gesture and role in a mythical perspective. Instead of hypocrisy in the original sense (play-acting) or in the ordinary sense (role-playing for practical reasons), we encounter self-hypocrisy: the attempt to identify oneself with the role. A mythical perspective confuses playful and practical: the role is a shelter and a justification (it masks incarnation and ethical responsibility); thus it is playful, and yet it is not (the role is assumed not to be fictional). Society allows us, even forces us, to adopt this perspective: we make images out of each other. In Cocteau's words, Victor Hugo was a madman who believed he was Victor Hugo. In this perspective, social roles are idols, instead of tools or toys.

In principle, the theater is opposed to this socioreligious conception of roles, since it rests on a clear trichotomy between spectator, actor and character.[10] But the dramatic treatment of the roles may still be such that it countenances idolatry. Not in *The Chairs*. The protagonists are themselves like actors playing roles. These roles are cynically garbled, mixed, caricatured. Their selection and multiplicity, also the theme of the social gathering, allow the play to appear as a global critique of the mythical perspective on social roles. I cannot object to that: mythical self-hypocrisy threatens both esthetic sense and moral sense. This kind of critique is quite banal; but the way it is done in *The Chairs* is not so banal. A fairly specific feature is that the attack concentrates on the cultural idol of the Artist, or Writer. And it might also be said that the atomization of roles corresponds to a cultural situation in which mythical blocks have disintegrated into a shower of fast-changing, and recurring, slogans.

But the most interesting thing, with respect to social resonances, still lies in the emphasis on blanks. The device of the invisible characters and the fact that the two protagonists exist only through their interplay are a potent illustration of the purely social aspect of our existence. As purely social beings (not physiological, not even economic), we are for and by each other. By this I do not mean that we need other people, among other things, to survive, project practical and ethical goals. I mean that, whether we like it or not, our purely social situation is not that of an incarnated creature, but that of an image painted by the others' verbal and non-verbal gestures.

Within this general situation, *The Chairs* also sketches a pattern of group dialectic: in this case, the couple and the rest of society. The protagonists are by each other. But it soon appears that they need a *They* to be a *We*. And the accumulation of the chairs between them also suggests that the *They* threatens the *We*.[11] However, this aspect is only sketched: regarding group dialectic, *The Chairs* cannot compare with, for instance, Sartre's *Morts sans sépulture* (translated as *The Victors* and as *Men without Shadows*) or Genet's *Les Nègres* (*The Blacks*).

My interpretation of the play and of its significance seems to run counter to some other comments: lack of communication, meaninglessness (or absurdity) of language, or existence; "ontological emptiness."[12] Such comments appear to be based on a lack of distinction between modes of existence and meaning. I am thus inclined to view them as incomplete formulas.

A question such as: "Why is there something, rather than nothing, or something else?" manifests ontological gratuitousness, which is the basic inescapable absurdity. In this sense, absurdity is not opposed to meaning, since it can be applied to anything, including purpose and reason: "Why is there meaning, rather than no meaning, or some other meaning?" Ontological systems may shift about this basic absurdity, or gratuitousness. But they have to rest on it, since it is nothing else than the absolute. Against this background, human understanding tries to compose figures: coherent totalities (meaning as immanent purpose), or their parts (meaning as transcendent purpose). Meaning and lack of meaning become polar: comprehension is more or less successful.

Animal existence, for instance a human life, partakes of basic gratuitousness. Besides, it cannot be reduced to one coherent configuration: if our life were a cosmos, or an organic part of a cosmos, we would have no need of a logos. Rather than death, which, in principle, would allow one to consider a life as a totality (this is what biographers try to do), suffering makes the lack of meaning acute. As it is lived, not glossed over, suffering is the radical lack of understanding, hence the basis of the need to understand: if feeling were without suffering, feeling would be understanding and we would not need thought and words to try to make up for the lack, or mask it with verbal make-up. Experiences other than suffering are amenable to understanding. But there is still the multiplicity of meanings to consider, in relation with the complexity, mutability and disparity of experiences. I have proposed a distribution of kinds of meaning; others can be devised. Various meanings can be enjoyed in various aspects of life: they show each other's insufficiency. Even discounting suffering and failures, there cannot be one and only one meaning for a life as a whole, or part of a whole. If there were, there would be no biographical and autobiographical urge. If a life were a well-made play, or part of one, there would be no need and no possibility of dramatic art.

To return to *The Chairs*. I have already noted how the episode of the orator might be interpreted as stressing a lack of communication on the gestural plane. On the same plane, however, the protagonists communicate extraordinarily well. In their case, "lack of communication" and "meaninglessness of language" could refer only to the designative aspect: they do not communicate coherent pieces of information; they are inconsistent autobiographers. But it is inappropriate to consider a play as if it were a narration. In spite of some gratuitousness, in spite of the instability and mixture of roles, the play does not suggest to me the meaninglessness of language: it shows that gestural value is one thing and designative value another. It does not suggest to me that human life has no meaning. It shows how the purely social aspect of existence can be playfully enjoyed and satisfy an understanding of some experiences as role-playing. Through the device of the blank characters, it also suggests that other data, other aspects of experience, could be taken over by other types of meaning. What drama leaves blank, narration could use. Some experiences may have dramatic meaning for us, others a poetic meaning: this is intimated by the use of mock-poetry.

The phrase "ontological emptiness" also appears to derive from the emphasis on blanks: neutralization of fabulation and invisible characters. But this does not annihilate dramatic existence. Of course, within the context of human life, this type of existence may be viewed as superficial, lacking in ontological roots, mere appearance: - *The Chairs* incites us to consider the purely social roles we play as fiction. On the other hand, however, we must incarnate ourselves, suffer and act practically, we must be non-fictional actors in order to play fictional roles.

True, as it strives to purify dramatic existence, *The Chairs* avoids representing suffering and practical action on stage: wisely, I think, for such representation can only have the effect of turning them mythically into gesture and role. And it also avoids suggesting that practical action and suffering lie beyond the dramatic field, on the other side of the play's horizon: it only suggests death. But, as a counterpart to the neutralization of fabulation, the play is led to present the protagonists as actors playing roles. And if, within the play, the chairs are simply the commodities of conversation, their materiality is suggested on the other side of the horizon. Note also that chairs are not mere lumps of matter, but products of practical activity.

In order to receive an impression of unlimited "ontological emptiness," we should have to retain a mythical perspective on social roles. The socioreligious goal is to absorb all aspects of experience into the social aspect, so that individual human lives may receive all the meaning and ontological grounding they need, as parts of a society turned into a totalitarian cosmos. All the world's a stage and all the men and women merely players. Except for the ambiguity of "players" (actors, or characters?), this could serve as a candid formulation of the socioreligious goal. But the conversion, or perversion, can have a chance of success only if the purpose is not stated candidly: "*merely* players" and "stage" would not do. *The Chairs* turns the myth into farce. Idols become toys handled flippantly. It does not show that the socioreligious project fails because we remain suffering animals and practical agents. It shows instead that, if the project were successful, it would turn us into fictional characters, in the way a rationalistic (not rational) interpretation of the world as a well-make play or narrative turns history into fiction. The socioreligious project fails in its very success because its goal is self-contradictory and can be pursued only through self-hypocrisy. It is the absurdity of this goal, not of language, not of existence, which *The Chairs* discloses in my opinion: in this respect, it proceeds as a *reductio and absurdum* argument.[13] The impression of ontological emptiness will extend to human existence (not just to purely social roles) only if we start from the assumption that myth, and myth alone, more precisely socioreligious myth, can provide us with an ontological ground.

NOTES

1.　The distinction between designation and gesture may bring to mind J. L. Austin's opposition between statement and performative utterance (*Philosophical Papers;* Oxford: Oxford University Press, 1961), also perhaps the distinction between "cognitive" and "expressive." "Engaged" and "disengaged" appear to correspond roughly to "transitive," as used ty linguists. "Gesture" is given a narrower range than is Richard P. Blackmur's *Language as gesture* (New York: Harcourt, Brace and Co., n.d.).

2.　"What is bothersome in society is that the person merges with the function, or rather, the person is tempted to identify himself totally with the function." Ionesco, in Claude Bonnefoy, *Entretiens avec Eugène Ionesco* (Paris: Belfond, 1966), p. 17.

3.　"Literary history as it is practiced is only a *concierge* story." Ionesco, in Bonnefoy (*op. cit.*), p. 67. Note also that literary criticism often prefers passwords to concepts, hence dramatic dialectic to analytic logic. Frequently, literary critics appear to understand each other better than themselves. Gesture stresses speaking to; designation speaking of; poetry speaking.

4.　Some stage-directors "wanted the old woman to be played by an old actress to look more real. But that was wrong, since her performance has to be athletic, a real ballet with chairs." Ionesco, in Bonnefoy (*op. cit.*), p. 112.

5.　The trouble with thematic criticism is that it makes no difference between newspaper article, sonnet, sermon, novel, play, or philosophical essay. As for structural analysis, it still has to take into consideration the difference between play and narrative, and between history and fiction.

6.　In the listing of guests, "there is obviously first of all a phonetic association. It is a game. Words come and link freely. There is a certain gratuitousness in this." Ionesco, in Bonnefoy (*op. cit.*), p. 155.

7. "*Les Chaises* cannot be understood, as Kenneth Tynan suggests, as a statement whose moral is that human beings cannot communicate with each other. The fact is that the Old Man and the Old Woman are so perfectly able to communicate with each other that they share the same consciousness. Our acceptance of their projection is proof of their ability to communicate with us." Richard Schechner, "The Enactment of the 'Not' in Ionesco's *Les Chaises*," in *Yale French Studies*, No. 29 (Spring-Summer 1962), p. 72. "My theater is said to be a lament of the solitary man who cannot communicate with others. Not at all. Communication is easy." Ionesco, in Bonnefoy (*op. cit.*), p. 69.

8. About the orator: "His visible presence is unavoidable. He has to be seen and heard since he is the last one to remain on the set. But his visibility is only an arbitrary convention, based on a technical difficulty which could not be solved otherwise." Ionesco, in *Notes et contre-notes* (Paris: Gallimard, 1962), p. 168. Still, the orator does not have to look human.

9. "The deaf and mute orator was to expose the impossibility of communication." Simone Benmussa, in *Ionesco* (Paris: Seghers, 1966), p. 109.

10. To me, the current slogan of "participation," as applied to the theater, smacks of socioreligious reaction, or nostalgia.

11. It might also be alleged that their suicide move confirms the destruction of the couple by society: each "dies" alone. But they disappear in unison. It is part of their game. They do not interpret the arrival of the emperor and of the orator as the destruction of their duet.

12. "The theme of the play was nothingness, not failure. It was total absence: chairs with nobody. [...] The chairs arriving at full speed, faster and faster, this expressed for me ontological emptiness, a kind of whirlwind of emptiness." Ionesco, in Bonnefoy (*op. cit.*), p. 84. This may have been the original vision. But it is not the whole finished play. On Ionesco as a dreamer, and as a dutifully Jungian dreamer, see Alexandre Rainof, *Mythologies de l'Etre chez Ionesco* (*diss.*, University of Michigan, 1969).

13. "What appears to me absurd, basically uncanny, is existence in itself.

[...] As soon as there is a discrepancy between ideology and reality, there is absurdity. It is not the same absurdity, it is a feeling of practical, moral, not metaphysical, absurdity." Ionesco, in Bonnefoy (*op. cit.*), p. 149.

"A PSYCHOLOGY BASED ON ANTAGONISM:"
IONESCO, PINTER, ALBEE AND OTHERS

by John Fletcher

> 'Il n'y a de théâtre
> que s'il y a des antag-
> onismes.' IONESCO,
> *Notes et contre-notes.*

I

Techniques special to comparative literature can help to clarify and situate accurately various literary relationships which are too often taken casually for granted or passed over without examination in an incidental phrase. Eugène Ionesco and Harold Pinter constitute a particularly interesting case of this, since they are frequently mentioned in the same breath but usually without much critical discernment of the similarities and differences existing between the two contemporary playwrights. When applied to specific texts, the comparatist technique which I term "confrontation analysis" can hope, through parallel and contrast, to define with a welcome degree of precision the specific qualities of a representative, even exemplary writer. In the present case I shall close in on Ionesco via a confrontation between his early work and that of Pinter, since the first "unsophisticated" phase in both playwrights shows an oneirical immediacy which is to some extent diluted and overlaid, in later, more "polished" works, by other considerations. I therefore refer mainly to Ionesco's *Victims of Duty,* written in 1952, and Pinter's *The Birthday Party,* written some five years later; and by way of contrast I shall also be looking at a few other contemporary plays, including Pinter's *The Homecoming* (1965) and Edward Albee's famous success, *Who's Afraid of Virginia Woolf?* (1961-62). All these works, we shall find, deal in antagonisms of one kind or another—in the contemporary myth of violence—so it is with this aspect that I shall particularly be concerned. But first of all, let us look a little more closely at what *Victims of Duty* and *The Birthday Party* have in common in terms of setting, plot, characterization, dramatic technique, and theme.

II

Although Pinter wrote *The Birthday Party* some years after Ionesco's *Victims of Duty*, there is no likelihood that he was influenced by it. It is probable that he had little or no familiarity with Ionesco's work at the time; and it is quite certain that the original image for *The Birthday Party* arose out of his days in repertory, touring south-east England. The initial impetus to write the play, in other words, was provided by a real event, and was not the result of a literary stimulus at all. This is how Pinter described that real event in an interview on BBC television with Joan Bakewell:

> It was a most miserable week at Eastbourn...I found digs in which a man had to share a room with a man in a kind of attic...There was a terrible landlady, and it was all quite incredibly dirty. And at the end of the week I said to this fellow, who turned out to have been a concert pianist on the pier: "Why do you stay here?" And he said: "There's nowhere else to go." I left with that ringing in my ears. Then about a year later or so I started to write *The Birthday Party*, but it has no relation to that original thing, that situation in Eastbourne, other than that there were two people who got me onto the first page.
>
> (*The Listener,* November 6, 1969, p. 630)

In fact, just as the atmosphere in *Victims of Duty* is of the sort of petit-bourgeois Paris apartment with which Ionesco is familiar, Pinter's play is redolent with the feel and smell of British theatrical "digs" in which a fair proportion of his youth was spent.

There are several other parallels between the two plays. Both open with reassuring, commonplace activities—in fact in both cases it is the reading of a newspaper and the discussion of its contents which provide the lead-in—but they soon veer off into the oneirical, *Victims of Duty* more so than *The Birthday Party*, which for all its disturbing overtones remains rooted in a recognizable contemporary situation. Both plays, in fact, are "thrillers" of the kind defined early on in *Victims of Duty* by Choubert: "the theatre's a riddle," he says, "and the riddle's a thriller" (p. 120).[1] The subsequent performance will constitute an ironic development of that remark: *Victims of Duty* is certainly a riddle, and the riddle is a thrilling one on the whole, though less so than in *The Birthday Party,* which is as suspenseful as a Hitchcock movie. It is very likely that Pinter was influenced by Hitchcock in the dramatic manner in which he springs surprises on his audience or introduces unexpected twists to his plot; certainly the way in which Stanley tries to detach McCann from Goldberg, then attempts to persuade Goldberg to give up his mission, and is finally pressed with the accusation that he "betrayed the organization" (p. 48), is all in the purest thriller tradition.[2] This impression is reinforced by a realization that the organization's representatives are not as fully in control of the situation in Act II as Goldberg in his briefing of McCann (pp. 29-30) had airily implied, for by Act III Goldberg betrays considerable irritability and his aide distinct signs of nervousness. Nevertheless they contrive to get Stanley out of the house, and Petey finally offers no resistance to the abduction, so that the play ends on a whimper—unlike *Victims of Duty,* which ends on a bang. Despite this, *The Birthday Party* is a distinctly more "exciting" piece of theatre, holding the spectator's attention in a way Ionesco often fails to do—in particular the middle sections of *Victims of Duty* tend to be rather slack, and to present the director with the problem of keeping alive the audience's interest in the situation. The play is saved by the timely entrance of Nicolas d'Eu and the virtually simultaneous recurrence (with the coffee-cups) of the familiar Ionesco "proliferation" motif and of the disturbing business of Choubert's forced feeding. From this point the play sweeps on to its dramatic close, incidentally picking up again the "duty" theme which occurs at intervals throughout the action.

In both works, then, the plot—the story of a witch-hunt, of the oppression, exploitation and subjugation of a weak individual—is similar in several respects, and the characterization is equally so. In both plays names tend to be uncertain: *Victims of Duty* centers on doubt whether Mallot is spelt with a "t" at the end or a "d," and Goldberg enjoys three forenames (Nat, Simey and Benny), as McCann is variously called Dermot and Seamus. The characters as such form in both works a tight, restricted group carefully patterned and balanced to produce torturer/victim and mother/son relationships. In the case of the respective torturers, Ionesco's Detective is very much a stage cop, as Goldberg is a stage Jew, with his "Gesundheit" and patter about his "old mum", who was wont to greet him on his return home with "the nicest piece of gefilte fish you could wish to find on a plate" (p. 43). Both roles, in fact, are to some extent caricatures, in Pinter's case a particularly comic one: Pinter himself is of Jewish origin, which helps explain why Goldberg is so much more convincing a creation than the Irish McCann. He is certainly a very flesh-and-blood torturer, and his blunt "Webber, you're beginning to get on my breasts" (p. 46) parallels the Detective's patronizing use of the familiar "tu" form in addressing Choubert.

In conjunction with this relationship, there is in both plays a deliberate confusion between the role of son and lover. Madeleine begins as Choubert's rather shrewish wife; she then becomes a provocative mistress, before being transformed into his mother (p. 135). Likewise Meg, ostensibly Stanley's landlady, is seen as bearing another relationship to him: early on she affirms that she would "much rather have a little boy" (p. 11), and it soon becomes apparent that Stanley is a kind of son to her, certainly dependent on her ("I don't know what I'd do without you", he says on p. 18). If anything she is even more dependent on him: "he's my Stanley now" she says in her toast to him (p. 55), betraying strong emotion verging on erotic involvement. Petey instinctively recognizes the extent of her attachment to their lodger by concealing from her, at the end of the play, that Stanley has been taken from her; we are left to imagine the shock she will suffer when she finally realizes that he has gone. Ionesco's Madeleine is more mercurial, less consistent in her roles, and even the Detective merges into Choubert's father, but both works are concerned with a return to childhood: Stanley and Choubert in the course of the action are reduced to childish imbecility and effectively suppressed by the machinations of their respective torturers. But even Meg suffers regression; this occurs during the party, when in one of the play's most poignant moments she reminisces about her nanny sitting up with her at night (p. 60). This is not the case with Ionesco's Madeleine, who is closer to Pinter's Lulu—both women reproach their respective lovers, the Detective and Goldberg, with "using" them or exploiting them sexually (*Victims of Duty* p. 134 and *The Birthday Party*

p. 80). In fact, Ionesco economizes a female part by combining Lulu and Meg in Madeleine; but he also differentiates Goldberg and McCann (very much two faces of the same character in Pinter) by making Nicolas usurp the Detective's role after his death. On the other hand, both plays have an observer figure, either almost totally impassive as in the case of Ionesco's inscrutable Lady, or largely impotent to influence events, like Petey.

In terms of dramatic technique, too, the plays employ much the same devices. Both exploit ritualistic games which have sinister overtones: Nicolas does a kind of Indian war-dance around the Detective before stabbing him to death, and the climax of the celebrations in Stanley's honour is blind man's buff with the "birthday boy" in the title role, made sightless not only by the requisite scarf but also by McCann's snapping of his spectacles. And both dramatists tend to use the device of "freezing" the action in order to emphasize certain moments of high tension, for instance when Nicolas takes control of the situation in *Victims of Duty* (p. 164) or when Goldberg enters to face a "reception committee" in the living-room (p. 70). Both writers, likewise, exploit the possibilities of blackout, though in Ionesco's case this is mainly used to change the personnel or modify their dispositions on stage; in Pinter's it is used to intensify a climax in the action: the timely cut-out of the coin-fed meter at the precise instant when Stanley begins to strangle Meg must rank as one of the most unexpected and startling—indeed most Hitchcockian—moments of crisis in contemporary drama.

In both cases, too, the writing is rich and baroque. As elsewhere, Ionesco uses here verbal prolixity to suggest in another dimension the same threatening anarchy as the proliferation of objects does. *Victims of Duty* is a very "wordy" play, with numerous lengthy tirades, especially in the middle sections when Choubert is recalling his early happiness with Madeleine, or the Detective is speaking as Choubert's father: it is significant that the lamentations of both characters go largely unheeded. In Pinter's case the range is equally wide, from Meg's commonplace "Here's your cornflakes" (p. 9) through Stanley's evasive rationalizatins of his failure in life ("All right, Jack, I can take a tip. They want me to crawl down on my bended knees," p. 23) to Goldberg's calculatedly mawkish affabilities:

Tonight, Lulu, McCann, we've known a great fortune. We've heard a lady extend the sum of her devotion, in all its pride, plume and peacock, to a member of her own living race. Stanley, my heartfelt congratulations. I wish you, on behalf of us all, a happy birthday. I'm sure you've never been a prouder man than you are today.   (p. 56)

Goldberg's language, in fact, is made up almost entirely of fluent clichés of this kind. "I swore on the good book." he says, recalling his father's deathbed blessing," and I knew the word I had to remember—Respect!" (p. 78). For a similar use of cliché, compare this advice from the glossy magazine *Homes and Gardens:*

Offset the basic apricot of the room with yellows and warm greens. An intricate floral vinyl wallpaper in tangerine, apricot, pale citrus and seaweed green on a background of golden amber could be highlighted with white ceiling and paintwork. Echo the wallpaper with a man-made fibre carpet in amber and have roller blinds in sunflower yellow.

Pale seaweed green or tangerine tiles could be used in the shower area and on the bath back provided they are plain or only slightly textured so as not to compete with the patterned wallpaper. Choose towels and bathmats in tangerine, seaweed and sunflower yellow to complete this unusual, yet feminine scheme;

with Mick's questioning of Davies in *The Caretaker,* where a similar home decorators' jargon is used as a means of attack:

I understood you were an experienced first-class professional interior and exterior decorator.

DAVIES: Now look here—

MICK: You mean you wouldn't know how to fit teal-blue, copper and parchment linoleum squares and have those colours re-echoed in the walls?

DAVIES: Now, look here, where'd you get—?

MICK: You wouldn't be able to decorate out a table in afromosia teak veneer, an armchair in oatmeal tweed and a beech frame settee with a woven sea-grass seat?

DAVIES: I never said that!

MICK: Christ! I must have been under a false impression!

DAVIES: I never said it!

MICK: Your're a bloody imposter, mate!   (p. 76)

Pinter's dialogue is continually modulating between the naturalistic and the contrived in this fashion. In the Joan Blakewell interview already referred to Pinter said: "I don't think that the language I use is naturalistic at all. It isn't naturalistic from one point of view alone, and that is that I take a good deal of trouble." Part of the "trouble" he takes is connected with editing. It is too often assumed that if you carried a tape-recorder on a bus you would collect a canfull of "pure Pinter" before very long. That this is not the case can be seen by comparing with Pinter's writing a fragment of genuinely unedited speech; the following is an extract from an interview with a Blackburn tramp:

> From fourteen to seventeen I was buried twice in Clifton pit. I was buried there twice. So I joined the Army for twelve years, and I went all over the world, every country you can mention. I fought for my country and I was a prisoner of war in Italy, in Syria, and I met the best people in the world when I was taken prisoner. I escaped out of that camp, and I come back, and my friend shot himself, a fellow called Tommy Aspic, he shot himself, definitely. Because he couldn't go through it again. And why couldn't he go through it? Because he got shell-shock, but that was my buddy Tommy, one of the best pals in the world, and I'm a real professional—machine-guns, anything. Them Germans wanted to kill us, but I killed them, and that was it. And I'll kill any German that comes on this foreign country, England, because I've fought for it, and I'll die for it again, and I'll say this, and I'll say it again, on my life: we beat 'em Germans fair and square—they treated us wrong. We didn't want to fight this war but we got them in, and that's it. And I'll say this: a German soldier is a good fighter, and I'm an Englishman, I'm Frankie Bennett, definite, a real tough sergeant, and I'm as tough as ever come in the desert, fought all the way through, I'm the toughest, roughest boy in the world.
>
> (*The Listener*, August 13, 1970, p. 207)

The interviewer, Jeremy Seabrook, describes the speaker, Frank Bennett, as a "confused personality" whose thoughts were "not

quite coherent." As one of the "lost and disorientated" rejects
from society, he resembles some of Pinter's characters—notably
Davies in *The Caretaker*—and, up to a point, even talks like
them. But Mr. Bennett's speech is rambling, aimless and—from
an aesthetic point of view—untidy, strewn with irrelevancies and
vacuous repetition. Pinter's Meg is roughly comparable with Mr.
Bennett in terms of class and education, but her longest sustained speech (the toast to Stanley in Act II) is a carefully developed piece of dramatic writing designed to betray her emotional involvement with her "boy". It makes this point with
economy and power, so that even her repetitions and seeming
irrelevancies have their purpose, although Meg herself is clearly
not fully aware of the implications of what she is saying even
when they cause her to break down:

> Well—it's very, very nice to be here tonight, in my house, and I want
> to propose a toast to Stanley, because it's his birthday, and he's
> lived here for a long while now, and he's my Stanley now. And I
> think he's a good boy, although sometimes he's bad. And he's the
> only Stanley I know, and I know him better than all the world, al-
> though he doesn't think so. Well, I could cry because I'm so happy,
> having him here and not gone away, on his birthday, and there isn't
> anything I wouldn't do for him, and all you good people here to-
> night...(*she sobs.*)   (p. 55)

In spite of appearances, therefore, Pinter's characters—unlike
real-life people—are going somewhere in their talk, even if they
do not always seem sure of where it is. As John Russell Brown
has pointed out, "on the printed page we read the smoke-screen;
we can analyse the diversionary tactics of two commanders who
are sometimes unaware of the combat that is taking place,"
since language is used, in often bewildering combinations, for
both evasion and attack.[3] The plays are not about the impossibility of communication, in fact, but the fear of it. Characters—like Aston talking of Guinness in his extract from *The
Caretaker*—use evasions and irrelevancies rather than mention
what really troubles them (in this case the fear of being sent
back to a mental hospital):

ASTON: Here's a few bob.

DAVIES (*taking the coins*): Thank you, thank you, good luck. I
just happen to find myself a bit short. You see, I got nothing for all

that work I did last week. That's the position, that's what it is.

Pause

ASTON: I went into a pub the other day. Ordered a Guinness. They gave it to me in a thick mug. I sat down but I couldn't drink it. I can't drink Guinness from a thick mug. I only like it out of a thick glass. I had a few sips but I couldn't finish it.

ASTON *picks up a screwdriver and plug from the bed and begins to poke the plug.*

DAVIES (*with great feeling*): If only the weather would break! Then I'd be able to get down to Sidcup! (p. 19)

The real action, indeed, often lies beyond or behind the words; the unexpected eruptions of strong feeling are the result of non-verbal movements which have been taking place as it were subterraneously, and the outburst, when it occurs, is liable to take both the characters and the audience by surprise for bringing out into the open the conflict that theretofore had been unspoken: Pinter's more recent plays *The Homecoming* and *Old Times* provided several striking examples of this. The spare simplicity of these later works is in marked contrast to the baroque elaboration of *The Birthday Party*—what Pinter described to Joan Bakewell as "a kind of no-holds-barred feeling, like diving into a world of words." Perhaps he was thinking of the formal balance in an exchange such as this:

GOLDBERG: Unfortunately we may be gone by then.

PETEY: Will you?

GOLDBERG: By then we may be gone. (p. 74)

There is an undeniable gusto about early Pinter, indeed, which one finds in early Ionesco also. Both writers are humorists who clearly enjoy the games they can play with words, and even with names: Choubert and Nicolas d'Eu are of course typical Ionesco puns on Schubert and Nicolas II, and one can imagine the relish with which Pinter invented the name of "Simey" Goldberg. Both writers, too, flaunt erudition: Ionesco's joke on Pascal's "thinking reed" (p. 156) is paralleled by Pinter's toying with the philosophical distinction between "the necessary and the possible" (p. 50), and both revel in the comic possibilities of bathos, as can be seen in the following examples:

> Played the piano? I've played the piano all over the world. All over the country. (*Pause.*) I once gave a concert.
>
> (*The Birthday Party*, p. 22)

> Nothing ever happens. A few comets and a cosmic disturbance somewhere in the universe. Nothing to speak of. The neighbors have been fined for letting their dogs make a mess on the pavement...
>
> (*Victims of Duty*, p. 117)

Pinter is the more consistently funny of the two dramatists, perhaps because his work derives the more directly and immediately from the music-hall tradition. (His ability to transform vaudeville into myths of power, fear, aggression and subjection is unfortunately not as prominently in evidence in the recent *No Man's Land*—at least not in the London first production, which over-emphasized the comic naturalism of two men returning from a pub to continue the night's drinking at the home of one of them.) When Lulu taxes Goldberg with teaching her things "a girl shouldn't know before she's been married at least three times" his answer is characteristic of the smutty repartee so many stand-up comics once delighted their audiences with: "Now you're a jump ahead!" he says; "What are you complaining about?" (p. 80). Similarly, Stanley savors the bawdy innuendoes the adjective "succulent" gives rise to in his banter with Meg (pp. 17-18). And just as Ionesco revels in exposing the professional jargon of the Detective, Pinter delights in showing the officialese with which Goldberg impresses McCann: "Certain elements might well approximate in points of procedure to some of your other activities" (p. 30), he pontificates. Such high-sounding verbiage, comically enough, "satisfies" McCann more than plain English would have done. Once again, this sort of thing was a staple of the comedy of the halls. The comedy even extends to a form of charade in Pinter's party games and in Ionesco's forcible feeding and pursuit of Choubert.

And both plays reveal considerable self-consciousness about theatre itself. *Victims of Duty* is on one level a manifesto for a new kind of theatre: Choubert frequently brings up the question of a possible renewal in dramatic art, and Nicolas's utterance, for all its apparent inconsistency, is a fair description of Ionesco's own attitudes:

> Drawing my inspiration from a different logic and a different psychology, I should introduce contradiction where there is no contradiction, and no contradiction where there is what common-sense usually calls contradiction...We'll get rid of the principle of identity and unity of character and let movement and dynamic psychology take its place...We are not ourselves...Personality doesn't exit.   (p. 158)

Pinter does not make direct statements of this kind, but he does rely self-consciously on techniques of popular entertainment, such as cross-talk. The "wooing" of Stanley by Goldberg and McCann in Act III is a case in point: the cross-talk extends over two pages (82-84) and no seasoned theatre-goer would miss the reference to familiar patter routines.

Finally, the two plays show distinct similarities of theme. In both there is a palpable sense of menace introduced early in the action: Choubert's description of the man in the photograph, "without a tie, collar torn, a face all bruised and swollen" (p. 126) as after a *passage à tabac,* ties up with hints about government pressure at the beginning and Choubert's own unpleasant experiences later. Likewise in *The Birthday Party* Stanley is disturbed to hear the news that "two gentlemen" are expected at the boarding-house, and there follows some play with the idea that they are coming with a wheelbarrow and are "looking for someone" (p. 24). Meg asks in Act III if there is a wheelbarrow in the boot of Goldberg's car, and later still Goldberg himself muses on the size of the boot in which there is "just room...for the right amount" (p. 71). Finally, as he and McCann remove Stanley, Petey is assured that "there's plenty of room in the car" (p. 86). Both plays, too, involve torture of one sort or another: Stanley is grilled by his two tormenters, his glasses are deliberately broken, and he is subjected to the notorious interrogation technique of having a torch shone in his eyes. Choubert is similarly pressurized by the Detective, who resorts, however, to the childhood trauma device of forcing his victim to swallow dry bread. And as we might expect, violence erupts in both plays: Madeleine's face is slapped by the Detective, Stanley kicks Goldberg in the stomach during the interrogation and attempts to rape Lulu during the blackout at his party. We have already seen that he tries to strangle Meg on the same occasion, but he had shown similar murderous instincts towards her at the end of Act I. There is of course accomplished murder in *Victims of Duty* when Nicolas stabs the Detective, but this action merely forms a climax to mounting hostility, expressed first verbally and then physically. It is no coincidence that among Nicolas's prerequisites for a new theatre should be "a psychology based on antagonism" (p. 158), a requirement he proceeds to put into effect: the Detective dies as much a victim of the clear logic Nicolas repudiates as of the duty for which he expects a "post-humous decoration" (p. 165).

The situation in Pinter's puzzling later play *The Home-coming* should now, I think, be clearer in the light of what has just been said. The sudden flashes of violence—verbal violence, reported violence—all of it of an extreme nature; the disturbingly aggressive eroticism; the way people dominate, bully and sacrifice each other—Lenny with Ted, Max with Sam—the disturbing confusions between mother-figures (Jessie) and whore-figures (Ruth); the painful vulgarities; all this we have seen in *The Birthday Party* and *Victims of Duty*, if in more muted form. The only difference, to my mind, is that in *The Homecoming* Pinter is being more consciously autobiographical—and this accounts for a certain extravagence, and for some of the vulgarities that are, as it were, extraneous to the play, gratuitous in fact. It can hardly be a coincidence that the household is North London Jewish, that an academically distinguished son (should we read successful playwright?) returns from America bringing home an attractive wife (played at the première by Pinter's own wife Vivien Merchant) who succumbs more or less willingly to the obscene blandishments of the father and brothers, ousting the legitimate husband. The violence done to the mother image near the end—"MacGregor had Jessie in the back of my cab as I drove them along" (p. 78)—is painful, but is consonant with the suggested reduction to whoredom of the hitherto respectable wife and mother Ruth and completes the desecration of that image. The language is more varied than in *The Birthday Party*— these people are more educated and articulate—but it still serves to mask the explosive hysteria and the ever-constant battle of wills which underlies the situation, and in this respect is no different from that in *The Birthday Party* and in *Victims of Duty*.

III

Since the earliest times drama has been concerned with the expression of conflict and antagonism, but usually in a fairly genteel manner, from Racine's Hermione to Ibsen's Hedda. Antonin Artaud, of course, is the great theorist of antagonism on the modern stage, and we should establish a distinction between the sort of inward-turned, ritualistic, almost balletic violence he insists upon in the theatre, and the more outward-turned, audience-directed violence—the violence of shock upon our sensibilities as well as our susceptibilities—which Brecht inaugurated, Genet elaborated and much very recent drama depends upon, including the *Marat/Sade*. Fernando Arrabal and Edward Albee, on the other hand, are, like Pinter and Ionesco, of the first sort, enacting a carefully orchestrated ritual of violence which we contemplate, concerned but not directly implicated in. So although physical violence—such as the blinding of Gloucester—has been a feature of some movements in the past, it has known a marked recrudescence in recent years in the plays—among others—of Arrabal and Edward Bond.

The dominant themes of Arrabal's drama—Arrabal is a Spaniard, now in his mid-forties, who writes in French—are childhood and lost innocence, cruelty and lust, sex and violence and death. Two figures haunt his world: one is the domineering, smothering, hypocritical mother, who does most harm when she professes the greatest affection and concern, and the other is the protean infant/virgin/whore, who is capable at one moment of great love, and at another of blatant infidelity. So we find that Arrabal's vision is at once childlike and sharply adult in its awareness. An instance of the childlike is when, in the one-act play *Picnic on the Battlefield*, the Tépans shield from the bombardment under an umbrella, and Zépo donates an artificial flower he'd made for every comrade who dies in action. In contrast with this sort of thing, you have the very adult awareness in *Fando and Lis* of the difficulty not only of conjugal relationships, but also of homosexual affairs: the play deals with terror, exploitation and brutality, and portrays the way a lover's fleeting tenderness may be swamped by the irresistible impulse to denude, chain up and flog his mistress. Arrabal's most subtle and complex work, *The Grand Ceremonial*, consists of a clear-sighted examination of the intimate relationship there exists between love and death, mother-fixation and violence, voyeurism and

impotence.   Another play, *The Solemn Communion,* explodes
the myth of youthful innocence by revealing that the little girl,
looking so sweet and demure in her white communion dress,
is a murderess.   This last play is characteristic of what Arrabal
has called the "half religious, half-obscene nature" of his theatre,
as it is typical of the intimate relationship he establishes between—to quote his own words again—"bad taste and aesthetic
refinement".

As in so much contemporary drama—Genet's plays are
another instance of it—there is not much in the way of plot development in Arrabal's theatrical works.   This gives the director
considerable scope for improvization, and indeed requires him to
exploit the possibilities open to him for elaborate ceremonial
and ritual.   The same is true of John Spurling's recent treatment
of the Che myth in *Macrune's Guevera,* a play in which considerable violence is distanced and orchestrated by the device
of putting it at two removes from the spectator—firstly through
the presentation by the playwright-within-the-play Edward
Hotel, and secondly through the inspired graffiti of the Scottish
artist Macrune, who is the immediate subject of the piece.   As a
result, the vision of Che's activities and legend, as seen through
these two deforming lenses, becomes a kind of elaborate charade
in which the lifelikeness of theatre and the theatricality of life
become inextricably confused.   This play, like Peter Weiss's
Marat/Sade which I mentioned earlier, is a complex ballet in
which the actors perform an elaborate, if controlled, dance of
the kind first used by Genet in *The Blacks,* in which a group of
black people conduct an effectively savage anti-white ritual
involving sacrifice and death.   So that we're not surprised to read
Peter Brook's assertion in the preface to the *Marat/Sade* that
everything about the play is designed to shake the spectator
forcibly out of his complacency and bring him back to his
senses again.   The idea of the play, Brook goes on, is the play
itself (something which, incidentally, can be said of nearly all
the plays I discuss in this essay), and this cannot, he says, be resolved in a simple slogan.   "It is firmly on the side", he suggests,
"of revolutionary change.   But it is painfully aware of all the
elements in a violent human situation and it presents these to
the audience in the form of a painful question."

The most violent moment in the *Marat/Sade* is not the
elaborate re-enactment in Charenton asylum of the assassination

of Marat by the ecstatic Charlotte Corday under the direction of the institution's leading patient, the Marquis de Sade, but rather the extreme brutality with which the nurses, on orders from the director of the mental home, restore order when the play breaks down at the end, and the patients, throwing off the discipline of the performance, run amock in the bath-house which is the makeshift theatre Sade has chosen. It is true that the translation published in this country (which reflects Peter Brook's Aldwych production) is more explicit in its stage-directions than the original German version, even at one moment requiring the disembowelling of a prisoner on the revolutionary scaffold; but the point still remains that the cruellest moments of all occur, as it were, between the "inner" and the "outer" envelope of Weiss's conception. It is as if he were saying that theatre cannot ultimately exorcise violence, since it may serve to exacerbate it. But then this *is* a revolutionary situation in more senses than one, Sade acting subversively, like a kind of Red Guard in the face of Governor Coulmier's assertion that the French Revolution, in 1808, has achieved all its aims and that its earlier excesses are to be repudiated. Sade's answer to this, in the teeth of Coulmier's rising dismay, is to set up a situation which, far from being therapeutic and restorative as the Governor intends, is openly disruptive and negative. As President Sadat of Egypt has found with his students, as Mao eventually found even with his devoted Red Guards, a revolution itself becomes an institution which must be preserved, if necessary at the cost of violence suppression, against those who will always assert with violence that it has not gone far enough in wiping out the old order. The Surrealists, after all, were not the first to dream of "permanent revolution". Sade antedated them by over a hundred years with his cry: "Frenchmen, one more effort if you wish to be truly republican!" When he seeks through ideal intermediaries—the patients at Charenton—to put this into practice, the reaction of the "achieved" revolution is as swift and effective as it is inevitable and totally foreseeable from the start.

A similar "social stalemate" obtains at the end of Edward Bond's controversial play *Saved*. Bond justifies the notorious central episode of the play, the stoning to death of Pam's baby by its putative father and his gang of toughs, by saying that "the scene is typical of what some people do when they act without restraint". It is a pity this episode is so often cited without

reference to the context, which, as Bond rightly insists, is that
of a morality play which shows that, in a situation in which, as
he tellingly puts it, religion can "never be more than the opium
of the intellectuals", "morals cannot be slapped on superficially
as a social lubricant". In the current anarchic situation, Bond
shows, horrors will be perpetrated out of cowardice, or for no
real reason at all.

This is also the message of the Italian playwright who enjoyed a brief vogue in the fifties but now seems to be unjustly
neglected, Ugo Betti (1892-1953). *The Queen and the Rebels*
is an overt political play which deals with the issues of human
dignity and bad faith in a context that is unspecified but accurately detailed, owing a clear debt, one feels, to Sartre. A
bloody revolution is in progress but things are not going too well
for the rebels entrenched in their mountain fastness. They must
capture the Queen of the ancient régime and put her to death
before she can be used as a rallying point of the counter-revolu-
tion. A group of travellers is stopped at a mountain village, and
detained on suspicion that the fugitive Queen is among them.
One of the women, Argia, is seeking to join her lover, who acts
as interpreter for the rebels while trying to keep his skin intact
and also feather his own nest in expectation of the time when,
inevitably, the revolution, after its indiscriminate orgy of violence, settles down into its own order and oppression. Argia, a
fairly common tart who as she puts it "was made a woman of"
at the age of eleven, is taken for the Queen. The real Queen
swallows poison before she can be unmasked. In the closing
scene, Argia's cowardly lover having been shot while attempting
to run for it, Argia proves false a cynical assertion (made by
the worldly-wise commissar) that even courage is "gratuitous
and false and easy". Like any Sartrian heroine, she fully assumes
her attributed identity as Queen, and it is in fact in truly regal
manner that she faces the firing squad with head held high.

We may be too cynical, now, to take Betti's confidence
that the rot always stops somewhere, just as we tend to find
some of Sartre's heroes too good to be true. It may be that the
cool unveiling of cowardice in Arthur Adamov's earlier plays is
more convincing, if less flattering to our egos. The plays I am
thinking of—*La Grande et la Petite Manoeuvre* and *Tous contre
Tous*—constitute a ruthless exposure of intolerance, cowardice
and the abuse of power by racial majorities, as well as of the

dishonest hollowness of the political rhetoric which covers such abuses and blatantly excuses self-interest. No specific enemy is mentioned in the speeches Adamov transcribes with Orwellian accuracy: the limping refugees the radio denounces could be Jews, gipsies or blacks, but they could equally well be liberals or revisionists, depending on the context. *Tous contre Tous* is about the cruelty of all political life; the refugees are alternately persecuted and flattered, with cynical opportunism, according to the sort of shifting political needs of the moment which Sartre pillories in *Les Mains sales*. In fact Adamov projects a world not dissimilar from that of the Hungarian film-maker Jancso, in which we witness the disgusting treachery of those who are politically afraid, and in which we observe too the shifting quicksands of political fortune, of anarchy and disorder, of rhetoric and menace, and the consequential spinelessness of all those involved. Adamov's conclusion is lucid and detached: in such a climate only shrewd opportunists survive, like Darbon. All the others, from courageous people like Noémi, to shabby and grovelling people like the refugee Zenno, go under. The play ends with a coda curiously like Ugo Betti's: the stage is cleared and four shots ring out, the last of which silences the Mother, who is perhaps the most loathsome character of all. "Whatever one does", Adamov concluded at this pre-Marxist stage of his career, "one is crushed". It is the message of so much political drama of our time. Even Che, as John Spurling shows, was betrayed. Political violence, it would seem—at least that is what these dramatists think—can only lead to the destruction of what little is good in the wake of so much that is bad.

With Edward Albee we move from the rather grey world of European drama to the vivid milieu of the American college campus. In *Who's Afraid of Virginia Woolf?*—this title is a pun on "who's afraid of the big bad wolf"—we have verbal clashes of extreme violence, explored with almost unprecedented psychological realism, but this very realism, I would suggest, lies at the root of the relative weakness of his play when compared with those I have been discussing: the exposition of the conflict, and its exorcism, are explicit, and must be assessed on that plane. What we find in Ionesco and Pinter, on the other hand, is antagonism of a secret and only half-understood kind, clashes at the subconscious level, in fact; the issue is less explicitly stated than it is in Albee, so that the resolution need not—indeed cannot—be explicit either. Because he adopts heightened naturalism,

Albee—like Ugo Betti to some extent—is faced with the problem of credibility. The "requiem mass" sequence, for instance, is somewhat weak, and the psychological transformation of Honey, who abruptly realizes that after avoiding children for so long what she now most wants is a baby, is rather sudden. Moreover the intellectual allusions in the play could be justified on grounds of realism (this being a college milieu), but equally they can be criticized for flattering the audience. No wonder, then, that Albee has been accused of a certain "flipness" in his dramaturgy and of a feeling that his plays are too "tightly 'wrapped up' "[4] in a way that is not unlike Tennessee Williams. There are human, even sentimental, revelations, such as the fact that apart from her father-fixation Martha loves George more than any other man: she torments him mercilessly, but she could not live with anyone else. Hence the longevity of their strange marriage. Nick and Honey, on the other hand, cohabit mainly for social reasons, with no genuine intimacy beyond a conventional and perfunctory one; they married because they were childhood sweethearts, she believed herself to be pregnant, and there was money on her side. Honey is bird-brained, Nick a social climber, a pro on the make, callow and inadequate under his physical and social assurance. The relationship of George and Martha is exceptionally stormy—positively Strindbergian—with no holds barred in their struggles, but they are bound as close to one another psychologically as the divorcees of Marguerite Duras's play *La Musica.* Martha at first appears the stronger personality of the two—but George reveals his true masculine dominance at the end when he takes the initiative of "killing" their "son". In fact, in the course of the hellish night the quartet spend together (Act II is called "Walpurgisnacht") George, at first sight weak and spineless, turns out to be the strongest of these lost souls. Who *is* afraid of Virginia Woolf? All of them, except George, the most cultivated, intelligent and articulate of the four. The play, in fact, is the story of his triumph. It might almost be seen as a "taming of the shrew"; except that this shrew keeps inventing new rules for their "game" and so continually needs to be retamed. There appears to be no end to the process: but a hint is given at the last that something has happened of a fairly definitive nature. George has killed the son, Martha's alibi, pretext, and hold on George. He took a risk in doing so, but a risk which pays off since Martha is finally not able—or not willing—irrevocably to "break George's back"; she thus concedes him the initiative. Her submissiveness at the end is in marked contrast to her aggressiveness at the start, when she has yelled "what a cluck you are." That, then, is the purpose of the "psychology of antagonisms" which we have seen at work in a number of contemporary plays? In *Who's Afraid of Virginia Woolf?* it is naturalistic, with naturalistic solutions and all that is implied by such in terms of theatrical strengths and weaknesses. But in *Victims of Duty* and *The Birthday Party*, for reasons which are now perhaps clear, this is not the case. We must go deeper to find a clue to the enigma—assuming there is such a clue.

In his critical notice of a Paris revival of *Victims of Duty* Bertrand Poirot-Delpech gave an explanation which may serve as a start. The play, he said, is a "psychoanalytical confession," and he proceeded to elaborate this idea in the following terms:

> In his natural submissiveness Choubert represents an ideal prey for violent people of all sorts, and like Bérenger in *Rhinoceros* can be seen as a martyr to individualism in the face of all coercive systems. But he is first and foremost a victim of duty...of the duty of existence. Whatever the régime, Ionesco's character is condemned all his life to equally absurd repentance and transcendence under the eyes of a father-God who takes refuge in the procreative instinct, and a spouse-mother who nags him uncomprehendingly. Treated by these two like a weak and wayward child, he is compelled all his life to seek their forgiveness for a forgotten offence, and to impress them by impossibly prodigious feats. (*Le Monde*, May 19, 1965, p. 16)

This interpretation is helpful as far as it goes, but it hardly accounts for the role of violence in other plays by Ionesco which also, like *The Bald Prima Donna* of which Poirot-Delpech is mainly thinking in this connection, presents analogies with *Victims of Duty*. In *The Lesson*, for example, a sexual aggression takes place—and a clearly phallic one—but the oral aggression on Choubert is just as sexual, if anything more disturbingly so. In both cases the rape implies a certain degree of assent on the part of the victim, as indeed does the abduction of Stanley in Pinter's play.

There, perhaps, lies the only key to the enigma that we can hope to find by rational analysis. In *The Birthday Party*, as in the work of another Jew, Franz Kafka, a man is recalled to order, a recreant is forcibly retrieved, and the machine of oppression achieves its object. So too with Ionesco's play: the Detective dies a "victim of duty," but his sacrifice has not been in vain, since the other characters unite to continue his efforts in reducing Choubert to order. The sinister thing is that, by this stage, Choubert has become a willing accomplice in the work: after Madeleine's revealing comment "We're all victims of duty!" he joins with the others in shouting "Chew! Swallow!" as the curtain falls.

These plays are therefore concerned with the objectification of a contemporary anxiety, with the subtle acceptance of exploitation and domination, and with extreme violence, the precise nature of which is not interpreted and situated by Ionesco and Pinter, as it largely is by Albee, Betti, or Weiss, but left broadly unassigned. Both *Victims of Duty* and *The Birthday Party* orchestrate with dazzling richness a central image: in Ionesco, the enforced quest for Mallot, in Pinter the running to earth of a fugitive. Are we then to read these two major modern plays as political, or as psychological allegories? As we will: in this sort of drama, for each individal spectator in these troubled times, in the last analysis it is a question of "If the cap fits..." And it is this open-ended ambiguity which gives the less naturalistic type of play—the sort written by Pinter and Ionesco—its extraordinary resonance, and will ensure its durability in the living theatre.

NOTES

1. Quotations are taken from *Amédée, The New Tenant, Victims of Duty* by Eugène Ionesco, tr. Donald Watson (New York: Grove Press, 1958); and *The Birthday Party* and *The Room* by Harold Pinter, revised edition (New York: Grove Press, 1968). References are to the page numbers of the respective volumes, and the difference will be clear from the fact that *Victims of Duty* runs from p. 117 to p. 166, and *The Birthday Party* p. 7 to p. 87. One small change in Donald Watson's translation of *Victims of Duty* has been made where I felt it to be unidiomatic. The quotations from Pinter's *The Caretaker* and *The Homecoming* are taken from the British editions published by Methuen.

2. See "The Gift of Realism: Hitchcock and Pinter" by Alan Brody, *Journal of Modern Literature*, III, 2 (April 1973), 149-172.

3. "Dialogue in Pinter and Others" by John Russell Brown, *Critical Quarterly*, VII, 3 (Autumn, 1965), 225-43 (234).

4. "Albee and the Absurd" by Brian Way, in *American Theatre*, ed. John Russell Brown and Bernard Harris (London: Edward Arnold, 1967), pp. 201 and 207. Earlier in his essay Way calls *Virginia Woolf*, somewhat unkindly, "a cross between sick drawing-room comedy and naturalistic tragedy" (p. 189).

HUNGER AND THIRST:
A CONVERSATION WITH SIMONE BENMUSSA
AND AN ANALYSIS

"I myself do not know whether I am a Christian or not, religious or not, a believer or not, mystical or not," said Ionesco commenting on the title of this play. *"Hunger and Thirst* is a biblical title and I am of a Christian background. We are all hungry, we all thirst. Our hungers and thirsts are manifold: earthly nourishment, water, whiskey; we hunger for love, for the absolute. The bread and meat and wine which Jean, the hero, longs for are only substitutes for what might satisfy a hunger and thirst for the absolute."

The play is an appeal, the story of an odyssey, a quest. Jean goes about the world trying to fulfill this need; only he is mistaken as to the roads, and even as to his desires. He gets nothing. He continues to be thirsty and hungry. His thirst cannot be slaked, his hunger cannot be sated. Why this emptiness? Because every man desires the absolute and the infinite but seeks them in what is relative and temporal. He is able to find nothing since all is wind and ashes. "King Solomon is my master," writes Ionesco in his *Notes and Counter Notes.* Ionesco is well aware that he is not the first to think this way, and that others will continue saying such things after him. There is a great truth in this fundamental banality. The nourishment offered Jean will prove inadequate because the getting of it is precarious, because it deteriorates and proves illusory.

The play is divided into three episodes: the Flight, the Rendezvous, and the Black Masses at the Good Inn. These represent three stages in Jean's quest.

THE FLIGHT

In the first act, Jean and Marie-Madeleine, his wife, return to a ground-floor flat in an apartment building they once occupied at some time in the past. They have a baby, they are young. Jean, however, does not want any part of these quarters which are dark, gloomy, damp, and which appear to be progressively sinking deeper and deeper into the ground. This apartment, a dwelling whose furniture is covered with slime, represents solitude, fear of death, death itself, the grave. Jean wants to escape; he can no longer bear to come close to the image of death he has created. He wonders whether "home" is not composed of the accumulated memories abstracted from one's childhood residences: that of one's mother, a prison for one who longs for adolescence, that which immured the adolescent longing for adulthood, finally that of the adult who dreams of adventure. These homes were jails wherein one envisions liberty, the result of painful, successive beginnings.

Ionesco draws this image from his own dreams. "I know this image represents my mother's house," he confides. "In Bucharest, mother had rented a mezzanine, such as exist in that city, and also in England, in those houses which are at ground level with kitchens located in the basement. She did not have time to live in it, she died just before the date arranged for moving in. The memory of the apartment to which Jean returns in the beginning of the first act represents for me, simultaneously, my mother's flat and her tomb. I believe she subconsciously knew that she was going to die, and her choice of that apartment when she could have rented others, on higher floors, always seemed bizarre to me, struck me as a premonition. It was if she accepted the tomb, as if she were resigned to dying. For me, the place where she never came to live has become the very image of a grave. Each time I think of a similar house, my mother is there."

Marie-Madeleine believes in salvation, and she tries to communicate that belief to her husband. First, she must convince him to enter the state of resignation. He has to be prepared. "This is a house of habit," she says. Does she fail to realize that this declaration strongly suggests her own death, as well as that of Jean? She understand and does not understand, she accepts and does not accept. "So long as I've got a bed, a glimmer of light, and you still at my side—it all seems beautiful." One must accustom oneself to death by habit, rather than face it as a sudden catastrophe; it overcomes you gradually, by successive alterations. It must be made tame. Later, she and Jean will meet with eternity, but imperceptibly, without realizing it, since there is no other way. Thus, the Jean of *Hunger and Thirst* echoes Bérenger the First vis-à-vis Marie and Marguerite in *Exit the King;* it is the same apprenticeship of death preached by women to a man who rejects resignation. Marie-Madeleine looks forward to being alone with her husband: "So long as I'm with you, I'm not afraid to die." Jean refuses. He yearns for youth, spring, adventure, freedom. He wants the Adventure. "Your hold on me is *great.* But the universe is greater, and what I need is greater still."

Thus, there begins between them that dialogue aimed at persuasion, preparation for death, supreme resignation, where everything can be cast in darkness or light, seen as bliss or its opposite. Each has his own point of view; no communication is possible. Jean interprets the damp blotches on the walls of his prison as so many bloody shapes. Marie-Madeleine calms his fears by describing them to him in terms of the colorful pictures in a child's book. One is not surprised by this maternal and "piously" false language used by Jean's spouse; one recognizes in fact the theme of the woman-wife-mother-goddess, the feminine plurality present in all of Ionesco's plays. The way to calm the child-Jean is simply to deny the event: "nobody dies." Or does Marie-Madeleine believe that every presence lives on forever?

As though in answer to this question a character materalizes on the stage, Aunt Adelaide. Ionesco specifies in the stage directions that Aunt Adelaide should first be seen arriving by means of her reflection in the mirror. The end of the act parallels the beginning: she departs but her image lingers in the same looking glass. This poetic device, well-known by phantom creators, makes us take cognizance that the character on the stage has come from another world. Ionesco relates: "My aunt, my mother's sister, wanted to be a vagabond, although she had everything she needed: a lovely apartment in Paris, a dentist's office (this was her profession). This was in 1958, some twenty years after my mother's death. She exercised her profession, and had a pension as well since she was a widow. She had a stroke, like my mother, but unlike my mother she survived it, remaining partially aphasic. At the end of her life, she began to dress in rags and go begging in the streets. She used to stand at the entrance of subway stations. Someone always brought her to the police station, but they never kept her. They would take her home, and in a little while she would start again. Gradually, the policemen became accustomed to seeing her; she was well-known in the district. One day they brought her to the hospital of Sainte Anne, but, soon, since she was unhppy there, she was allowed to go back home. She promised to behave, but she was still roaming the street. Finally, she set her own house on fire. The firemen arrived, and the fire was put out at once. When they questioned her as to who might have done this deed, she answered it was a neighbor. At the time, she was seventy-nine years old. Aunt Adelaide is a very specific memory."

Further in act one, Marie-Madeleine participates actively in Jean's visions. This time the character is voluntarily imagined. Jean's wife lights a fire to dispel his gloom and make him feel nice and warm. Jean sees a woman's face in the flames: "That's how I always see her, desperate, holding out her arms, in agony... there she is again, rising like a phoenix, an eternal reproach... Yes, I know you're frightened, I know you're in pain. If only I could help you. But I can't. Forgive me."

The dead wander through the apartment but they are not benevolent spirits intent on protecting the living; they are Jean's agonizing obsessions made flesh. Marie-Madeleine addresses the woman in the fires as though she could see her as clearly as does her husband: "It's not his fault, my dear..." Jean's wife will not leave him to his solitary state. By associating herself to his most intimate fears and remorses, she slides into his psyche, his memories and is able to intervene in the dialogue he is holding with himself. Ionesco relates: "One night I dreamt I saw a woman caught within a fire. I can still see her terrified expression, her flaming hair. In the dream I tried to jump in, to pull her out of the blaze, but I could not do it, seared by the flame. I woke. The next morning I learned that the woman in my dreams had died in the course of the evening. I was filled with guilt: I imagined I had failed to do all I could have in order to save her. The woman Jean sees in the fire is that very woman."

When Aunt Adelaide appears in the first act of *Hunger and*

Thirst, she does so as the embodiment of a precise memory which, brought to life upon the stage, reawakens in turn a whole series of related memories, remote yet linked through dream. In particular, there is the remembrance of the mother—Ionesco's mother died in 1936 in Rumania—and of her home, both seen through the fiery glow of nightmare. Twenty years after the loss of his mother, the playwright is able to fuse dream and event into the single image of Aunt Adelaide, her personal peculiarities transformed into the fantastic stage gesture of thrusting a knife into her head whence flows a colorless gelatin. The "real" phantom has a double, its reflection in the mirror. It is also her coming on stage which seems to summon the figure in the flames. Thus, the burning building of Ionesco's dream, and the real fire set by his aunt to her own house come together to form an alloy within the crucible of poetic imagination. The characters of Ionesco's world represent in their metamorphoses the writer's private desires, remorses, regrets: they are living concretizations of the questions arising from the playwright's metaphysical anguish.

The theme of encirclement, of asphyxiation, dominant in Ionesco's entire theatre, reaches its greatest intensity in *Hunger and Thirst.* Thought vacillates when the perception of the impossible reaches this degree of sharpness. An answer is no longer possible since the question cannot be formulated; the blind aspirations of a being become the question. The voice suffocates in the relative and the contingent. Can only God question God?

It is necessary for Jean to retrace his steps. Perhaps he does not feel for Marie-Madeleine a love as strong as the one she has for him. As he looks around the home he shares with her, he seems to see only the humidity clinging to the walls. His wife reflects: "I'm joined to him for all eternity. Why do these bonds seem like chains to him?" Jean does not grasp this language. He fails to understand that Marie-Madeleine represents austerity, purity, the asceticism needed for salvation. She is both queens of *Exit the King,* lovely Marie who stands for light in life, but also Marguerite who initiates Bérenger the First to the acceptance of death through which he will, once again, rejoin the light and "take his place" in eternity.

As to the luminous garden not only does it exist, but it is within the house, and Jean could have seen it. For his wife, this garden is love, paradise, but it is enclosed and she wants to keep

Jean there. He, however, because he feels only the threat of imprisonment, does not see the garden. Were he to do so, he would
consider the garden a jail, as he sees the house as a tomb. His
claustrophobia prevents him from believing in a possible freedom
so long as he stays with his family.

Jean is unable to resign himself to the human condition. He
cannot accept being born, living, dying. Thus, it is impossible for
him to cherish the world, or be reconciled to his destiny. A victim of this predicament, he finds that he no longer loves his wife,
at least not in the way she loves him. This is the chain of the
pain of being and of the impossibility of experiencing an absolute
love.

Jean wishes to escape, to run away, and he will finally do
so, but like a child, because he is full of fears and old guilts
which have a strong hold on him. He is afraid of making Marie-
Madeleine unhappy. Also he fears he might need her; he is her
child, he has transferred his filial love onto his wife. There is a
trinity of mothers in the house: his own mother in the flames
of the fireplace, his "second mother," Aunt Adelaide, and his
wife, "a true mother to him." This is what Jean has turned
Marie-Madeleine into, and she allowed this to happen, enjoying
the role. Now he must flee from home. The device he uses to
make his escape is the childish game of hide-and-seek. His wife
accepts to play the game; she is obviously used to it which suggests that it is not the first time. She has had to play games
with her child-like husband in order to demonstrate her understanding, her love, and to make herself loved. She clearly believes that this is the way to keep him calm, to dissipate his
fears; she alone knows that he has never become a grown-up.
Following the "impossible persuasion" dialogue, the game of
hide-and-seek is Ionesco's scenic concretization of Marie-Madeleine's own solitude, of her quest of her own absolute which
lies, for her, in Jean's love. He, however, proves elusive, escaping
her understanding. Other hands will grasp him, hold him.

Does Jean escape through the door, or could it not rather
be that his body is dispersed among the objects in the room?
His head appears from behind a piece of furniture, then in a
corner of the stage, in another,...etc. Let us recall the pantomime in which Harlequin, pursued, becomes elusive by reappear-
ing in all the objects within the house. These become the hiding

place for Harlequin's head, for his foot, but they disappear as soon as the pursuer touches them. Harlequin sprinkles with mischief this bit-by-bit dismemberment of his person. Thus, one could say that Jean does not flee through a door, but through a dream. He is not as elusive, as he is invisible. Marie-Madeleine experiences this invisibility before the actual departure. As she puts on her glasses, then picks up a magnifying glass to look for her vanished husband, the harlequinade ends in a naively nostalgic Pierrot pantomime: Jean reappears, literally carrying the flower of love which his wife claims cannot be plucked from his heart; he has torn off the branch, and sets it on the table. Once again reality and unreality are visibly joined.

THE RENDEZVOUS

Outside, there are roads. Jean wanders along them, through marshland, through arid plains. He reaches, at last, a plateau on which stands a museum. He does not enter the latter since the doors are closed. The musuem cannot be visited; "At the moment it's not the season," explain the two watchmen whose exterior appearance is identical. In any case, Jean cannot go in for he is waiting for someone to arrive. He has a rendezvous with a woman he loves, or perhaps has loved, or will love. This act is one of expectation, or perhaps one ought to say it is itself "in expectation," in the sense of "in suspension."

Following the threat of suffocation which pervades act one, the second episode is one of brath, of respiration, and thus, for Ionesco, of theatricality. "Happiness uplifts me...No, it's more than that, it's a rising tide of irresistible joy, a great wave that sweeps through me and makes the desert fertile. "This episode evokes a rush of love, as one speaks of a "rush of air," one of the most magnificent in the history of dramatic literature. Jean having left his dwelling—tomb or egg—is on his way to hell. This central episode is out of time (or, at least, as we will see later, in an accelerated time, so compressed that it seems timeless), out of space, suspended like a drop of water. Jean uses the word "brought" to describe his journey to that spot: "Somehow I seem to have been brought here." This is a stationary point where lines of force come together, reach a kind of balance: the rush of love, the refusal of love, remembrance and forgetfulness, desire and sin, exaltation and anguish, distance and the fixed point, acceleration and immobility, meet half-way in perfect equilibrium. Here, contrary propositions are equally true, and opposite emotions equally sincere. It is of course from these opposite threads that Ionesco weaves the fabric of his plays. Events cross each other, cancelling one another out. This is a juncture, the fusion of opposites into frozen waves.

Cosmic dynamism is the very essence of Nature. This formula recalls Marie-Madeleine's exclamation: "Why does he get in a state? All houses are tombs." Why be surprised by a particular *locus* of death, since death is everywhere. Is this not merely a tautology? Could one not make a case for Jean reliving the obvious which he envisions in a luminous present whereas the response he receives is tautological? In this sense one could say that Marie-Madeleine, like the two watchmen, is deaf to Jean. One of the watchmen does not understand Jean's lyric outburst; it suffices him to know that this man is happy: "Well, that's all right then! Good...I'm glad, for your sake, to see you so happy...This gentleman is happy." One could say with greater precision: this gentleman is happy for the moment; when anguish will overcome him again, dust and derision will be "Nature."

Will a shadow obscure this miraculous clarity? "Though I can almost feel her presence, behind it there's a void. But it's sure to be filled in the end..." "If the impossible were to happen, and she didn't get here today, could I leave word with you?" The watchmen require "some means of identification" since Jean does not carry "a photograph" of this woman. The total similarity of uniforms and appearance deprives the guards of individuality. Ionesco suggests in this scene the faceless impersonality of the law as well as the concomitant sense of guilt experienced by us in the face of authority. This time, however, the power of authority is used gently, helpfully. Yet, one cannot help feeling that if these identical twins, the guards, were to multiply, to proliferate, turning into a throng, the multitude would crush Jean.

The two watchmen represent the beginning of a geometric progression, the image of a regular, mechanical oppression, the kind of malady which afflicted the corpse in Amédée's apartment. The underlying impression of a repressive authority, still barely concretized in the insignificant persons of the museum guards, is nevertheless insidiously disquieting. The seed of tyranny is ready to flower as the uniformed guards insist on an identification of "this lady." How can Jean, dreaming of an invented memory, provide them with anything so precise? He has forgotten the name of this woman. He can evoke her only through images, impressions: a glance, a smile, the love she inspired. He no longer remembers the color of her eyes, her hair, her height. The essence of love has come to replace the identity of the woman he loved. Is she a being he has loved, or is he waiting for a love still unknown to him? Isn't his whole being composed of the will to love? Again both propositions are true: the "lady" is at the same time a guilty, forbidden past love, its face erased or disappearing under the layers of overlapping memories, and a projection of an impossible, longed for love, the symbol of the thirst for timeless passion. A stage direction at the beginning of the second act bears out our opinion; it is specified that "the light will be cold, an empty brilliance, without shadow and without sun." The impossibility of shadow, therefore of any contrasts, transports the viewer into an ideal, divine place. When more precise memories of the beloved arise, Jean will again see the contrasts, watch the movement of the sun: "I can see us walking side by side in the sunshine...I can still see our two shadows." He will also be able to describe the road with a certain amount of precision, unlike a man who finds himself "brought" to a certain place. With the return of memories, we become convinced that love was present, and that we were led into the very image of love. There was a beloved, but, transcending her, there was a vision of absolute love, glowing in the past, extending into the future, omnipresent. The awareness of this kind of passion fills Jean with the nostalgia of fullness. "A case of burning nostalgia," Marie-Madeleine called it. The gradual, gentle loss of happiness is modified by the suggestion of consummation. Here one finds the theme basic to all of Ionesco's works: the duality which the writer cannot reconcile within himself and which makes for "ardent" suffering.

Jean has condemned himself to love not at all, if not absolutely. All earthly love, all human love implying death cannot fulfill him. When he refused love, claiming that he had to be free, was he not deceitful? Is he not rather afraid to suffer, yet ready to carry the greater burden of nostalgia? To love absolutely is to be liberated from death, and that cannot be granted a mortal.

Who then is this woman Jean seems to have lost? Is it indeed a woman? Jean's evocation is a liturgy of love. This goddess, revealing herself miraculously in a clearing of a virgin forest, grows, merges with nature, yet remains a spiritual creation. She is earthly and heavenly, rising towards the skies and spreading in space at the same time. She is outer abundace and the inner sanctum of the temple; she is both sanctuary and cult. Jean calls her "my home, my haven." She is a divinity who "used to adorn herself with bracelets," sailing proudly "in a blue embroidered dress." "Misty eyes...no, black...no, very bright...and penetrating, no elusive...with a present, no, absent look, the color of certain dreams, as gentle as the touch of a warm river in summer. You see? She's easy to recognize!" Perhaps so, since she is Nature in all her seasons, the incarnation of the miracle of Being. But also this love is a mass Jean forbids himself to celebrate. Nor can this love story ever succeed either on the psychological or metaphysical plane. Psychologically, if Jean loves someone he destroys the attributes of that person; he kills Marie-Madeleine within his heart, thus stilling the ancient echo of his mother's voice. Metaphysically, fullness becomes vacuity as guilt bores a hole through which all must trickle into the world.

Having left home, Jean finds himself in a state of sin, and thus already in hell. For a while he will continue to wander in between a lost paradise and a promised land. Act Two, like the First Act, ends with the same chain woven from a double impossibility: that of existing and that of loving absolutely. Whether in the damp basement, slowly sinking in mire, or on the airy terrace suspended between heaven and earth, Jean has been travelling in circles. He must now explore Hell.

THE BLACK MASSES

The last episode takes place in a dubious inn, run by fake monks. A kind of black mass will be celebrated. There, everything is trickery. The devil is legion.

Jean makes his way there through roads that vanish, and the place he reaches seems strangely deprived of any surround-dings. From the moment the curtain is raised, even before we hear the explanations offered by Brother Tarabas, whose task it is to welcome visitors, we feel the hostile atmosphere of the place, contrasting with the fawning speeches of the brother. This is a prison, barracks, a hospital, an inn, stratifications of a single establishment used at different times for a variety of purposes; such is the deliberately mollifying explanation proffered by Brother Tarabas, but we cannot help but think that it is rather an ever growing, threatening multiplication of punitive places: hell.

Brother Tarabas calls it an "establishment," proud of the fact that he uses an exact word. Isn't the exact word often the most indefinite? Memories of disciplinary institutions going back all the way to grammar school crowd in. Jean is far from "home." He has an inkling that he is not welcome, no matter what they try to make him believe. The hearth has no fire, the door creaks. Yet, Brother Tarabas' first words are: "Come in and welcome, guest. Come in." It seems strange indeed that in such a place, so overcast with mist, there should be so many passing travelers that the function of "brother in charge of welcoming strangers" should exist. They were expecting Jean, however; they knew that he would, of necessity, reach this inn. It is the garrulousness of Brother Tarabas who eagerly provides bits of harmless information which makes us uneasy about this false inn. His explanations are of the familiar, fairy tale type: If I've got large ears, my child, it is the better to hear you. The homespun cassock? "We wear these habits for the sake of convenience," says Tarabas. Another brother enters, clenching a carbine; during the entire scene he will remain seated, his rifle directed toward Jean. "That's our hunting brother," Tarabas ventures politely. "We do our own hunting, our own fishing." Jean, confident, calm, pleasant, does not sense anything, and thanks the brothers for all the attention they lavish upon him: bread and water which he devours greedily, and which is brought him at an ever quickening rhythm. The two actions are connected: he eats because food is brought endlessly, the food is being offered because he is not sated. We receive the distinct impression that Jean will never break out of this circle.

This episode is constructed as a series of successive, cross-reflected interrogations. In this game of questions and answers,

the answers can only be inadequate since the questions are
faked. We are reminded of extorted confessions, of trials where
the final decision has been arrived at before the facts. These
false, God denying monks, will force Jean to admit that he has
seen nothing of the world since artistic creation is doomed to
failure; in this void, memories are empty of content. The tor-
mentors' method rests on their ability to make Jean believe
that his memory is faulty. "He's inventing new words, so we
don't notice the ones he's forgetting." As soon as he acknowledges the existence of nothingness, Jean becomes one of them,
a member of the order; henceforth he will be addressed as Brother Jean.

The powerful Tarabas, the play's principal character, employs methods of seduction. His plaything, now Jean, will be
caught in the web and brought to confession. He owes the
brothers a debt of gratitude—they have been good to him—and
so he will relate, since they wish it, the story of his travels.
Little by little all the brothers appear on the stage. A feeling
of uneasiness, brought about by the increasing restlessness of
the crowd, pervades the atmosphere without Jean realizing it
at first. The monks fuss over him obsequiously, washing his
feet, applying warm towels to his face—this last deed is done at
the precise moment Jean tries to speak. "You're lucky to have
the chance to travel...," says Tarabas, admiringly. Made uncomfortable through excess of generosity on his hosts' part, Jean in-
quires how much he owes them—This is, after all, an inn. "Don't
bother about it," is the answer. He insists he would like to pay.
Smothering him with hot towels, they assure him: "It doesn't
cost much." It will cost him his existence. The only alarming
hint can be read into the fact that one of the brothers stands
before the door, blocking the exit.

Tarabas himself must obey the Brother Superior. The
latter is a character larger than life. Ionesco specifies that he
should be on stilts. His appearance is fantastic: a nude figure
in white robes. Tarabas will often turn toward him, interpreting
what is believed to be the opinions or directives of the Brother
Superior. For Ionesco, this character does not exist. He represents the parody of the tyrant, and perhaps, the parody of a
false priest of God. Dogma is caricatured here, Godless dogma,
dogma turned by men into a divinity. This kind of false creation
needs an interpreter. Tarabas who seems to decipher Brother

Superior's impassive face is well suited to his function, and he in turn, has assistants of lower rank which reveals the powerful hierarchial structure of this establishment. Yet this social pyramid does not rest on anything solid. The display of rank and power allows the audience, represented on the stage by the monks come to view the play within the play presented for the visitor, to imagine a veritable force of fear, artificial fear, founded on a void, yet-generating ever greater anguish. Tarabas makes use of all the sadistic methods of political interrogations and brainwashings. He is the examining magistrate, the torturer, the policeman rolled into one. He is always able to prove that the other is in error, and thus, in the end, he will ensnare his victim, just as every tyrannical regime triumphs where it can establish its domination.

Ionesco portrays fake monks because the Inquisition is the archetype of the Gestapo, the N.K.V.D., of all police brutality. It is the image par excellence of the dark times, the middle ages of the mind, when all ideologies became extreme, aggressive and criminal. Whatever form tyranny assumed, Tarabas represents them all, including the tyranny of conformity. One must distrust false saviors, affirms Ionesco. "We wish you to be saved," echoes Tarabas.

The first comedy of questions imposed on Jean is the tale of his journey. What has he seen on his way? What has he done with his life? All is a failure. As to the monks, they know in advance what they want to hear. Jean has surveyed the world, seeing it in all its insignificance, in its hazy daily routines. The brothers reproach him for having failed to encounter fabulous cosmic events, yet they know that he would have seen nothing of the sort, and they are gald of it. In a negative kind of way, Jean is guilty, and thus he belongs to them. A fallen angel, like themselves, Jean will bring proof of the fact that creation is a derision. He should have seen 'the crystal wolves, the petrified hag, and the airy temples." He saw nothing of the sort. They corner him. He is forced, over and over again, to transcend personal memories and enter the realm of dreams and light where the marvelous can be glimpsed. But Jean has only seen life: men and women passing by, children with satchels on their backs. He is condemned unless he can go further, will himself beyond the confines of this world. Pressed in this manner, Jean loses all presence of mind: as he describes the

fragments of the world he has glimpsed his anxious replies become no more than strings of words, meaningless nouns.

It is too late when Jean understands why he has seen
nothing. His whole life could have been a continuum of vital
moments—a possibility denied by the false monks—if he had
only understood that light can be found everywhere and in
everything, if he had only believed Marie-Madeleine. The policeman in *Victims of Duty* says to Choubert: "I should have
liked to fill the emptiness with life." Two views of the world
were possible, one of disgrace and one of grace. We find these
two polar states in all of Ionesco's plays: one of euphoria in
which light is diffused over the world, making trivial events
appear miraculous, objects of awesome wonder, where the
child passing with a satchel on his back becomes a miracle of
creation as fabulous as the crystal wolves or the shining knight;
and the other, gloomy, heavy, where nothing stands out on the
immense gray plain. He has vaguely glimpsed—perhaps it was a
trick of his imagination—the face of old age itself.

Ionesco's theater is one of poetic confession, confession of
a time beyond dream, as "the dreamer withdraws from his
dream," a fact which is revealed only through writing. And when
the world is no longer adequate, then there are the simplest, the
most primitive gestures, for they, the ancient ones, render the
world concrete again upon the stage. And when these will no
longer suffice, there are objects which begin to act, and subjects
that translate remote obsessions. Everything is mobilized so that
this confession can be made to us. Then, finally, all the roads
disappear. Nothing remains.

After his examination by the Inquisitors, Jean recognizes
his failings. It is at this moment that the monks choose to present a show to their guest who is now one of them. To illustrate
this "didactic entertainment," produced by the Pedagogical
Brother in charge of "education and re-education," two men
are brought in, imprisoned in two cages. Jean is told that they
are old clowns, former professionals. They play respectively the
parts of Tripp and Brechtoll—the word Tripp suggests "les
tripes" (the bowels) of one who is perpetually hungry; the name
Brechtoll is a portemanteau word à la Lewis Carroll, a combination of Bertolt and Brecht.—These two comedians will eanct a
frightful farce, a mock-ceremony of a false trial preceding the

final judgment. The audience itself is conditioned, breaking into teams: on one side sit the red monks, on the other the black; each group will react according to its allegorical ideology. The game of faith denial, and compromises begins. There is no enigma, no truth to discover. Everything is false, anything is true. The two clowns are starving men, and they are ready to exchange their beliefs with one another, shifting their ideology to the opposite ideology for a bowl of soup. Tarabas plays his cat and mouse game. Dishes are held out to them, then removed from their reach. Tarabas does not act directly; he is assisted by two brothers who add their dose of sadism to the proceedings, denouncing the clowns, altering their words and meanings, turning a deaf ear even after they have exacted a renunciation of former beliefs. This play within the play is a spectacle on many levels. Above all Ionesco mocks political trials, revealing the vitiated mechanism of justice.

What roles do these old clowns, and false monks play? "Brechtoll is Brecht," Ionesco says, "with his false certitudes, his fanaticism which can shift to the opposite fanaticism, with his truth which is neither better nor worse than another, and with his cowardice." The two characters are interchangeable. He who believes in God will give up his faith. He who does not believe will turn to religion. An extreme ideology can easily become anoher extreme ideology. Thus, neither message has any value since each is the product of certain interactions at a given historical moment. Brechtoll will make concessions he maintains are necessary, and these, in turn, will lead him to total repudiation. He will repeat, after Brother Tarabas: "Our Father...Give us our daily bread." After this treatment for ideological detoxification, the spectacle will culminate in the final brainwashing: the demystification of the ideal of Freedom.

Horrified by the violence and the cowardice he has been made to witness, Jean expresses the wish to see the show stop. He is asked whether he enjoyed it. They could repeat the performance, shifting roles since each clown has "learnt the two parts." Brechtoll could play Tripp; Tripp, Brechtoll. "Thank you, it would give you too much trouble," Jean ventures. The Third Brother is disturbed: "Trouble? Why did you say trouble? It was for *our* pleasure and for *your* pleasure."

Now that Jean has been fed and entertained he will have

to pay back his debt to the monks. How long will this take?
The duration of Hell. The manner in which he will repay the
order for its kindness will be by serving it. Since he is at the
lowest echelon of the hierarchy, his job will be to pass food
to the perpetually famished monks. As he begins his penance,
he is dressed in monk's habit. "It's so you won't dirty your
clothes, Brother Jean," is the deceitful explanation. As the
members of the community go through the ritual of placing
the hood up on his head, Jean is told: "It's so the smell of
cooking won't get in your hair." Thus, he will pay with the
coin of Eternity. Time is fragmented into infernal minutes,
their numbers appearing on illuminated screens. A choir of
monks chants the figures. As the immense gear is set in motion, Jean passes the platters at an increasingly staccato rhythm.
As early as 1959 in the n°15 of *Cahier des Saisons*, André
Breton wrote about one of the early Ionesco plays the following which, when seen in connection with this play, acquires
its full impact: "Let us savor, led by Ionesco's masterful hand
to the confines of spasmodic laughter, the bitter pleasure of
witnessing the stripping of our privileged-subordinate condition
which allows us to participate at once in the madman's mass
and the prisoner's rounds."

Is Jean in Hell or Purgatory? During the black mass, the
luminous garden of the first act reappears, with its Jacob's
ladder rising to the sky. His wife and daughter (the latter is
grown, indicating the passage of time) are there, calling to
him. Jean exclaims: "I'd never noticed the light all round
you before; you've always been in that light. I hadn't realized."
Is this his guilt, the sin which has brought him to this Hell?
"Wait for me," he cries out, "now I understand."

Ionesco once wrote: "The fact that we are filled with
an inexplicable nostalgia might after all be the sign that an
elsewhere exists."* This sentence might lead us to believe that
there is still a hope of light. Perhaps an answer can be found
in the exclamation of the Guard in *Exit the King:* "Oh, you,
great Nothing, help the King.!"

Translated by Judith Kutcher and Rosette C. Lamont

*   Revue de métaphysique et de morals.   Simone Benmussa's analysis of
Hunger and Thirst was based on the list of the play as it appeared in numbers 146, 147 and 148 of the NOUVELLE REVUE FRANÇAISE (Febru-
ary-April 1965).

Editor's note: In the summer of 1969 Ionesco came to Stockbridge to
overlook the production of his *Hunger and Thirst*.   One morning he began
to discuss this scene with a group of friends.   "Aunt Adelaide," he said
"is at once a ghost and a real person. The ambiguity must be carefully preserved. I had such an aunt, my mother's sister. She was married to an un-
frocked priest. She herself was a professional woman, a dental surgeon.
When she sold her dentist's office she went off the deep end. She took to
begging. It was she, however, who helped my mother when our father left
her. This was of course before she went mad. As to my mother, she brought
me and my sister to Rumania after my father, a lawyer, had won a custody
case despite the fact that he had abandoned us. My father was remarried,
and his new wife was not at all pleased at the idea of having us, but she
could not say so. Our mother began to look for an apartment for herself.
One night I dreamt she was caught in a burning building and I was unable
to pull her out; the following morning we found out she died that night."

MACBETT IN THE LIGHT OF *VERFREMDUNG*

by Edith Kern

Ionesco's *Macbett* might well be called a masterpiece of *Verfremdung*. While Martin Esslin's designation of Ionesco's early plays as theater of the absurd seemed felicitous, the term no longer appears to fit his more recent theater. Indeed, if one wishes to characterize all of Ionesco's theater, from *The Bald Soprano* to *Macbett,* with one word which would also relate this theater to the world view predominant in our time, one might well use that of *Verfremdung.* Yet is seems almost sacrilegious to do so, since Ionesco has ridiculed the term as vehemently as he has attacked the German playwright who made it famous. Ionesco's barbs against Brecht and the Brechtian notion of *Verfremdung* (or what he seems to have considered it to be) are to be found mainly in his satiric play *L'Impromptu de l'Alma* (1956) (*The Shepherd's Chameleon*); in his *Notes et contre-notes* (1962) (*Notes and Counter Notes*), a collection of essays, talks, and notes, some of which had appeared in print earlier; and in his play *La Soif et la faim* (1966) (*Hunger and Thirst*). Before looking, therefore, at *Macbett* in the light of *Verfremdung,* one feels the need to find the reasons for Ionesco's antipathy against the German playwright and his theatrical theories and to ascertain their validity.

It is *The Shepherd's Chameleon* which is most revealing in this respect. Ionesco himself described it as "une mauvaise plaisanterie" ("a rather wicked joke") and continued to explain: "I put on the stage friends like Barthes, Dort, etc. ...To a large extent this play is a *montage* of quotations [compiled] from their erudite studies: it is they who wrote the play. There is also another character that is Jean-Jacques Gautier. I have not made a success of that character [...] . And yet he is the most dangerous of dramatic critics: not because of his intelligence, for he is not intelligent; not because of his severity for which there is no foundation; but because one knows when he attacks an author, that author is ready to believe himself a genius."[1] As these statements reveal, the play was conceived as a satire against a number of contemporary critics, two of whom, Roland Barthes and Bernard Dort, had been favorably inclined toward Ionesco's early plays, while the third, Jean-Jacques Gautier, the critic of *Le Figaro* and defender of bourgeois boulevard theater, had been his natural opponent. What is, of course, significant is that both Barthes and Dort had been among the founders of the bi-monthly *Théâtre Populaire,* which had become one of the staunchest defenders of the Berliner Ensemble in the wake of its success during the international theater festival in Paris, in 1954. Together with other members of the journal's editorial staff, they had also become admirers of its director Brecht, praising him as playwright and theoretician of a new *engagé* and Marxist theater. A take-off on their theatrical criticism involves, thereby, willy-nilly a take-off on Brecht as they interpreted him.

In 1955, the January/February issue of the *Théâtre Populaire* had been dedicated to a presentation of Brecht and his dramatic theories. It contained an unsigned Editorial, most likely written by Barthes, contributions by Michel Habart, Walter Weideli, René Leibowitz, and Bernard Dort as well as excerpts from Brecht's theoretical treatise "Petit Organon pour le théâtre" (*Little Organon For the Theater*) and from a few of his minor plays, such as *Grand'Peur et misères du Troisième Reich* (*Great Fear and Misery of the Third Reich*). Ionesco seems to have been annoyed, and perhaps felt threatened, by this unbridled admiration which was leveled at a theater that was presented as both political and Marxist, for his *The Shepherd's Chameleon* (not unlike an article written almost simultaneously by his friend Lemarchand)[2] lashes out against the dogmatism of the *Théâtre Populaire* which intended—as Lemarchand put it—to "muzzle young authors, as do bourgeois critics for other reasons."[3] The *dramatis personae* of Ionesco's play—whose title was obviously inspired by Molière's *L'Impromptu de Versailles* and Giraudoux's *L'Impromptu de Paris* and which, like them, represents the author's attempt to defend his theater—consist of a fictitious author by the name of *Ionesco,* three critics, and the maid Marie. *Ionesco* is shown writing a play when, one after the other, the three critics invade his study. Called, respectively, *Bartholoméus I, II,* and *III,* the critics obviously share the root of their name with Barthes, while its Latin suffix and their costumes designate them as pedants, and the threefold repetition of name and costume makes them ridiculous. It was in an answer to questions, subsequently asked by the periodical *Bref,* that Ionesco stated, with tongue in cheek, that this "wicked joke" was actually written by the critics whom he ridiculed in it. Peter Ronge's careful research has revealed the extent to which Ionesco's claim is justified.[4] He found that the play's dialogue is largely Ionesco's own free invention, although it follows Moliéresque—and one might add Commedia dell'Arte—schemata and grotesquely employs the jargon of Brecht's French admirers. In a lecture which Ionesco presented at the Sorbonne, in 1960, and which he entitled "Propos sur mon théâtre" ("Remarks on my Theater and on the Remarks of Others"), he spoke with even more resentment of Brechtian critics as those "docteurs" who "wish to be obeyed. They are furious if they are disobeyed. They do not like you to be what you are, they would rather you were what *they* want you to be."[5] What he referred to was an article, allegedly written by Dort about himself and Adamov, wherein the critic had said of both playwrights: "They have 'destroyed' a certain theatrical idiom, now they must reconstruct it; they have criticized, they have rejected, now they must take a positive line."[6] Ionesco concluded that Adamov, having followed the route suggested by Dort, i.e. having embraced the notion of engaged theater, retained the critic's favor, while he, having insisted on mapping out his own itinerary, was excommunicated by the *Théâtre Populaire.* It was in the same lecture that he referred to a conversation he had had with a British critic and during which it was intimated to him that there was an ingredient which would turn him into "the greatest writer in the theater to-day," if he were to avail himself of it. Eager to find out about it, he was told: "We are only waiting for you to deliver us a message. Up to now your plays do not have the message we were hoping from you. Be a Marxist, be Brechtian!"[7]

One would hardly expect a playwright of the power and imagination of a Ionesco to look with favor upon critics who wished to turn him into another, or upon the other whom he was to emulate, and one is not surprised that he delighted in caricaturing these critics as well as Brechtian ideas as they were filtered through their writings. But this disfavor alone does not account for his antagonism. In his article "Une Nouvelle

Dramaturgie" ("A New Dramaturgy"), which had appeared
in the Brecht issue of the *Théâtre Populaire,* Dort had stated
that the German playwright had broken with traditional historical theater wherein "history was simply presented as a condition of the plot and society, as the background against which
the action whose eternal character and universal value the author carefully establishes unfolds."[8] He has maintained that
"Brecht had precisely challenged such eternal and universal
aspects of actions, which for him are always in functional relationship with the society wherein they take place. His theatrical
universe does not consist of a tragic action seen in a certain
historical milieu. It is a whole wherein all elements act upon
each other—a 'social gestus' in relation to which the spectator
must consciously situate himself."[9] The editorial of the same
issue had summarized in terms which seem to echo Diderot that
Brecht does not think of art as essentially eternal but rather
as something each society must invent according to its own
needs.[10] The impression one gains, moreover, from an excerpt
of Brecht's *Little Organon,* included in this issue, is that all
theater previous to that of Brecht is faulty. But it is the translation and the excerpting which are at fault: they convey a misleading emphasis. Brecht had simply advocated the search for
new theatrical patterns that would correspond to and reflect
our changed conceptions of man and the universe—something
Diderot had advocated for his time and Ionesco and the French
avant-garde were equally striving for. One has but to reread
Ionesco's "A Talk about the Avant-Garde" in order to be reassured on this point. "At the beginning of this century and in
the 1920's in particular, a vast universal avant-garde movement
was felt in all domains of the mind and human activity. An
overthrowing of our mental habits. Modern painting from Klee
to Picasso, from Matisse to Mondrian, from Cubism to Abstrac-
tionism expresses this overthrow, this revolution. It emerged
in music and films and it affected architecture. Philosophy and
psychology were transformed. Science [...] gave us a new vision
of the world. A new style emerged and continues to emerge.
[...] Literature and drama from André Breton to Maïakovski,
from Marinetti to Tristan Tzara or Apollinaire, from the Expres-
sionist drama to Surrealism, down to the most recent novels by
Faulkner and Dos Passos and quite recently those of Nathalie
Sarraute and Michel Butor, have all shared in this surge of new
life. [...] The theatre is the most behindhand."[11]

What Brecht meant by *social gestus* is also so distorted by the French translation that the simple advice to the actor which it was meant to be is lost; namely, that he was to create onstage not merely an isolated, self-contained character but rather the social attitude people assume toward each other through the movements of their bodies, their tone of voice, their facial expressions, and which changes according to the social relationships established among them.[12] To realize the significance of this *social gestus* would seem of particular importance to the actors and actresses of Ionesco's plays. A good performance of *La Cantatrice chauve* (*The Bald Soprano*), for instance, would seem impossible without it. Yet what Ionesco gleaned from texts available to him induced him to have *Bartholoméus I* and *II* mock Brecht by declaring him their "God," according to whom Shakespeare was to be condemned as insignificant for having a foreign name which the *Petit Larousse* lists as Polish, and Molière to be denounced as "a bad actor," a reactionary, who since he is still appreciated, could not have expressed "the social gestus of his era."[13]

Ridiculing the very existence of Brecht's *Little Organon,* Ionesco has *Bartholoméus I* order *Ionesco* to open "the treatise of the great doctor Bertholus." In reality, Brecht's treatise was only a small volume wherein he formulated with the forceful simplicity of his later style some theoretical and practical concerns of what he considered modern "scientific theater." To *Bartholoméus I* this implies that he can promise *Ionesco* for his new play "a new theater, a scientific director, a company of young scientific actors who wish to usher it in with you. You will be treated scientifically." (12) When Brecht spoke of scientific theater, however, he had in mind a theater intent on conveying a vivifying experience rather than on lulling the spectator's senses. Fundamental to his notion of art is *Staunen* (Engl.: wonder, being astonished), which is also a crucial aspect of the scientific attitude. And he explains that "neither he to whom the equation two times two equals four appears commonplace nor he who does not understand it at all is a mathematician."[14] Galileo, who did not find it commonplace that a lamp would swing on a rope, recognized the special nature of the pendulum and "came thereby close to an understanding and thus a mastery of the phenomenon."[15] He was a scientist.

It is in this context that Brecht's notion of *Verfremdung*

assumes its importance, and one regrets that Ionesco had to be introduced to it in so incomplete and thereby misleading a fashion. Dort, for instance, describes it in "A New Dramaturgy" as follows:

> Rejecting all theatrical "illusion," Brecht bases his theater on *distance,* an alienation (*Verfremdung*): distance of the author from the reality from which he extracts his work, distance of the actor from the action (in the tradition sense) and from the character he plays, distance of the audience from the spectacle. And this distance is not an aesthetic one: not the effect of a style of writing or staging which would bring about the integration of the work in a literary rite...It is *historical,* the product of a divided society and a moment in history where all contradictions coexist.[16]

What this presentation overstresses are the practical effects Brecht, undoubtedly, had in mind. What it totally omits is the highly artistic attitude fundamental to the concept and central to the way in which Brecht envisioned the functions of playwright, director, and actor. Quite likely, Brecht derived the term *Verfremdung* directly or indirectly from the Russian Formalists' concept of *priem ostrannenija,* English: "making strange," German: *"verfremden."*[17] Since 1919 and throughout the twenties (which were also Brecht's own twenties), the Formalists had maintained that the function of the poetic image was not that of bringing us closer to a thing but rather of presenting it in a novel light by "making it strange." Shklovskij, the foremost spokesman of this poetic school, had declared that "the poetic use of the image, as distinguished from the 'practical,' lies in a 'peculiar semantic shift,' in the transfer of the object depicted to a different plane of reality. The habitual is 'made strange'; [...] the chain of habitual associations and automatic responses is broken: thus we become able to *see* things instead of merely recognizing them."[18] To make us *see* things has, in one form or another, always been the concern of poets, but the Russian Formalists had consciously singled it out during the twenties, and it was re-echoed by Cocteau's attempts to astonish, by those of the Surrealists and the Cubist and Abstract painters to create ("a fantastic world of new relationships"), and even by the Existentialists, e.g. by Sartre in his *La Nausée.* Brecht's poetry (including tht of the theater) with its startling juxtapositions of words and images is expressive of such *Verfremdung.*

However, Brecht was also the first among modern playwrights to see the implications of the concept for the theater. "A presentation which estranges (*verfremdet*) is one which lets us recognize an object but makes it appear strange at the same time," he states in his *Little Organon.*[19] While he introduces the term *Verfremdungseffekt,* or V-effect, he assures us that such forms of presentation had already been experimented with at the Theater of the Schiffbauerdamm in Berlin during the period between the first and second World Wars. At the same time he is fully aware that the tradition of *Verfremdung* is actually an even older one: "Ancient and medieval theater made its characters strange through masks of man and animal, and the theater of the Orient still uses musical and mimic V-effects;"[20] So does the circus clown. Since astonishment and wonder were to make visible what had been concealed under the veil of habit and the customary, guidelines for the organization of a theater, its writing, its staging, its acting, had to be developed so as to produce this effect. They had to be developed in contrast to the prevailing Aristotelian type theater as well as to Oriental theater which had become rigid in its patterns of *Verfremdung.* While Brecht did not specifically mention the Commedia dell'Arte, he seems to have espoused its spirit,[21] as did such French contemporaries as Jacques Copeau, who were also in search of a theater that defied Aristotelian rationalism and mimesis.

Despite the rigidity which Chinese theatrical *Verfremdung* had assumed, Brecht thought its techniques useful in the developing of his own. He found that the Chinese actor behaved on the stage in a manner that made it obvious that he was aware of being watched by an audience. This removed the illusion, created on the European stage, that the spectator is actually hidden behind a fourth wall and is, thereby, an invisible onlooker, a witness to a real event. As a consequence, the Chinese actor could consciously choose his stance of *actor* and in plain view of the audience select the manner which best conveyed what he wished to present. Such staging, however, becomes ironical and self-conscious. The actor "looks at himself" as it were and is fully aware of the use of his body, an awareness he does not have to conceal because his aim is not to create an illusion. Such an ability to "stand outside himself" is considered by Brecht a highly artistic achievement. It creates that distance between the actor and the part he portrays that Diderot had already considered essential to good acting, and it may, at the same time, create a distance between the audience and the actor. As a consequence, the emotions presented by the actor and those experienced by the audience might well be very different from each other.

This was not Ionesco's understanding of Brecht's notion of *Verfremdung,* and in his attempt to demolish what he considered it to be Ionesco opened up, in his *The Shepherd's Chameleon,* all the registers of his sarcasm, making the three "docteurs" look like the donkeys whose masks they don and whose demeanor they actually assume at the end of the play. What *Ionesco,* the author within the play, is engaged in writing is the very play the spectator sees unfolding before his eyes, namely, *Ionesco* beleaguered by three critics who wish to teach him how to write his play. Ironically, their very didacticism is thus concretized onstage, and they are truly *writing* the play with their dialogue: their dialogue is the play. Such a situation is, as all characters realize, "a vicious circle," and a way out of it is sought by the playwright or "playwrights." By means of a burlesque jargon, the way out (French: s'en tirer) is found through a mere juggling of words, suggested by the critics in concerted effort: "Substitute for the expression 's'en tirer,' the expression 's'en distancier' which means 'to keep one's distance,' and you will understand. To be more precise: one can distance oneself from the vicious circle only by not leaving it; one gets out of it, on the other hand, only by staying within it. [...] For the more distant one is...the closer one is...and the closer...the more distant...This is the electric shock of distancing or the Y-effect." (18-19) The concept of "distanciation" is absurdly concretized onstage when *Ionesco* is made to break the vicious circle of his play by opening the door for Marie, who has been clamoring to be let in, and is directed by *Bartholoméus I* and *Bartholoméus II.* "But be careful when you open the door. Play the scene according to the principle of distancing. [...] Do not identify with yourself. You have always been wrong to be yourself. [...] Keep your distance. [...] Observe yourself while acting. [...] Look at yourself out of one corner of your eye, listen to yourself with the other! [...] Be crosseyed, be crosseyed...!" (49)

Ionesco's outrageous parody is, unfortunately, a fight against windmills in more than one way. In its basic Brechtian sense, the notion of *Verfremdung* is instrumental in Ionesco's own conception of art. This is clearly revealed in his Conversations with Bonnefoy.[22] He describes, for instance, his moments of artistic conception in the following manner: "I have the feeling of being among extremely polite people, in a more or less comfortable world. Suddenly something breaks loose and rips, and man's monstrous nature is revealed, or else the décor takes on an inconceivable strangeness, and perhaps in this way men and décor reveal their true nature." And he compares this moment to the nature of theater: "Perhaps that's what theater is: the revelation of something that was hidden."[23] Ionesco's own definition of avant-garde theater even contains the germs of *Verfremdung* through dialectics. Ths is how he expressed it with regard to his play *La Cantatrice chauve* (*The Bald Soprano*): "It was by plunging into banality, by draining the sense from the hollowest clichés of everyday language that I tried to render the strangeness that seems to pervade our whole existence. The tragic and the farcical, the prosaic and the poetic, the realistic and the fantastic, the strange and the ordinary, perhaps these are the contradictory principles [...] that may serve as a basis for a new dramatic structure. In this way perhaps the unnatural can by its very violence appear natural, and the too natural will avoid the naturalistic."[24] These statements, to which might be added many more from among Ionesco's writings and interviews, easily serve also to describe Brecht's theater. If Ionesco failed to recognize the common denominator in their conceptions of art, this is perhaps also due to the manifold translations of the German term *Verfremdung*. Peter Ronge compiled a list of the French equivalents used by different translators, who chose them depending on the aspect of the term they wished to emphasize.[25] He found such translations as "éloignement," "étrangeté," "dépaysement," "distanciation," and even "aliénation." One can only agree with Hartwig Hanstein that it is "aliénation," with its Marxist overtones, that most strongly perturbed Ionesco and prompted him to assert the importance of man's innermost being as against any "social alienation" and to declare society itself as "alienating."[26]

How foreign this conception is to Brecht's theory becomes obvious when we look at his discussion of the "street scene," one of the many examples he had chosen to explain to his actors the techniques of acting necessary to achieve *Verfremdung*. Brecht had published it under the title of "Theatrical Experiment 10."[27] It had been singled out in Dort's discussion of the

the playwright's dramaturgy,[28] and had achieved a certain notoriety because Adamov, speaking of his own development as a playwright, also referred to a scene he observed on the street and which made him realize the importance of simple, everyday occurrences as inspiration for his work.[29] (Ronge reminds us that Diderot had likewise made mention of a street scene in his *Paradoxe sur le comédien* in order to exemplify the difference between nature and art.) Aiming his sarcasm at Dort's discussion of both Brecht and Adamov, Ionesco ridiculed the "street scene" in his *The Shepherd's Chameleon.* Upon being pressed by *Bartholoméus I* to tell him what the subject of his "play" is, *Ionesco* describes it as follows: "I saw once upon a time in a large provincial town, in the middle of the street, in the summer, a young shepherd who embraced a chameleon, at three in the afternoon. ...This moved me very much...I decided to make a tragic farce from it." (13-14) *Ionesco* even chooses as title for his play *The Shepherd's Chameleon.* Here, then, is an absurd street scene, used by *Ionesco* as "inspiration" for his play. To Brecht, however, the "street scene" exemplified what he considered "epic" theater—a concept which was also developed in the theater of the Schiffsbauerdamm in Berlin and of which this non-Aristotelian element of *Verfremdung* formed a crucial element. Essential to the scene is the fact that an accident has happened on the street and is reported by one of the bystanders. The form of his story may differ depending on such hypothetical questions as "who was at fault?" "why was the driver drunk?" etc. His comments are determined by them and aimed at answering them. At the same time, he is not personally involved in the events but merely demonstrates them as he comments upon them. He may even at times turn directly to the spectators and thereby interrupt his demonstration. If an actor onstage wishes to produce a similar effect, he has to study the art of *Verfremdung.* What he creates in employing it is epic theater.

But while Brecht conceived *Verfremdung* first of all in artistic terms, it is also true that he thought of it as something which de-emotionalized theater and made spectators not only *see* but also come to certain conclusions and possibly assume certain attitudes and actions. One is reminded of the Sartrean notion of the writer as "revealing" the world and of writing as a secondary mode of action. Dort was certainly correct in presenting the V-effect as something which would permit the spectator to disengage (literally, "unglue") himself from the spectacle and to understand it, "by deducing from it the great structures along which the society presented is organized and, through reflection upon them, grasp the historical significance of the fatality which crushes him, today,"[30] Brecht did, indeed, distinguish between old techniques of *Verfremdung* and new ones, maintaining that the new techniques aim not merely at description but beyond that at a kind of description which forces the spectator to *see* and think. The Editorial of the January/February issue of the *Théâtre Populaire* was justified in concluding that to Brecht the world seemed "maniable" (manageable) and that "Art can and must intervene in history."[31] But except for a brief period in his life when he was consciously didactic and Communist—although he did not even then succeed in pleasing the Communists—Brecht did not conceive of theater in terms that would have justified Dort to claim that his dramaturgy, in postulating the spectator's freedom, envisions theater as truly polemical.[32] It is doubtful, moreover, whether his mature plays with their theatrical dialectic convey anything comparable to a politically definable attitude. In retrospect, even his consciously didactic plays, such as *The Measures Taken*, appear to have shed their historical aspect and assumed universal overtones. Like Ionesco, Brecht had always insisted that theater must be entertainment and should be enjoyable. By taking their cues from the critics of the *Théâtre Populaire* rather than Brecht himself, the critics of *The Shepherd's Chameleon* grotesquely distort Brechtian views. *Bartholoméus I*, for instance, demands that theater be "a lesson on an instructive happening, a happening capable of teaching"; *Bartholoméus II* maintains that "one should go to the theater in order to learn"; *Bartholoméus III* that "an author must be a teacher" and is obligated to be boring; all three agree that theater should be "a required course" for which notes are to be given. (28-31)

Ionesco apparently was so irritated by what he considered to be Brechtian didacticism that he decried it as "an attitude of mind and an expression of the will to dominate."[33] He referred to all Brechtians as "terrorists" because, in his view, they wished to suppress all diversity in the theater.[34] Even a decade later, looking back at the time when he wrote his *The Shepherd's Chameleon*, he speaks of it as "the days of Brechtian tyranny, or of a tyranny that the Parisian Brechtians—revolutionaries without an army and one or two revolutions behind the times—were trying to impose."[35]   The revulsion he felt for "Brechtianism" was clearly transferred to Brecht himself.   In his *La Soif et la faim* (*Hunger and Thirst*), he portrayed him under the name of Brechtoll as one of the grotesque clowns that act out the play within the play.   The entire plot of this interior play is a droll take-off on the refrain of the *Threepenny Opera* "Erst kommt das Fressen, dann kommt die Moral" (Food first, morals later!).   In order to eat, the imprisoned clowns are forced to change their beliefs as completely as does the protagonist of Brecht's *A Man Is a Man.*

Yet Ionesco himself has been accused of didacticism and has even admitted to having written *engagé* theater.   In his Conversations with him, Bonnefoy had rightly pointed out that his *The Shepherd's Chameleon* is a thesis play, although written in defense of the freedom of creation and freedom from didacticism. When he was asked in an interview with *Cahiers libres de la jeunesse* whether his notion to make the spectators of his plays feel ill at ease wasn't a didactic aspect of his works which he denied nevertheless, he answered somewhat evasively: "I think I did say that once: in the stage directions written for the actors in *Jacques ou la Soumission.*   I wanted something 'painful' in their acting in order to convey to the audience a kind of unease that would correspond to the absurdity of the characters."[36] In the same interview he admitted to having contradicted himself by having attempted with his *Rhinocéros* (*Rhinoceros*) to write "engaged" theater.[37]   Most critics are agreed that the direction of Ionesco's theater has fundamentally changed since his *Tueur sans gages* (*The Killer*).   There are others who find germs of didacticism even in his earliest plays in the sense in which they make the reality they present to us "strange" and thereby make us *see* for the first time our language, our institutions, and our beliefs.   Julian H. Wulbern has gone so far as to claim that *Le Roi se meurt* (*Exit the King*)—perhaps Ionesco's most metaphysical play—"has achieved *Verfremdung* in the most Brechtian sense."[38]   As for *Macbett*, Ionesco has clearly stated that it was conceived as an attack on the violence that he finds rampant everywhere these days.[39]   While he considers it naïve to assume that such violence can be solely explained by social and economic reasons, he thinks, nevertheless, that it is man-made and might be avoided.   This is what he says in the program notes he wrote for the play: "Nevertheless, quite contrary to what one

might think, essentially my latest play is not truly concerned
with death but with murder and genocide. Murder can be
avoided—death not." But even in his contradictions and in his
insistence upon his right to be contradictory Ionesco shows an
amazing kinship with Brecht and the Brechtian conception of
theatre.

It is, therefore, doubly regrettable that Ionesco saw Brecht's
theories and practice only through a glass darkened by understandable exaggerations and generalizations of journalism. As
one rereads his *Conversations* with Bonnefoy and finds recorded
there his own regret that no real discussion was possible between
himself and the Parisian "Brechtians," one wonders what it
would have been like if the two playwrights had ever met to exchange ideas on the theater. But it is unlikely that Brecht was
even aware of the barbs Ionesco directed against him in his
The Shepherd's Chameleon, since the play was first presented on
February 20, 1956, thus only six months before the German
playwright's illness and death. At any rate, no reaction on
Brecht's part is extant to my knowledge. Wulbern tells of
attending a meeting of the Berliner Ensemble troupe in East
Berlin, in 1965, when the newly published German translation of
Notes and Counter Notes was read and discussed. Helene Wei-
gel's strong reaction to it, which Wulbern describes as one of
dismay and anger, seems to imply that Ionesco's views had been
unknown to her.[40] While a confrontation of the two authors
would not have shown them to be in full agreement in either
theory or practice, it would have brought to the fore the strong
anti-Aristotelian attitude which they share and which was nourished by and has in turn contributed to one of the most powerful
ideational currents of our time. *Verfremdung,* replacing Aristotelian empathy and individual catharsis is, as we have seen,
one of the essential ingredients of that current. So is the attempt
to create a theater no longer based on Aristotelian *mimesis* but
rather on a stylization that, defying the faithful imitation of
nature, makes the accustomed seem strange, new, and illogical.

In what sense, then, is *Macbett verfremdet?*

Ionesco explains in his Program Notes for the play's performance at the Théâtre Rive Gauche, that he called it *Macbett*
with two "t's" to differentiate it from Shakespeare's *Macbeth,*
which—he added with tongue in cheek—"will obviously be

known to quite a few." The two "t's," however, already announce that *Verfremdung* which, according to Brecht, lets us recognize an object but makes it appear strange at the same time. *Verfremdung* prevails in the play's plot and characters; they are based on those of Shakespeare and yet are different and appear, thereby, strange and startling. Ionesco presents no logical plot in the Shakespearean sense. He alters the composition of those participating in the action as well as their relationships. The significance of these changes becomes apparent as soon as one compares Shakespeare's list of *dramatis personae* with that of *Macbett.*

Duncan appears in both plays as King of Scotland, although his personality is altered by Ionesco. He portrays him not as a good man but as one full of contradiction. Of Malcolm and Donalbain, who are listed by Shakespeare as his sons, only the older appears in *Macbett,* but his name is distorted to Macol and he reveals himself miraculously not as the King's real son but rather that of Banco. "I am the child of Banco and a gazelle," he explains to Macbett, "which a sorceress had metamorphosed into a woman. Banco did not know that he had impregnated her. She became a gazelle again after having given birth to me."[41] Lady Duncan, for reasons that remain unexplained, had merely pretended that he was her and the King's son. By means of this altered relationship, Ionesco can make the Witches' prophecy concerning Banco's offspring grotesquely come true, while Shakespeare leaves this question unanswered. Macol's implausible origin creates a certain plausibility: Macol will be able to kill Macbett, because he is not born of woman. He can lawfully succeed him, since he is thought to be the son of Duncan. And he will be the founder of a new Banco dynasty. Since he is the son of Banco and resumes his real name, he will be Banco I, to be followed in due time by Banco II, III, IV, and so forth. Duncan's second son Donalbain, omitted from Ionesco's list of characters, is, nevertheless, briefly alluded to within the play. The First Witch, informing Macbett that Duncan has a younger son by the name of Donalbain, assures him at the same time that there is no need for him to remember this name, as Donalbain will not play any part in the unfolding of events. Ionesco thus ironically alludes to the fact that in Shakespeare's *Macbeth* he is merely a stage presence but never assumes the dimensions of a character. With slight alterations of their names, Macbett and Banco are retained in Ionesco's play and so is their basic relationship, although their function in the drama has been essentially altered, as a discussion of the play's structure will reveal. It is also significant to mention that many supporting characters, who in Shakespeare's *Macbeth* bear names and are thereby individualized, appear anonymously as "officers" and "generals" in Ionesco's version. Shakespeare's Sergeant has become a mere Soldier in *Macbett*. Lady Macduff as well as her son have been entirely left out by Ionesco who has thereby also omitted the murderous episode in their house. But what is more significant is that, while leaving out Lady Macbeth, he added the *dramatis persona* of Lady Duncan, who to some extent assumes the character of Lady Macbeth and, indeed, marries Macbett—or so it seems. The play's two Witches (not three as in *Macbeth*) prove, moreover, to be identical with Lady Duncan and her Lady-in-waiting. Still more significant is that the rebel Thane of Cawdor—merely referred to in *Macbeth*—assumes as Candor stage reality in Ionesco's play, together with the rebel Glamiss, while, in Shakespeare's play, "thane of Glamis" is one of the titles of Macbeth. It is as if through this sleight of hand Ionesco implied that each new title added to the name of the protagonist represented a traitor killed.

The French play is essentially non-Aristotelian.

It has no beginning, middle or end. Macbett is circular in structure, though in a more intricate manner than most of Ionesco's theater preceding it. One might think of it almost as a series of events, each closed upon itself and, like links of a chain repeated an infinitum. The play begins with the simultaneous entrance, from opposite sides of the stage, of Glamiss and Candor, the stage representing an open field. Since the two noble warriors move in a symmetrical pattern towards the center of the stage and stand there silently side by side, facing the public without apparently recognizing each other, a comic element attaches itself to them and counteracts their dignity: In their near-identity of exterior and action, they resemble the *zanni* of the Commedia dell'Arte. Their mask-like doubleness is intensified through the mechanical quality of the ensuing stage-play and dialogue. They simultaneously turn to face each other, greeting each other by uttering each in turn: "bonjour, baron," followed by "listen, Candor" and "listen Glamiss," respectively. Stage directions indicate that they are furious, and that in the scene which unfolds their anger and derision grow steadily. The target of their growing fury is Duncan, whom they accuse of being: "A tyrant, an usurper, a despot, a dictator, an infidel, an ogre, a donkey, a goose, worse even." (15)   As they conclude their list of insults and swear each other loyalty in their common aim to dethrone Duncan, Banco and Macbett—one after the other—cross their path and give expression to their faithfulness and admiration for Duncan.   This symbolical crossing, which is both visually and verbally established in this scene, is shown in the subsequent one as having resulted in war, although in non-Aristotelian fashion Ionesco omits all logical links and merely indicates through visual and aural means that a battle is raging. War is suggested through light and sound effects as well as through soldiers passing by, and wounded men and women dragging themselves across the stage.   From Macbett and Banco we learn that they are fighting for their King against the rebels. As they arrive onstage, one after the other, to pause momentarily in their battle, they not only look alike, wearing the same costume and beard, but also behave and speak alike: "Macbett enters from the back," the stage directions read.   "Macbett and Banco look alike.   The same costumes, the same beard.   Banco enters from the right.   He is tired; he sits down on a stone.   He holds his sword in his hand.   He looks at his drawn sword." (21) This is exactly what Macbett had done when he had come onstage before him, and the words spoken by Banco, as he looks at his sword, are identical to those Macbett had uttered before him.   While these words are meant to be a recital of their achievements, they are also grotesquely descriptive of war.   Without intending to do so, the two "heroes" make war appear strange and make it emerge in all its horrors.   The effect of *Verfremdung* is intensified by the fact that situation and words are thus twice repeated.   One is reminded of Brecht's advice to his actors to rehearse creating the V-effect by having them meet a character looking like them.[42]   But Ionesco creates an even more profound sense of *Verfremdung* in this scene because the comedy inherent in doubleness is juxtaposed with the hypnotic power inherent in the mechanical repetition of the terrors of war.   The image which emerges is imbued with surrealistic horror.   A few lines may suffice to convey the power of such *Verfremdung:* "The blade of my sword is red with blood.   I have killed dozens of men with my own hands;" Macbett realizes proudly.   "There isn't enough land left to bury them all.   The bloated bodies of those who drowned have drunk all the water of the lakes into which they had been thrown.   There is no more water, not even polluted

water. [...] The cut-off heads of our enemies, of whole batal-
lions, brigades, divisions, service corps with their leaders, from
the brigade generals hierarchically down to the division generals,
the 4-star generals, and the marshals spit on us and insult us.
Arms severed from bodies continue to brandish their swords or
to draw their pistols. Feet torn out still kick us in our behinds.
It is true that they were traitors. Enemies of the country. And
of our beloved sovereign Duncan, the Archduke. May God pro-
tect him. They wanted to overthrow him. [...]" (21-23) While
Macbett is certain that his cause is just, he feels at the same
time inexplicably nauseated, as does Banco in his turn.

But the technique of *Verfremdung* excludes any cathartical
identification with either Macbett or Banco. Their victories and
doubts remain subservient to the structure of the play and are
metaphysical rather than psychological. What was represented
visually in the first scene, namely their physical and verbal
crossing of the paths of Candor and Glamiss, now has assumed
dramatic proportions: the axis of their fidelity to Duncan has
cut across that of the traitors. A symbolical cross has been
formed, representing "the combat of two powers, the one above
and the one below," as Lady Macbett expresses it later in the
play. (85) The combat results in the destruction of the rebels
and their followers. But as the traitor-axis Candor-Glamiss is
destroyed, it is diabolically replaced by another consisting of
Macbett, Banco, and Lady Duncan. Due to the prophecies of
the Witches, to the tyranny of Duncan vis-à-vis Banco, and the
temptations Lady Duncan puts in the way of Macbett, relationships are abruptly changed. The shift is concretized in a conversation between Macbett and Banco, wherein expressions of
admiration and loyalty for Duncan become more and more
ambivalent and, finally, as did those of Candor and Glamiss at
the beginning of the play, turn as openly into expressions of distrust and rebellion. Their violence grows like that of an ava-
lanche, words engendering new words and new emotions:

Banco: Never seen such a thing.

[...]

Macbett: With all those who rummage and reach about him.

B: Who get fat by the sweat of our brow.

M: By the fat of our fowl.

B: Our sheep.

M: Our pigs.

B: This pig!

M: Our bread.

B: This blood we have spilled for him...

M: The dangers he involves us in...

B: Ten thousand fowl, ten thousand horses, ten thousand young men. What does he do with them? He cannot eat all. What is left over rots.

M: And a thousand young girls.

B: We know well what he does with them.

M: He owes us everything.

B: Even much more.

M: Without counting the rest.

B: My honor...

M: My good name...

[...]

B: [We demand] the right to increase our wealth.

M: Antonomy.

B: To be the only master of my territory.

M: He must be driven from it. (70-71)

The dialogue culminates in the description of Duncan as "the

tyrant," "the usurper," "the dictator," "the despot," "the infidel," "the ogre," "the donkey," "the goose"—as had that of
Glamiss and Candor. Ionesco's dramatization of these two characters thus served him to establish a parallelism which is both
dynamic and "estranging." It underlines the rôle of ambition
leading to treason and murder, while detracting from individual
motivation. A study of character is superseded by a mythical
constellation of forces that are perpetually destroyed and reborn.

For as soon as the opposition Candor-Glamiss/Macbett-
Banco has come full circle, a new circle starts, wherein Macbett
is accused by the ghost of Banco of the very tyranny of which he
accused Duncan and is finally killed by the son of Duncan and
Banco, who has become a new axis in the cross of opposing
forces. Ionesco's Macbett, unlike Shakespeare's Macbeth, kills
Duncan with the help of Banco and Lady Duncan. It is only
after Lady Duncan has revealed herself as identical with the
Witch, who had foretold his accession to the throne, and now
promises him her hand in marriage, that Macbett considers Banco
a rival and kills him. To Banco's ghost, who appears to him during the wedding feast, it is now he who is "a traitor, a scoundrel,
a killer" (91) and to Macol, who later kills him, "a tyrant."
(102) Again a circle has been completed and a new link in the
chain of violence started.

For at the very moment that Macol kills the tyrant, he him-
self becomes a tyrant and states this in no uncertain terms.
Candor and Glamiss, Macbett and Banco as well as Lady Duncan,
to justify their betrayal of Duncan, had employed a verbiage
similar to that of the public relations offices of governments.
The second Witch, having revealed herself as Lady Duncan's
Lady-in-waiting, had put it most succinctly when reassuring
Macbett: "Tell yourself that we want to save the country.[...]
You are going to build a better society, a new and happy world."
(61) Even if Ionesco's stage directions ask for a progressive darkening of the scene as a symbolic punctuation of the treacherous-
ness of her words, these words presume Macbett's hesitancy to
accept evil in its starkness. Macol, on the other hand, while
greeted by all as the hero and liberator, leaves aside all pretense.
He bluntly announces himself as being the scoundrel that Shakespeare's Malcolm only pretended to be. Ionesco merely translated Shakespeare into French and turning Shakespearian dialogue into monologue, deprived Malcolm's words of their attenu-

ating context:

> Myself [...] in whom I know/All the particulars of vice so grafted/
> That, when they shall be open'd, black Macbeth/Will seem as pure as
> snow, and the poor state/Esteem him as a lamb, being compared/With
> my confineless harms. [...] I grant him [Macbeth] bloody,/Luxurious,
> avaricious, false, deceitful,/Sudden, malicious, smacking of every sin/
> That has a name! but there is no bottom, none,/In my voluptuous-
> ness; your wives, your daughters,/Your matrons and your maids could
> not fill up/This cistern of my lust, and my desire/All continent imped-
> iments would o'erbear/That did oppose my will; better Macbeth/Than
> such a one to reign. [...]/With this there grows/In my most ill-com-
> posed affection Such:A staunchless avarice that, were I King,/I should
> cut off the nobles for their lands,/Desire his jewels and this other's
> house;/And my more-having would be as a sauce/To make me hunger
> more; that I should forge/Quarrels unjust against the good and loyal,/
> Destroying them for wealth. [...] I have none [of] the king-becoming
> graces/As justice, verity, temperance, stableness,/Bounty, persever-
> ance, mercy, lowliness,/Devotion, patience, courage, fortitude,/I have
> no relish of them but abound/In the division of each several crime,/
> Acting it many ways [...] (Shakespeare, *Macbeth*, IV:3 lines 50-97.)

While Ionesco clearly states his source he obviously does not
mention that he *verfremdet* this speech when employing it in his
own play. For what was Malcolm's psychologically calculated
misrepresentation of himself in Macbeth, has become, in *Macbett*, a structural necessity. In Shakespeare's tragedy, Macbeth,
a good man, led astray by the powers of evil, turned murderer
of a good man and was in turn destroyed by a better man. In
Ionesco, it is evil itself that, in the form of ambition and lust
for power, instigates an unending chain, a dance of death, wherein each individual becomes wittingly or unwittingly a participant.
As Macol reveals himself a villain, all those that had celebrated
his victory desert him one after another, so that their physical
departure from the stage, concretizes the inevitable isolation of
the tyrant, whose vocabulary abounds in such terms as "power,"
"overthrow," "destroy," "king," "empire," "super-majesty,"
"emperor of all emperors." One realizes that new rebels will
soon materialize who will overthrow Macol only to become
tyrants in turn and be overthrown. There is no end to this plot
as there was no beginning. Parallelism and circularity create a
dynamic pattern of war and violence that is *verfremdet* by means
of the comic mechanism of *zanni*-doubleness and repetition.

It is not accidental that Macbett stresses the resemblance between himself and Banco. When Lady Duncan first addresses Banco as Macbett, the latter himself explains that he looks at times like his own twin and sometimes like that of Banco. (29: 30) In the quasi-comic, Commedia dell'Arte-like pursuit, Macbett and Banco are forever calling out to each other and forever failing to meet during battle. It is as if the mechanism of ambition and power had usurped all individuality. Speaking with Bonnefoy about his film *La Colère* (*Anger*), Ionesco observed—employing the words of Bergson—that "a little of something mechanical encrusted on the living" is comical. But he maintained that things become stifling and tragic, "if the mechanical gets bigger and bigger and the living shrinks and shrinks."[43] In another of these Conversations he referred to Feydeau's gratuitous "mechanics of proliferation" and "geometric progressions." In *Macbett* the result of the mechanic foisted on the living has such vast and mythical implications that the tragic wins out over the comical, as both are *verfremdet* in this process of proliferation. Duncan, having rebuffed Banco's rightful claim to have his services rewarded, admits: "I don't know what got a hold of me. I should have made him a baron," only to conclude that "he also was desirous of wealth. [...] But if he becomes dangerous, one must be careful." (63) And to the officer who eagerly agrees with him, he shouts: "You, too, are a little ambitious, aren't you? You would also want, of course, that I strip Macbett of his tithes and wealth to give them to you, at least in part." (64) The pattern of ambition, avarice, and ensuing danger is further reinforced as he realizes that "Macbett also is becoming dangerous. Perhaps he would like nothing better than to have this throne in my place." (64) But when Macbett has actually usurped Duncan's place, he, too, learns that "History is sly. Things escape us. We are not masters of what we set in motion. Things turn against us. All that happens is the opposite of what we wanted it to be. To govern, to govern.[...] Events govern man—not man events." (89) The serious mood which has been created is dissolved and *verfremdet*, however, when Macbett imagines that someone has put in the place of his portrait that of Duncan and calls the action a sinister farce—an episode which makes his guests wonder whether "accession to power entails...myopia," thus stressing the farcical aspect even more with their pun on *myopia*.

Similar *Verfremdung*, permitting of no Aristotelian identifi-

cation or illusion of reality, is created by the figure of Lady
Duncan. As mentioned before, she is a weak reflection of
Shakespeare's Lady Macbeth, undoubtedly one of the most
interesting characters of world literature. Jan Kott, the Polish
critic whose interpretation of *Macbeth* allegedly inspired Ionesco,
presents her as the moving force of all the horrors perpetrated
in the tragedy, since it is she, the childless woman, who perpetually fans her husband's ambition by questioning his mascu-
linity and desiring the murder as proof of her love for her.[44]
Lady Duncan, though partly resembling her and assuming some
of her gestures, is, however, never motivated by psychological
necessity. All her actions seem gratuitous. After having stabbed
her husband, for instance she looks at him and finds that, in
death, he resembles her father. This seems but a weak and futile
echo of the episode in *Macbeth,* where the Lady is unable to kill
because the sleeper resembles her father. The famous sleep-
walking scene in Shakespeare's *Macbeth,* which shows Lady
Macbeth washing her hands, is also alluded to in Macbett, although its function is changed altogether. Duncan asks his wife
to be present during a scene when all those who betrayed him
are guillotined. As more and more guillotines appear on the
stage, Lady Duncan has tea served and has a basin of water,
soap, and a towel brought to her. According to stage directions,
she is to wash her hands as if to remove a tenacious spot. The
psychological gesture has been *verfremdet* but, in its grotesque
contrast to the beheading scene, serves to underline the horror
of the latter. So do Lady Duncan's counting of the heads that
fall and the simultaneous advances she makes to Macbett "to
the point where she becomes excessively and grossly indecent."
(38) Not unlike Lady Macbeth, Lady Duncan arouses Macbett's
ambition by linking it to sexual prowess. Yet, unlike her prototype, she does not bring into play allusions to conjugal relationships, but, while coarsely enslaving him, reveals herself identical
with that monstrous Witch that sends him on his road to murder
and perdition.

In establishing this unity which underlies the double figure
of Lady Duncan-Macbeth and the Witch, Ionesco achieves a number of V-effects:

The three Shakespearean witches are reduced to two: Lady
Duncan and her Lady-in-waiting, and are thereby deprived of the
magic that the number three entails. Their metamorphosis places

them within the realm of probability, that is, it makes them appear like real persons in disguise. Simultaneously, their witch-
ness is *verfremdet,* as it seems to be contained mainly in their
attire which they may put on or take off. Paradoxically, their
droll departure on flying suitcases ironically counteracts all
probability. At the same time, they seem to be theatrical concretizations of ambition and lust, "non-representational forms,"
exteriorizations of passions.[45] In that respect they belong to
the realm of myth where witches exit, one exclusive of probability. As such they are *verfremdet* from any logic or psychology. Ionesco leaves us in doubt as to whether they are intended
to be forces of evil and whether Lady Duncan actually assisted
in the murder of her husband and later married Macbett or
whether the Witch kept her emprisoned and usurped her place.
He suggest no reason why she killed her husband and fails to
explain her attitude toward violence and power. Ionesco apparently aimed at contradiction and paradox. It is as if he had
adopted one of the tenets of Brechtian *Verfremdung,* namely,
that the unity of a character is established by the manner in
which man's qualities contradict each other.[46] *Verfremdung* is
further created through the unexpected metamorphoses before
our eyes of two ugly Witches into the beautiful Lady Duncan and
her Lady-in-waiting and of two charming women into ghostly
hags. These transformations destroy theatrical illusion and in-
duce irony and *Verfremdung* in the manner of the Commedia
dell'Arte, a manner often practiced by Brecht, for instance, in
The Good Woman of Setzuan.

By altering character relationships and plot, Ionesco thus
seems to have clearly put into practice what he envisioned in a
"Note on Theater" written in 1953. He dreamed then of stripping "dramatic action of all that is peculiar to it: the plot, the
accidental characteristics of characters, their names, their social
setting and their historical background, the apparent reasons for
the dramatic conflict and all the justifications, explanations and
logic of the conflict."[47] What he wanted to emulate was the
"dramatic quality" of paintings which, like those of Van Gogh,
were expressive "of a clashing of forms, of lines, of abstract
antagonisms, without psychological motivation."[48] Crucial in
this statement is Ionesco's desire for abstraction, stylization, and
absence of psychology. To call theater thus envisioned merely
absurd would be absurd in itself. It is rather a theater that,
moving away from mimesis and empathy, speaks to the spectator

through the techniques of irony and *Verfremdung*. As such it belongs to the non-Aristotelian tradition of the Commedia dell'Arte, whose most salient trait is—quite contrary to common belief—by no means improvisation. While techniques of irony and *Verfremdung* may become highly intellectualized, they may also relish in the concrete, as they do in the theater of both Ionesco and Brecht. It is not surprising, therefore, that the "abstract antagonisms" that pervade *Macbett* are also rendered concrete through stage play and stage properties.

Décor and lighting have an essential part in this play in terms of irony and *Verfremdung*. I have already mentioned the proliferation of guillotines and fallen heads which symbolize tyranny and through their grotesquesness make it "strange." The mechanical entrances and exits of characters as well as the masks seem to stem directly from the Commedia dell'Arte world and introduce laughter where seriousness is expected. The detached episodes of the lemonade vendor and the butterfly catcher are like *lazzi*. The dance-like movements of the Witches that seem to enfold and engulf Macbett and Banco are what I have called elsewhere "concretizations of metaphor," frequently found in the Commedia dell'Arte.[49] It is Commedia dell'Arte-like *Verfremdung* that emanates from the Soldier scene which was, no doubt, inspired by the beginning of *Macbeth*. In Shakespeare's tragedy, the Sergeant praises the protagonist's bravery in battle. But in *Macbett*, the Soldier rather resembles the figure of a *zanno* who utters wisdom unwittingly. As he arrives onstage, Duncan first believes him to be drunk, then, having learnt that he is wounded, asks him for news of the battle, only to be told: "What does that matter?" Not only does the soldier not care, but he does not understand at all what is going on. He does not even know the names of his generals: "I do not know. I came out of the inn, a sergeant on horseback caught me with his lasso. He was the one who enlisted me. My pals who were with me could get away. [...] I tried to resist, they beat me, bound me, led me away. They gave me a sabre. Well, I no longer have it. Then a pistol. [...] They made us yell: 'Long live Glamiss and Candor!' [...] And then they made us prisoners. And then they said to me: if you wish to keep your head on your shoulders instead of seeing it rolling at your feet, march with us now. They told us to cry: 'Down with Candor and Glamiss!' Then they were shot at, and then we were shot at. [...] And then there were only masses of dying men every-

where [...]." (26-27)   This is the naïve irony of the Soldier
Schweik whom Brecht dramatized.   Filtered through the eyes
of this "simpleton," this Commedia dell'Arte *zanno*, war appears
strange and we are made to *see* its horror.

What seems to place this and others of Ionesco's plays
likewise within the realm of this type of non-Aristotelian theater
is the pattern of its dialogues.   The dialogue between Macbett
and Banco already quoted might serve to illustrate how close
the techniques utilized by Ionesco are to those of the Commedia
dell'Arte repartee, as preserved in the model books for actors.
Here are for comparison a few lines from a model dialogue,
entitled "Dialogue of Scorn Against Scorn":

The woman - The ties...

The man - The chains...

W - What do you tie?

M - What do you link?

W - This soul.

M - My heart.

W - Tear yourself apart!

M - Break!

W - If faithfulness...

M - If love...

W - Bound you...

M - Welded you...[50]

The two characters to whom any name might have been assigned are clearly juxtaposed rather than engaged in true dialogue.   Their conversation works itself into a pitch similar to
Macbett's and Banco's when they shout: "Our sheep."—"Our
pigs."—"The pig!"—"Our bread."—"He owes us everything."—

"Even more."—"Without counting the rest."—"My honor..."—
"My name..." etc. It is equally *verfremdet.*

Verfremdung, then, is but the old-new technique and essence of a theater that in its very make-up is non- or anti-Aristotelian (both Brecht and Ionesco have designated their theater
as such); does not strive after classic rationality and unity of
action; does not aim at *mimesis* or *catharsis,* relies on verbal
and stage play, *jeu,* and shows human conflict as inherent in a
web everyman (not an individual character nor a God) has
woven. To thus see himself, man must look at himself, a stranger
—*verfremdet.*

NOTES

1. Eugène Ionesco, *Notes and Counter Notes*, tr. Donald Watson (London: John Calder, 1964), p. 133.

2. Peter Ronge, *Polemik, Parodie und Satire bei Ionesco* (Bad Homburg v.d.H., Berlin, Zürich: Gehlen, 1967), p. 88, n. 235.

3. *Ibid.*, p. 90, n. 238a.

4. *Ibid.*, p. 203.

5. *Notes and Counter Notes*, p. 64.

6. *Ibid.*, p. 68.

7. *Ibid.*, pp. 66-67.

8. *Théâtre Populaire*, Jan-Féb. 1955, *11*:34.

9. *Ibid.*

10. *Ibid.*, p. 2.

11. *Notes and Counter Notes*, pp. 50-51.

12. Bertolt Brecht, "Kleines Organon für das Theater," in: *Schriften zum Theater* (Frankfurt a.M.: Suhrkamp, 1957), No. 61. Translations from this work are my own.

13. Eugène Ionesco, "L'Impromptu de l'Alma," in: *Théâtre II* (Paris: Gallimard, 1958). The translations are my own. All page references are to be the original and will appear as numbers in the text.

14. *Schriften zum Theater*, p. 84.

15. *Ibid.*

16. *Théâtre Populaire, op. cit.*, p. 29.

17. Edith Kern, "Brecht's Epic Theatre and the French Stage," *Symposium* (Spring 1962), p. 33.

18. *Ibid.*

19. "Kleines Organon," No. 42.

20. *Ibid.*

21. The costume and character changes of the *Good Woman of Setzuan* are typical Commedia dell'Arte *lazzi*, for instance. A similar technique was also employed by Molière in his *Dom Juan* and his *Malade imaginaire*.

22. Claude Bonnefoy, *Conversations with Ionesco*, ed. Claude Bonnefoy, tr. by Jan Dawson (Paris: Pierre Belfond), 1966. English tr. (London: Faber and Faber, 1970). All references are to this translation.

23. *Ibid.*, p. 143.

24. *Notes and Counter Notes*, pp. 26-27.

25. *Polemik, Parodie*, p. 155.

26. Hartwig Hanstein, *Studien zur Entwicklung von Ionescos Theater* (Heidelberg: Carl Winter, 1972), p. 26.

27. Bertolt Brecht, "Die Strassenszene: Grundomodell einer Szene des epischen Theaters," in: *Schriften zum Theater, op. cit.*, pp. 90-105.

28. *Théâtre Populaire, op. cit.*, pp. 28-29.

29. *Polemik, Parodie*, pp. 117-118.

30. *Théâtre Populaire, op. cit.*, p. 32.

31. *Ibid.*, p. 2.

32. *Ibid.*, p. 36.

33. *Notes and Counter Notes*, p. 119.

34. *Ibid.*, p. 229.

35. *Conversations*, p. 139.

36. *Notes and Counter Notes*, p. 118.

37. *Ibid.*, p. 120.

38. Julian H. Wulbern, *Brecht and Ionesco: Commitment in Context* (Urbana, Chicago, London: University of Illinois Press, 1971), pp. 208-209.

39. *Figaro Littéraire* (May 6, 1972), 1355:15-18.

40. *Brecht and Ionesco,* pp. 3-4.

41. Eugène Ionesco, *Macbett* (Paris: Gallimard-NRF, 1972). All page references are to the French edition and are indicated in the text. The translation is mine.

42. "Kleiness Organon," No. 59.

43. *Conversations*, p. 108.

44. Jan Kott, *Shakespeare notre contemporain*, tr. from Polish by Anna Posner (Paris: Julliard, 1962), p. 105.

45. *Notes and Counter Notes*, p. 187.

46. "Kleines Organon," No. 53.

47. *Notes and Counter Notes*, p. 225.

48. *Ibid.*

49. Edith Kern, "Concretization of Metaphor in the Commedia dell'Arte and the Modern Theatre," in: *Actes du IVe Congrès de l'Association de Littérature Comparée* (Fribourg 1964, The Hague: Mouton, 1966), pp. 1232-1242.

50. Edith Kern, "Beckett and the Spirit of the Commedia dell'Arte,"

Modern Drama (1966), pp. 266-267.

TOWARDS A DREAM THEATRE

by Eugene Ionesco

A psychologist, one of the great masters of psychoanalysis, once stated: "A dream is a drama of which we are at one and the same time the author, the protagonist and the spectator." Indeed, when we dream we are always in character. It is theatre *par excellence*. We witness the surging of events, the birth of astonishing, utterly surprising *dramatis personae,* and yet these amazing creations come from us. We discover ourselves in and to ourselves. We also discover objective truths. There are some famous examples: Descartes' dream, or the fact that Henri Poincaré, the famous mathematician, made his most important intuitive discoveries in the state of dream. It is in the latter, sheltered from diurnal activity, retired within oneself, that one collects one's thoughts in meditation. The outside world is closed to us, but it is the essential aspect of the outside world which falls under our gaze, and the scrutiny of our consciousness. We do no always envision a solution, but what comes to us is what is most important, not the solution but the problem, or the major problems.

It is often, it is above all in the dream state that I experience a fundamental anguish: the sense of danger, my coexistence with others, my condition in this world, the knowledge of death. And this comes to me in such a sharp form, with such immediacy, as something so obvious, that it could never happen in the false light of day.

If only I could recall all my dreams, if I could reproduce the stuff of dream in its language, with its words, what amazing things I would say! We do nothing but translate, as best we can, the language of dreams. Logical, rational coherence is nothing compared to the coherences of oneiric images and symbols.

In my preceding plays, I had already attempted to use symbolic dream images. I did it in *Amédée or How to Get Rid of It,* in *Hunger and Thirst,* and *A Stroll in the Air.* Still, the situations, the plot line remained more or less logical, coordinated, as one would expect in a rational universe. I would use a situation out of dream, but the characters would never speak as they do in dreams. Or, as in *The Bald Soprano,* I made use of a non-logical language, but the behavior of the characters and their situation seemed realistic.

This time, however, in *L'Homme aux valises,* I am trying to use elements drawn from dreams, dream images and situations expressed in an oneiric language. In short, I have tried to substitute for rational coherence another form of coherence which appears incoherent in the face of rationality.

Translated by Rosette Lamont

L'HOMME AUX VALISES:
IONESCO'S ABSOLUTE STRANGER

by Rosette C. Lamont

On Satruday, November 29, 1976, the day of the opening of his new play, *L'Homme aux valises,* Eugene Ionesco granted an interview to Françoise Varenne of *Le Figaro.* In the course of a meandering, allusive if not elusive conversation, the playwright declared: "It is one of my pleasures to toy with what is most serious, even awesome." Nothing could define more clearly Ionesco's recent dramatic work, and in particular this play, his most tragic and, at the same time, most anarchically comic creation.

L'Homme aux valises is a dream play. As such it is projected out of linearity onto the vertiginous spiral of the time/space continuum. This does not mean, however, that the atmosphere is unreal, vaguely symbolist; on the contrary, it is characterized by that peculiar sharpness and vividness of detail which is inherent to the dream state. In the latter, we are not surprised to meet our ancestors and talk with them as though they were contemporaries, and we can be at the same instant in Paris and Venice simply because Paris is Venice and Venice Paris. As Jung explains: "Dreams...are the facts from which we must proceed."[1]

Ionesco who is deeply indebted to Jungian analysis is aware that he is working with archetypes. In this play, however, he is conscious of dealing with, what he calls "cultural archetypes." Jung defines the archetype as a pre-existent form that is part of an inherited structure of the psyche. He compares the form of a primordial image to the axial system of a crystal. The archetype is a *facultas praeformandi,* a form which can be filled with content only when the conscious mind brings the material of experience to bear upon the psyche. Jung states that, although

"the self is the principle and archetype of orientation and meaning,"[2] it is essential for the individual to emerge out of personal
myth, and rejoin the collective unconscious on the deeper
levels of the psychic life, that is in those regions that can be
considered "the world." The way both into the outer and the
inner *unknown* is perilous and slow. To go beyond the *persona*—
the mask worn by the actors we pose at being in our confrontations with society—we require the assistance of the *mandala,*
the magic circle which appears before us, or rather arises out of
us, whenever we find ourselves in situations of psychic confusion.
In Lamism and Tantric Yoga, the mandala is an instrument of
contemplation as Jung found out when, after drawing a strangely
Chinese-looking design which he called "Window on Eternity,"
he received from a friend the manuscript of a Taoist-alchemical
treatise entitled *The Secret of the Golden Flower* which was so
close to his own cryptogram that he welcomed it as a confirma-
tion of synchronicity. In both drawings, the psychiatrist recognized a center, a golden castle, marked by a cross radiating into
four parts. It is in these parts that we find constellations of
archetypes which represent a pattern of order. The archetypal
image which is not ourselves appears to us to instruct the self
in objectivity, in psychic reality. Jung stresses that the archetype
is not "an inactive form, but a real force charged with a specific
energy."[3] These mysterious figures cannot be disregarded for
they are able to tell us things we do not know; they are psycha-
gogues, ghostly gurus. The fact that the unconscious personifies
itself may be uncomfortable for those who like to feel in control
of themselves, but the very autonomy of unconscious contents
allows us to differentiate ourselves from our subconscious.
Above all, it is important to develop techniques of dealing with
dream images, to become directly aware of the ideas they try to
communicate. For the dramatist, Ionesco tells us, the process
ought to be a familiar one since dreams are a sort of dramatic
enactment in which we play at one and the same time the roles
of director, writer and actor. The flow from subconscious to
conscious mind can also be reversed; a dream can be concretized
upon the stage, and address the audience in a much more direct
manner than when a writer dramatizes an idea, when he tries to
convince, to teach, to preach. As Ionesco writes in *Fragments of
a Journal:*

> The language of literature, particularly of dramatic literature, is by
> no means an illustration or a vulgarization of some other, superior,

language. A concrete thought, a thought by means of images, of happenings, of movements, is a valid, that is to say it is just as proper an instrument of research, as conceptual and discursive language.[4]

There are times, however, when the dream is a nightmare, when we are filled with anguish at the thought of our powerlessness. Ionesco is keenly aware of those moments when we feel that we are not directing our dreaming, but are instead being led, being dreamed. Not is this any kind of vague *angst,* the product of hysteria. Too often in the course of the twentieth century men have experienced the horror of being caught in a nightmare not of their making. Hitler dreamt millions into concentration camps, as did Stalin into the death camps of slave labor. And in a way, is it not true that these monstrous, mad dictators were themselves nothing but incarnations of Lenin's infinitely cruel reveries? We live in a house of mirrors; we project reflections on the stage of our theatres. The reign of modern tyrants created new myths, myths having to do with the extremes of the biological human condition. When, as Jerzy Grotowski writes in his *Poor Theatre,* only the human body is the last bastion of dignity, of man's particularity, then we must go beyond literature, find archaic, eternal images to express this situation. Incantation, dance, gestures, rhythmic patterns constitute a new language. Then we witness the metamorphosis of humans into rhinoceroses upon the stage. This kind of image can be defined as the content of a form assumed by what Ionesco calls "cultural archetypes." As to the latter, they can be also seen to be the result of "amplification" (Jung's term), that is the elaboration of a dream image by means of association.

The man carrying luggage is an eloquent symbol for the state of estrangement and spiritual exile which characterizes contemporary man. To wander aimlessly, to be exiled and self-exiled, to lose one's roots, one's papers, one's name and identity, such is our lot. We are all men without shadows, like Chamisso's Peter Schlemihl. Indeed, today's shadows are not cast by our own bodies as much as by those of our vigilant doubles. In such circumstances, the anguished sleep of a Vietnamese refugee in America is not different in essence from that of a Tatar deprived of his native Crimea, or of an Angolan Portuguese for whom Lisbon is *terra incognita.* This is the century of displaced nations, of uprooted classes. Farmers are being made to cultivate a strip of soil with which they have no spiritual, ancestral connections, while others till the very earth from which the former have been driven. Town dwellers die along the road, marched towards distant rice fields. Even in our democracies, the bulldozer of progress levels familiar neighborhoods, robbing citizens of memories, of their history. The state of homelessness is our common plight. Dissident poets from Moscow or Leningrad live in Jerusalem, New York, Paris, Frankfurt, Milan. As Slava Rostropovich, the great cellist who harbored Solzhenitsyn in his *dacha,* put it to a journalist: "It is not my fault that I must realize my life's dreams not in my homeland but in the theaters of New York, San Francisco, London, Paris, Milan, Vienna and Zurich."[5] Even those of us who enjoy travel would not wish to be condemned to an eternity of journeying. Who could understand this better than a dramatist born of a French mother and a Rumanian father, forced by his parents' separation, and by the rise of fascism during the Second World War to shift from one country to another, to go into hiding in the countryside, to shuttle between languages? *L'Homme aux valises* is both Ionesco's personal myth, his life history concretized upon the stage, and the story of twentieth century man as "wandering Jew," as Leopold Bloom-Ulysses.

The man—he is never given a name so that he is both Everyman and NoMan, the latter being the way in which Odysseus identifies himself to the Cyclops—is first seen walking out of nowhere, a valise in each hand. He looks lost upon the bare stage. As the lights gradually bring part of the latter out of darkness, the audience notices another man, sitting at stage left, in front of an easel. With his blue beret and box of paints, the latter is a caricature of the French Sunday painter, an occupation traditionally as peaceful and devoid of risks as fishing. In this wasteland of a spot, one can nevertheless hear the lapping sounds of running water, as though an invisible river flowed across the stage. "This is the Seine,"[6] the painter tosses out, never turning around to look at the traveler. As he enters into conversation with this strange guardian at the gate of dreams, the man embarks in the time capsule of Ionesco's play.

A rumor of voices rises, seeming to waft from the other bank of the invisible river. We are reminded of the dead, crowding together to see Odysseus. The sound effects suggest a throng, and something vaguely menacing fills the air reminding the protagonist of massacres, those of the Reign of Terror, or, of all manner of terrorism. The painter attempts to reassure his interlocutor, but only succeeds in deepening the foreboding atmosphere:

> You're mistaken. This is 1938. Of course the great breath of the French Revolution is still blowing through the people. But, at the present time, France still exists, and her citizenry believes in her. It is fortunate indeed that we're still in 38, and that 1944 hasn't happened yet.

But 1944 is sure to roll around, "as sure as God made little apples" and men big guns, for, despite Giraudoux's optimistic title for his 'entre deux guerres' play, *La Guerre de Troie n'aura pas lieu*, we know that the Trojan war took place, and so did the Second World War. With 1944, as Ionesco reminds us bitterly, will come the rest: loss of faith in one's country, loss of nerve, recriminations, the ghosts of a shameful period of collaboration. Thus, the painter's ambiguous response constitutes the teasing leader of the time spiral. The voices of the invisible people reach a crescendo as they are described waving "flags of fire, flags of blood." These are the eternal emblems of wars, revolutions, catastrophes. The protagonist of *L'Homme aux valises* is doomed to travel through all of those in search of his personal and ancestral past. As though summoned by an inner need, a gondola appears upon the invisible river the painter calls the Seine. Paris and Venice are "twin cities" is the explanation given for this strange concretization. The gondolier extends a helpful pole for the man to jump in. Whether he hails from Paris, Venice, Ur, or Babylon, this voyager must cross the river, be it the Seine or the Styx.

Ionesco's latest metaphysical farce may be *engagée* in the Sartrian sense of the word, but it is above all, as the dramatist points out in his program notes, a dream play. If one of André Breton's noble obsessions was the creation of "the dream-text," then it can be said that in *L'Homme aux valises* Ionesco pursues his self-declared program of creating an oneiric universe upon the stage. Like the Surrealists who where his master, the dramatist believes that an interpenetration occurs between the conscious day life and the subconscious night existence, for dreams contain fragments of the day's impressions, and the latter are encrusted with bits and pieces severed from the psyche's intense activity in its nightly revels. To use one of Breton's own titles, the two modes of apprehension must be viewed as "des vases communicants."

As to Surrealism, it would be an error to study it as a school of literature, as a literary movement. It owes a great deal to the admiration Breton had for Freud, as well as to the former's study of medicine. It is therefore a method of investigation to be compared with that of psychoanalysis, except that its aim is not to effect cures, but to travel out to unexplored regions of the mind. For the Surrealists, the basic instrument of research is the image. Perhaps it would be more accurate to state that for them the image constitutes an atom of mental energy. As images generate other images, energy mounts, and an explosion may occur. This is devoutly to be wished, and pursued through the practice of automatic writing and the accompanying experimentation with the speed of free association. By means of the latter in particular, the Surrealists felt they could realize Rimbaud's hope of acceding to "the unknown," that is the very source of the metaphor. There, one could transcend personality, and find, under the multiple layers which constitute individuality, the irreducible self, at once individual and part of the collective subconscious. As Sarane Alexandrian states in his magnificent book, *Le surréalisme et le rêve,* André Breton, Philippe Soupault, Péret, Crevel, and the poet Desnos can be said to have lived hypnodramas; they were in some ways forerunners of Jacob Moreno's psychodramatic sessions, with the difference—and it is an essential one—that they sought to inoculate themselves with "the immortal malady, the fever of imagination."[7]

Unlike psychoanalysts, poets do not try to make their way back to the rational state; they dwell in the realm of Hypnos whence they send coded messages, mysterious iconographies. There have been analysts, however, who risked madness in order to travel both outward, and into the depths of the mind. C. G. Jung was this kind of scientist, and he has become of late a spiritual guide for students of myth, or comparative religions, and for artists.

In *Fragments of a Journal,* Ionesco writes that he prefers "Jung to Freud, (because) Jung does not ban religion."[8] By religion, the dramatist means that "numinosum" (Rudolf Otto's term) which Jung defines as "a dynamic existence or effect, not caused by an arbitrary act of will."[9] When Jung speaks of

religion he is careful to differentiate it from creed. As he points
out, "it is unquestionable that not only Buddha or Mohammed
or Confucius or Zarathustra represents religious phenomena, but
that Mithras, Attis, Kybele, Mani, Hermes and many exotic
cults do so as well. The psychologist, in as much as he assumes
a scientist attitude, has to disregard the calm of every creed
to be the unique and eternal truth. He must keep his eye on the
human side of the religious problem, in that he is concerned
with the original religious experience quite apart from what the
creeds have made of it."[10] It is in this sense that Ionesco is
able to reconcile Freudianism with Buddhism, for, as he says:
"The connections between Buddhism and the thought of Freud
seems to me all the more convincing because Freud himself,
towards the end of his life, discovered and asserted that we
have within us, that our whole being bears within itself a death
instinct, a longing for rest, the "Nirvana instinct'."[11] One of
Ionesco's illuminations, what a friend teaches him to be "a
sartori,"[12] has to do with the feeling that death, "this non-
self, is (his) truest, most essential self, his 'atman'."[13] Such a
discovery cannot be made while words lie like masks upon the
images of our subconscious mind. Chatter, verbiage must fall
away like dead leaves to reveal the tree of life at the center. It
stands rooted in our ancestral past, reaching beyond the self;
the fruit it bears are archetypal images.

In the book he dictated shortly before his death, Jung
recounts his encounter with the latter: Siegfried whom he has
to kill in order to transcend heroic idealism, Elijah and a blind
Salome—she is an anima figure—and finally Philemon, a force
that taught psychic objectivity. As he was writing down these
visions, the scientist could not help but think that it was ironical
that he, a psychiatrist, "should have run into the same psychic
material which is the stuff of psychosis and is found in the insane."[14] He realized, however, that if these apparitions confuse
the patients, they also issue from the "matrix of the mythopoeic
imagination which has vanished from our rational age."[15] Although to allow oneself to discourse with such apparitions is
considered the path of error, Jung felt that he could not avoid
it, for it would take him on "a voyage of discovery to the other
pole of the world."[16] Through the anima, a relationship was
established with the dead, "the land of ancestors."[17] Jung
speaks of writing at that time his *Septem Sermones.* The following passage is particularly important for it provides a key to

the understanding of the first scenes of *L'Homme aux valises:*

> From that time on, the dead have become ever more distinct for me
> as the voices of the Unanswered, Unresolved, and Unredeemed; for
> since the questions and demands which my destiny required me to
> answer did not come from me from outside, they must have come
> from the inner world. These conversations with the dead formed a
> kind of prelude to what I had to communicate to the world about the
> unconscious: a kind of pattern of order and interpretation of its
> general contents.[18]

In Act I, scene 5, the man meets with a group of people
who claim to be his maternal ancestors. He does not recognize
the place, although an old woman, his grandmother, tells him it
is their country of origin. An old uncle, dressed as a beggar, but
who claims that the king conferred a title of nobility on him on
account of his self-made wealth, questions the man about the
latter's mother. The answer: "I have no news of her. I don't
know where she might be." The old woman's husband walks
off the stage, and a strange conversation ensues:

The Man: Why is grandpa backing away?

The Old Woman: He's crawling off to die.

The Man: I thought it was over and done with, but now I recall he
died in a ground floor room, one with a singularly low ceiling. He was
stretched out on a pallet, a black skull cap on his head. Yes, I was
present at his agony. And you, granny, are you dead or alive?

The Old Woman: I'm dead?

The other "ghosts" beckon to the Man to join them, whispering
enticingly: "We're nice and cozy together, aren't we? Come
close to us, dear. We'll face the world together. Let's close
ranks." One of the women in the group is the Man's wife, or,
as he thinks at first, his mother. In point of fact, a loving wife
becomes a kind of mother to her husband. The attention she
lavishes upon the latter makes him forget his loss: "My poor
darling mother, my mummy. You've been gone twenty years,
thirty, forty, I don't know how many years. I've been sleep-
walking. How could I have forgotten?" He's also forgotten the
others: the young man in black, his son killed in the war, and

his small daughter. The latter is a rag doll tightly clasped by the young man in black. With its "Egyptian" eye, and rag body, the doll suggests a mummy, one that must make the journey described in the Egyptian *Book of the Dead.* The son and daughter look indivisible; they form a hermaphroditic archetype. The limp, exteriorized *anima* of this "homo Adamicus" concretizes the protagonist's bewilderment, his inability to remember the departed: "One ought never to leave anyone. They die the moment you turn your back." Only in dreams does one know the full extent of one's solitude.

In Mauclair's production, the dead ancestors were shown herded together in a kind of tumbril, or a gigantic miner's wagon traveling on invisible tracks which appeared to run on the very spot where the Seine crossed the stage in the first scene. Clearly, there is more than one way of crossing the Styx. The dead wave cheerfully to their living descendant, urging him to jump aboard their conveyance. As it lurches forward, the man springs onto the back of it, like a youngster hitching a ride on a trolley. The gigantic urn/wagon gathers speed, and rolls towards the wings. Just as it is about to disappear, the man lets go and lands on the ground. He is obviously terrified, like one recalled from the brink of suicide. "No, not yet, not I," he whispers, watching the wagon tumble forward, pouring its load of bodies into an invisible pit. It has been a narrow escape. Ionesco's protagonist remembers the two valises he has had to set down when he considered joining his ancestors. "I'll let you know when my time's up, "he shouts in the direction of the void.

As a maker of modern myths, Ionesco creates a powerful picture language. In this way, he fulfills what Jung defines as man's task: "to become conscious of the contents that press upward from the unconscious."[19] The latter possesses, according to Jung, better sources of information as to the relationships between life and the after life than the conscious mind. In one of the Terry Lectures delivered by the great psychologists in 1937, he suggests that the human personality is made up of consciousness which is limited, and the unconscious psyche, an "indefinitely large hinterland."[20] This is the space in which one of the most touching scenes of Ionesco's *L'Homme aux valises* takes place.

We see an old scarecrow of a woman seated in a wheel-chair.

At the sight of a radiant girl walking in, the aged creature exclaims: "Mummy, my little mother!" The latter, without a
moment's hesitation, clasps the bag of bones in her round, soft
arms, whispering: "My child, for me you will always be my
little girl!" If the audience begins to smile, assuming that it is
being treated to "typical Ionesco nonsense," the snicker fades
as we find out that the aged invalid we see was separated from
her mother in early childhood. We are not told whether the
mother died, or left the family, but what is clear is that the
wound caused by her absence has never healed. Thus, the
memory of the absent mother did not fade, preserving her
forever in the guise of a beautiful, young woman. In the dream
confrontation Ionesco presents on the stage, the survivor is true
to her age, but her vision is as old as she was on the day of
separation. Now that she is close to senility, the old woman
is as helpless in her wheel-chair as a babe in its carriage. The
dialogue which ensues is one between past and present:

The Old Woman: When I was a good girl you used to buy me candy.

The Young Woman: I'll buy you candy.

The Old Woman: Chocolate?

The Young Woman: Chocolate.

The Old Woman: At the corner sweet shop, in a lovely box?

The Young Woman: They still have lovely boxes there.

The Old Woman: Will you buy me a lovely dress? I promise to be
good.

The Young Woman: The loveliest of dresses.

The Old Woman: You'll walk me to school, won't you? I want so
much to show you off to my little friends. They said you'd never
come back.

The Young Woman: We've got to go, but this time I'm taking you
with me. We'll never part again.

The Old Woman: Never, never.

The Young Woman: Never.

If the mother has disappeared it may be on account of a secret connected with her origins. The man is searching for the real name of his grandmother's mother. Her maiden name was changed, and it has become impossible to find its trace. The clerk being questioned ventures an explanation: "Is it likely that she belonged to a persecuted ethnic category? To a condemned race? In this case, it would be better to discontinue the inquiry..." This is sound advice, but not easy to follow for a man who has doubts as to this own identity. Suddenly, as though emerging from his minds, the grandmother materializes on the stage. In her lacy white frock, her floppy garden party hat, she seems to have stepped out of a daguerreotype. The man cannot get over her youthful beauty, but the town hall clerk has a ready explanation: "She's grown younger since she got rid of a name which set her apart from other people and rooted her to the Ages."

Two themes constitute the leitmotivs of Ionesco's *L'- Homme aux valises:* the loss of one's identity, and the hope of survival on the very brink of dissolution. Both of these come together in Act II.

The protagonist has arrived as a tourist in a foreign country which is clearly on the other side of the Iron Curtain. Although it is the country of his birth, the man can no longer read the street signs, or find his bearings. "A new city is rising behind the old one even before the old city is torn down." Childhood friends appear; they have become pale faced bureaucrats, and they do not recognize, or pretend not to know their erstwhile companion. The latter is being watched by the police, and since he has somehow misplaced his passport, and lost all his papers, he must contact the French consul. This proves to be quite difficult, and when at last the protagonist reaches him, he finds a man on the brink of a break in diplomatic relations. The consul is quite willing to issue some papers, any papers in fact, to his frantic visitor. It is obvious that these documents will be so much paper. Nor does this empty shell of an official lose his diffidence when it becomes clear that his visitor has forgotten the name of his father together with that of his mother, and that he has no clear notion of his age, size, or profession. The only definition he is willing to offer is that he considers himself to be

"an existing person." When the consul draws his attention to
the fact that he shares this identity with many, he is happy to
amend it to "a person who specializes in existing."

There are places, and countries where this specialty is not
easy to pursue. When the man, finally armed with worthless
documents, reaches what he takes to be a hotel, he is surprised
to see that his room has four beds, and that all four are occupied;
the inn is a hospital, not unlike the psychiatric wards in which
dissident thinkers are being held for "re-education" in the Soviet
Union. In this particular clinic patients linger, or rather are
allowed to linger till one of their beds is needed. Then, the
occupant of the bed is dispatched from this world by virtue of
a perfected system of euthenasia.

Euthenasia will be practiced upon one of the four patients,
an old woman who complains of feeling that her flesh is being
pierced by the branches of a tree shooting up within her body
cavity. It is an evergreen, coniferous tree, with needles for
leaves. As she sits up on her bed, arms stretched out in agony,
as though crucified upon her inner growth, one of her companions in misery seeks to reassure her: "My wife had the exact
same thing. It goes away if you diet." The sick creature in-
quires: "Was she cured?" The man answers ambiguously: "She
grew younger. It's a sign of Spring." We know the man is
lying for his wife is dead, yet it is also true that it is not uncom-
mon for the dead to look touchingly young and at peace after
the final agony. His lie covers a deeper truth. This is no consolation, however, for the tree-filled woman who prefers suffering to death, a trait she shares with La Fontaine's "bûcheron"
(wood-cutter), and with most of Ionesco's other *dramatis personae,* particularly King Bérenger Ier. She cannot hide her fear
and horror of death when the hospital doctor approaches her
for the final injection. Even his promise that the drug will make
her feel wonderful cannot calm her. In a scene of extraordinary
violence, the "doctor" kills the woman twice for good measure,
first by injecting her with a poison, then when she is clearly gone,
by shooting her in the head. To find a key to the dramatist's
attitude towards this atrocious murder committed in the name
of euthenasia, one has only to read his description of the death
of a friend:

Our friend Sorana Gurian died some years ago after a serious illness.

Day after day, for months, for a whole year or two, injections kept her alive, granted her reprieve from one day to the next.

Michel M., the psychotherapist, thought that the anguish in which Sorana lived was cruel and intolerable. He decided to do something for her, to help her as best he could. He went to the nursing home one day, then the following day, then every day for two or three months. He had resolved to teach Sorana how to die, to teach her death. He succeeded in this difficult undertaking. One morning, Sorana calmly told the doctor who came to give her the daily injection that she did not want it, that she did not want to be put to sleep, ·so that she might keep her consciousness intact until the last moment. A week later she died, with dignity, as she had wished it.[21]

The last weeks of the run of Ionesco's *L'Homme aux valises* coincided with the arrival in Paris of the Ukrainian scientist Leonid Plyusch who had been confined for three years to the mental hospital of Dniepropetrovsk. The press, the intellectual elite, as well as the French communist party, had pressed for his release which brought him to France in time for the XXII Congress of the Communist party. Plyusch disclosed to a huge audience gathered at the Paris Mutualité the conditions of his internment following his arrest for "anti-Soviet propaganda." Drugged, held tight by what the French call "la camisole chimique" (the chemical straight jacket), brought to a comatose state through powerful doses of insulin ("shock therapy"), he was brutalized, beaten, and finally confined to ward 9, among the criminally insane. He told of his progressive loss of memory, his sinking into apathy. Yet, all along he was fighting to hold on to the details of his torture in order to communicate them to the world at some future time.

For many years now, Ionesco has written in defense of those he calls "les fous de la liberté": Solzhenitsyn, Sakharov, Amalrik, Siniavsky, Bukovsky. A number of these witnesses for truth have escaped the hell of death camps, or the far more terrifying death of consciousness. Others are still suffering: Mihajlo Mihajlov in Yugoslavia, the biologist Sergei Kovalev, the physicist Andrei Tverdokhlebov, the Tatar Mustafa Kzhemilev, and many others. In the hospital scene, Ionesco has succeeded in fusing his political preoccupations with his metaphysical concerns. The latter have to do with the unavoidable absurdity of personal mortality, and the isolubility of certain questions: What is Being? Why Being? As the dramatist states again and

again in his Journals, there is no answer to the latter, except
perhaps the one lying at the very core of "the impossibility of
answering."[22]

It is not easy for Man to exist without answers; it is virtually
impossible for him not to question. The quest for truth is the
essence of tragedy from *Oedipus Rex* to *L'Homme aux valises*.
Ionesco's protagonist, another one of his numerous *Oedipes
manqués*, also finds himself at the crossroads, facing a perverse
female Sphinx and her riddles. The latter, thrown out with professional rapidity, sound like the ridiculous questions of a French
quiz program, one of the latest aspects of the *cocacolonization* of
Europe. Here are a couple of examples:

> Sphinx: What cannot touch the heart without blushing?   In the
> plural.
>
> The Man: Razor blades.
>
> Sphinx: Noble when fine?
>
> The Man: The soul.

There are also echoes from the games played by the Précieuses
Ridicules and their coterie. So far so good. Next, our hero is
required to name "a writer in three letters." Without a moment's
hesitation he exclaims: "SUE. Eugène Sue." Wrong. It was
supposed to be POE, the perfect name for a Mystery Woman
such as the Sphinx. The mistake, however, is revealing. There
is the joke of the Christian name of the French nineteenth century novelist, identical to that of the dramatist, but, beyond
the *boutade*—Ionesco enjoys his little jokes—there is also the
fact that Sue is not only the author of *Les mystères de Paris*
(still part of the fun and games perhaps), but also that of *Le Juif
errant*. The "cultural archetype" Ionesco was referring to
suddenly becomes obvious. The "Man with the suitcases," the
inveterate tourist, is twentieth century man as "wandering Jew."

One of the striking phenomena of our epoch is the metamorphosis undergone by the myth of the Jew. Never had the
victims of the Diaspora been anything but the Other to the rest
of society. With the Holocaust, and its succeeding mass decima-
tions and expatriations, the Jew has become the symbol of

universal persecution, the essence of human suffering. The pictures we have seen of prisoners, heads shaven, eyes widened by starvation, make of Ivan Denisovich a brother of the living dead of Auschwitz and Dachau. Ionesco who is a friend of the little state of Israel often says that a world without Jews would be both harder and sadder. It is good to live with a hope of the coming of the Messiah, and the vision of the rising of the New Jerusalem. Paradoxically, the Jewish people represents the deepest pain, and the most radiant hope.

Hope is at the heart of every man who has retained something of the grace of childhood. The latter signifies for Ionesco a lost Paradise, one of those rare states of plenitude which can be recaptured only by a miraculous epiphany. In the village of La Chapelle-Anthenaise where Ionesco spent some time as a little boy, he felt safe, "outside of time."[23] He can never recall without emotion the village square, the tiny church, the radiant light of a summer Sunday. Then his world was complete, and he stood at the center of the mandala. The rest of his existence is a quest for that space of time, that blessed moment lost in the past. As to writing, it is an attempt to find one's way through the labyrinthine forest by means of words.

For the writer, words are the instrument of reaching the *unknown*, and of *ingathering*. Through their incantatory power a center, or goal, can be attained. As Jung says: "The center is the goal, and everything is directed toward that center... The self is the principle and archetype of orientation and meaning."[24] This realization came to the psychoanalyst as a result of a dream so vivid, and so final that he knew that a personal myth emerged from it. The experience is described in almost mystic terms as "a stream of lava" whose fires "reshaped (his) life."[25] The dream, as Jung tells it, represents a mandala with inner and outer circles. The dreamer is making his way through a dirty, sooty city, on a rainy winter night. His companions are Swiss like himself, but the city is Liverpool. It seems, however, that the true city is elsewhere, "up above, on the cliffs."[26] The companions make their way up to a plateau where they find a square into which streets converge. The city is arranged radially around the square, and in turn, at the center of the square there is a round pool, and therein an island. On the island which seems to have its own sunlit climate stands a radiant magnolia tree, covered with reddish blossoms. This vision seemed to obliterate the rain, fog, smoke of the city, and convey the very reason for the dreamer's existence. Jung reminds his reader that Liverpool is "the pool of life," and that "the liver, according to an ancient view, is the seat of life."[27] Thus, the dream depicts "the climax of the whole process of development of consciousness."[28]

The magic tree of life, a kind of ladder going from the earth to heaven, appears in a number of Ionesco plays, particularly in *Hunger and Thirst,* and *A Hell of a Mess.* It is connected with his remembrance of La Chapelle-Anthenaise. In scene XVI of *L'Homme aux valises,* just as in Jung's primal dream scene, another town, the true city, no larger than an architect's maquette, appears at the back of the stage. The man recognizes it at once, and tries to rush in its direction, but realizes that he does not know the way. Strangers appear, dressed in period costumes. As they turn, bend, point, offering directions in the stylized diction we associate with recitative, we are reminded of a mechanical ballet, as though we had walked not through a mirror, but rather into the display window of a department store, at Christmas. This is the path to the wizard of Oz; it runs through Alice's Wonderland:

> This isn't the real town...The true city, the ancient one, is a tiny hamlet two kilometers from here...It's in the opposite direction. On the road to Poitiers...You'll reach it by passing the washouse to the right, then a vegetable garden, and the château. After that, on your left, you'll see a meadow with sheep grazing...You'll get to a tiny wooden bridge over the small Garonne...On the other side of the bridge there's a path which leads through the rue de la Vierge to Saint-Jacques bridge. Straight ahead there's another meadow, and, on one side of it, a narrow walk, climbing through hawthorn, pink, white, blue, green.

If the pink and white hawthorn bushes have been transplanted from *Swann's Way,* the blue and green ones clearly grow *du côté de Ionesco.* The man, however, has not reached his destination. He must walk on, along gravel paths to a pool, and then a garden where "strawberries, wild strawberries" grow. He has to continue turning round and round through present past past present (the title of one of Ionesco's journals) until at last he stumbles on "the village, the church, the Chapelle Anthenaise."

When, after the end of the First World War, Ionesco's

mother came to take her little boy back to Paris, she promised him many sophisticated pleasures to replace the simple joys of country living: "The war's been over for a long time, it's quite different, quite different. There are fêtes going on all the time, it's lots of fun: roundabouts, shows, lights, lots of lights. It's all lit up at night. And Aunt Sabine has a fine drawing-room. She entertains fashionable people. She gives parties."[29] The little boy envisioned a story-book Paris of "merry-go-rounds, all lit up," a dazzling metropolis inhabited by "ladies in fine dresses, people singing in the streets," an eternal Quatorze Juillet with its "fireworks."[30] How could he have guessed that he would be projected into Time, that centrifugal force, and out of the immutability of things standing still? As he writes with profound nostalgia: "At fifteen or sixteen, it was all over, I was in time, in flight, in finiteness."[31]

L'Homme aux valises is an attempt to dramatize the search for the presentness of life, such as it was experienced at the Mill, with its seasons "spread out in space."[32] Even Baudelaire, Ionesco's favorite poet, could not persuade the dramatist that "this world is a hospital where everyone is possessed by the desire of exchanging his bed."[33] Yet, both poets—Ionesco is a poet of the stage—know that "speed is not only infernal, it is hell itself, it is the Fall, accelerated."[34]

In Mauclair's production, *L'Homme aux valises* ends with a fête, a particularly threatening one, at once a child's vision of post-war Paris, and an intimate sexual fantasy.

The action takes place in a large, formal garden, a park à la Versailles with fountains, fireworks, dance music, champagne. The man stumbles in, still carrying his suitcases which seem to have grown heavier, in proportion to his weariness. A magnificent young woman walks up to the stranger, enjoyning him to rest, and promising food and drink. "What will she bring me," the Man muses. He is filled with expectation, and a tremulous kind of hope. When the lovely woman returns she is offering herself, nor does the presence of her husband lurking in the background deter her. As to the latter, though accompanied by two men who look like body guards, he does not seem to notice, or mind, his wife's flirtation. In fact, in a manner typical of the *mari complaisant* of French farce, he suggests that he will keep an eye on the luggage. The park, however, is full of policemen.

'Homme aux valises*

As the protagonist follows—one can hardly say he is leading—
his forceful partner, both of them describing ever widening circles to the strains of Sibelius' *Valse Triste,* armed men spring
from behind columnar trees, or out of thickets. There is no
place for the would-be lovers to hide. Our truly sad Olympio
cannot forget that he is in a police state, or that perhaps these
cops are concretizations of his own sick conscience. Time is
also at his heels: "We don't have time. I've got to catch a train,"
he whispers. The lady's husband appears, carrying both bags.
Time has run out, and yet the park fills with people ready to
dance. Fireworks begin to explode, the stage is filled with
couples and laughter. "Come and join us," says the lovely
woman to the man. Others invite him also to take part in the
festivities, but he refuses. It is not that he is excluded, but that
he excludes himself: "I can't enter the dance. I haven't come
to this country to dance." One recognizes here a state of mind
Ionesco describes in his confessional journals: a desire to enter
life, society, to immerse himself in friendship, contradicted by a
darkening pessimism. Yet, there is something else, something
which is not negative; it is the need for the artist to safeguard his
integrity, to remain an observer.

The final image of this play is that of the man sitting on
one of his valises in the midst of a busy throng. Suddenly everyone of the dancers turns into a traveler, each carrying one suitcase. They seem terribly busy as they rush from one side of
the stage to the other. Some begin to pile up their luggage
around the protagonist who does not move, watching this hustle
and bustle with a bemused smile. A Ionescologue is reminded
of the end of *The New Tenant,* with the latter literally buried
under the pile of furniture carried up by the movers. Here,
however, the familiar mechanism of proliferation, one of Ionesco's favorite devices, is used to a different end. The sudden
immobility of the man does not suggest death as much as a
state of contemplation. It is as though, after much searching
and running, the protagonist had at last reached the center of
the mandala, and this only as a result of his final renunciation,
his transcendence of desire. The suitcase carried by the others
symbolize their life. Some are still rushing headlong, others set
down their existence at the feet of the sage. He watches, at once
solitaire and *solidaire* like Camus' Jonas. It is a splendid image
of the artist as the eternal Adam. Ionesco and Mauclair, the
dramatist's principal interpreter, have succeeded in creating

on the stage the ultimate metaphysical image, that of Man as inveterate dreamer, and by this very fact perfect mediator. As Wandering Jew, he brings to his fellow-creatures the wisdom of centuries of suffering, and the knowledge that comes from a refusal to be committed to the transitory. To be truly present to oneself, and to others, one must be of No Place and of Every Place, to be No Man and Everyman. Only then can one found relations based on mutual reverence for the spirit, though it be assigned to this grotesque and vulnerable dwelling, mortal flesh. As Ionesco declared in the course of an unpublished lecture delivered in March 1976: "The reason for writing is to cast up to heaven our cry of anguish, and to let other men know that we have existed."

NOTES

1. C. G. Jung, *Memories, Dreams, Reflections* (New York: Vintage Books, 1965), p. 171.

2. *Ibid.*, p. 199.

3. *Ibid.*, p. 352.

4. Eugene Ionesco, *Fragments of a Journal* (New York: Grove Press, 1969), pp. 129-130.

5. Susan Jacoby, "We Love you Slava," The New York *Times Magazine*, Sec. 6, April 18, 1976, p. 70.

6. Eugène Ionesco, *L'homme aux valises* (Paris: Gallimard, 1975), p. 9. All quotations from this play have been translated by the writer of this essay. All future quotations from the play come from the same edition but will not be footnoted.

7. Sarane Alexandrian, *Le surréalisme et le rêve* (Paris: Gallimard, 1974), p. 131. The quotation has been translated by the writer of this essay.

8. See 4, p. 60.

9. C. G. Jung, *Psychology and Religion* (New Haven and London: Yale University Press, 1938), p. 4.

10. *Ibid.*, p. 7.

11. See 4, p. 51.

12. *Ibid.*, p. 69.

13. *Ibid.*, pp. 58-59.

14.   See 1, p. 188.

15.   *Ibid.*

16.   *Ibid.*, p. 189.

17.   *Ibid.*, p. 191.

18.   *Ibid.*, pp. 191-192.

19.   *Ibid.*, p. 326.

20.   See 9, p. 47.

21.   See 4, p. 112.

22.   *Ibid.*, p. 43.

23.   *Ibid.*, p. 11.

24.   See 1, p. 199.

25.   *Ibid.*

26.   *Ibid.*, p. 198.

27.   *Ibid.*

28.   *Ibid.*, p. 199.

29.   See 4, p. 7.

30.   *Ibid.*, p. 8.

31.   *Ibid.*, p. 11.

32.   *Ibid.*

33.   Charles Baudelaire, "Any Where Out of This World, N'importe où hors du monde," *Le Spleen de Paris.* This quotation was translated by the writer of this essay.

34.   See 31.

BIBLIOGRAPHY

BOOKS

Abastado, Claude. *Eugène Ionesco.* Paris, Bordas, 1971. 287 p.

Benmussa, Simone. *Ionesco.* Paris, Seghers, 1966. 192 p.

Boisdeffre, Pierre de. "Bu baroque au classicisme: L'aventure d'Eugène Ionesco." *In his: Une histoire vivante de la littérature d'aujourd'hui.* Paris, Librairie Académique Perrin, 1958. p. 929-934.

Bondy, François. *Ionesco.* Reinbeck bei Hamburg, Rowohlt, 1975. 157 p.

Bonnefoy, Claude. *Entretiens avec Eugène Ionesco.* Paris, Editions Pierre Belfond, 1966. 221 p.

Bradescu, Faust. *Le monde étrange de Ionesco, essai d'explication d'un théâtre qui s'impose sans se définir.* Paris, Promotion et Edition, 1967. 220 p.

Büttner, Gottfried. *Absurdes theater und bewusstseinswandel, über den seelischen realismus bei Beckett und Ionesco.* West Berlin, H. Heenemann K. G., 1968. 233 p.

Clurman, Harold. *The naked image: observations on the modern theater.* New York, The MacMillan Company, 1966. 312 p.

Coe, Richard N. *Ionesco.* London, Oliver and Boyd Ltd., 1961. 120 p. (New ed.: *Ionesco, a study of his plays.* London, Methuen and Co., Ltd., 1971. 206 p.)

Cole, Toby. "Eugène Ionesco." In: *Playwrights on playwriting.* New York, Hill and Wang, 1960. p. 282-284.

Dickinson, Hugh. "Eugène Ionesco: The existential Oedipus." In his: *Myth on the modern stage.* Urbana, University of Illinois Press, 1969. p. 310-331.

Donnard, Jean Hervé. *Ionesco dramaturge ou l'artisan et le démon.* Paris, Lettres Modernes, 1966. 196 p.

Duckworth, Colin. *Angels of darkness, dramatic effects in Samuel Beckett with special references to Eugène Ionesco.* New York, Harper and Row, 1972. 153 p.

Esslin, Martin. *The theater of the absurd.* London, Eyre and Spottiswoode, 1962. 344 p.

Falabrino, Gian Luigi. *Ionesco.* Florence, La Nuova Italia, February 1967. 154 p. (Il Castore, 2).

Fowlie, Wallace. "Ionesco." In his: *Dionysus in Paris.* New York, Meridian Books, 1960. p. 229-237.

Frois, Etienne. *Rhinocéros.* Paris, Hatier, 1970. 80 p. (Profil d'une oeuvre, 2).

Glicksberg, Charles. *The ironic vision in modern literature.* The Hague, Nijhoff, 1969. 268 p.

Gluckman, Marta. *Eugene Ionesco y su teatro.* San Francisco, El Espejo de Papel, 1965. 163 p.

Gros, Bernard. *Le roi se meurt.* Paris, Hatier, 1972. 80 p. (Profil d'une oeuvre, 32).

Grossvogel, David J. *Four playwrights and a postcript.* Ithaca, N. Y., Cornell University Press, 1962. 209 p. (New ed.: The Blasphemers. Ithaca, N. Y., 1965. 209 p)

Guicharnaud, Jacques. "A world out of control: Eugene Ionesco." *In his: Modern French Theatre from Giraudoux to Beckett.* New Haven, Yale University Press, 1961. p. 178-192.

—. "The weight of things: Eugene Ionesco." *In his: Modern French Theatre from Giraudoux to Genet.* New Haven and London, Yale University Press, 1967. p. 215-229.

Hanstein, Hartwig. *Studien zur entwicklung von Ionescos theater.* Heidelberg, Carl Winter Universitatsverlag, 1971. 125 p. (Annales Universitatis Saraviensis Philosphie-Lettres, Band 12).

Hayman, Ronald. *Eugene Ionesco.* London, Heinemann, 1972. 114 p. (Contemporary Playwrights).

Jacquart, Emmanuel. *Le théâtre de dérision.* Paris, Gallimard, 1974. 313 p. (Idées).

Jacobsen, Josephine and William R. Mueller. *Ionesco and Genet: Playwrights of silence.* New York, Hill and Wang, 1968. 242 p.

Lamont, Rosette C. *Ionesco, a collection of critical essays.* Englewood Cliffs, N. J., Prentice-Hall Inc., 1967. 188 p. (Twentieth Century Views).

—. "The double apprenticeship: life and the process of dying." *In: The Phenomenon of Death* ed. by Edith Wyschsgrad. Harper and Row, 1973. p. 198-224.

Laubreaux, Raymond. *Les critiques de notre temps et Ionesco.* Paris, Garnier Freres, 1973. 188 p.

Lécuyer, Maurice. *Le langage dans le théâtre de Ionesco.* Houston.

Lewis, Allan. *Ionesco.* New York, Twayne Publishers Inc., 1972. 119 p.

—. "The theatre of the 'absurd'—Beckett, Ionesco Genet. In his: *The contemporary theatre.* New York, Crown Publishers, 1962. p. 259-281.

Liour, Michel. "La prolifération dans le théâtre d'Eugène Ionesco." *In: L'onirisme et l'insolite dans le théâtre français contemporain,* ed. by Paul Vernois. Paris, Editions Klincksieck, 1974. p. 75-158 (Actes et Colloques n 14, Actes du Colloque de Strasbourg).

Mauriac, Claude. "Ionesco." *In his: L'allittérature contemporaine.* Paris, Albin Michel, 1969. p. 200-207.

Mikheeva, Agnessa Nikolaevna. *Kogda po stene khodiat nosorogi.* Moscow, The Arts, 1967. 176 p.

Monférier, Jacques. "L'insolite dans La soif et la faim." *In: L'onirisme et l'insolite dans le théâtre français contemporain,* ed. by Paul Vernois. Paris, Editions Klincksieck, 1974. p. 159-179 (Actes et Colloques n 14, Actes du Colloque de Strasbourg).

Pronko, Leonard Cabell. *Eugene Ionesco.* New York, Columbia University Press, 1965. 47 p. (Columbia Essays on Modern Writers, 7).

—. *Avant-Garde, the experimental theatre in France.* Berkeley and Los Angeles, University of California Press, 1962. 225 p.

Ronge, Peter. *Polemik, parodie und satire bei Ionesco. Elemente einer theatertheorie und formen des theaters uber das theater.* Bad Homburg, V.D.H., Berlin, Zurich, Gehelen, 1967. 291 p. (Romanische Versuche und Vorarbeiten, 14).

Roud, Richard and Charles Marowitz. *Ionesco: ironia y compromiso.* Buenos Aires, Charles Perez, 1968. 60 p.

Saint Tobi. *Eugène Ionesco ou à la recherche du paradis perdu.* Paris, Gallimard, 1973. 218 p. (Les Essais CLXXVII).

Sandier, Gilles. *Théâtre et combat.* Paris, Stock, 1970. 368 p.

Seipel, Hildegard. *Untersuchen zumexperimenellen theater von Beckett und Ionesco.* Bonn, Romanisches Seminar Der Universitat Bonn, 1963. 291 p. (Romanische Versuche und Vorarbeiten, 14).

Sénart, Philippe. *Ionesco.* Paris, Editions Universitaires, 1964. 128 p.

Serreau, Genevieve. "Eugène Ionesco." *In her: Histoire du*

nouveau théâtre. Paris, Gallimard, 1966. p. 37-65.

Styan, John Louis. "After Godot: Ionesco, Genet and Pinter." *In his: The Dark Comedy. The development of modern comic tragedy.* Cambridge, Cambridge University Press, 1968. p. 234-250. (Orig. ed.: Cambridge, Cambridge University Press, 1962).

Surer, Paul. "Eugene Ionesco." *In his: Le théâtre française contemporain.* Paris, Stoiété d'édition et d'enseignement supérieur, 1964. p. 479-498.

Tarrab, Gilbert. "Eugène Ionesco: sa place dans le Nouveau theatre et le Nouveau Roman." *In his: Le theatre du nouveau langage.* Tome I. Ottawa, Le Cercle du Livre de France, 1973. p. 90-206.

—. *Ionesco à coeur ouvert.* Montreal, Cercle du Livre de France, 1971, 120 p.

Taylor, John Russell. *The angry theatre.* New York, Hill and Wang, 1969. 391 p. (Orig. ed.: NewYork, Hill and Wang, 1962).

Vernois, Paul. *La dynamique théâtrale d'Eugène Ionesco.* Paris, Editions Klincksieck, 1972. 308 p.

Voltz, Pierre. "Eugène Ionesco." In his: *La comédie.* Paris, Librairie Armand Colin, 1964. p. 183-185.

Wellwarth, George E. "Eugene Ionesco, the absurd as warning." *In his: The theater of protest and paradox.* New York, New York University Press, 1964. p. 51-72. (New ed.: New York, New York University Press, 1971. 409 p.).

Williams, Raymond. "Tragic Deadlock and Stalemate: Chekhov, Pirandello, Ionesco and Beckett." *In his: Modern tragedy.* Stanford, Stanford University Press, 1966. p. 139-155.

Wulbern, Julian H. *Brecht and Ionesco.* Urbana, University of Illinois Press, 1971. 250 p.

BIBLIOGRAPHY:
SPECIAL ISSUES OF PERIODICALS

Cahiers des Saisons 15   Hiver 1959
    William Soroyan   Ionesco
    Jacques Lemarchand   Les débuts de Ionesco
    Jean Anouilh   Du chapitre des Chaises
    Pierre Aimé Touchard   La loi du théâtre
    Jacques Brenner   La vie est un songe
    Philippe Soupault   Eugène, mon ami'

    Georges Neveux   Soux la loupe
    Quatrezoneilles   Le verbe se fait cadavre
    Alain Bosquet   Se débarrasser du personnage

    Nicolas Bataille   La bataille de la Cantatrice
    René de Obaldia   Ionesco de Cerisy
    Jacques Mauclair   Une aventure fantastique
    Kenneth Tynan, Philip Toynbee and Orson Welles
        Controverse londonienne

TDR   7, n 3   Spring 1963
    Genet-Ionesco Issue

    Ionesco   Notes on my Theatre
    Richard Schechner   An Interview with Ionesco
    Martin Esslin   Ionesco and the Creative Dilemma
    Jean Vannier   A Theater of Language
    Richard Schechner   The Inner and the Outer Reality

Cahiers Renaud-Barrault 29   February 1960
    Jean Duvignaud   La Dérision
    Alfred Kern   Ionesco et la pantomime
    Marcel Moussy   De Victor a Jacques, ou de la revolte a la
        soumission
    Pierre Aimé Touchard   Un nouveau fabuliste

Cahiers Renaud-Barrault 42   February 1963
  Henry Miller   De Dié à Carmel
  Richard N. Coe   La farce tragique

Cahiers Renaud-Barrault 53   February 1966
  Maurice Lécuyer   Ionesco ou la précédence du verbe
  Abirached, Robert   Le duel et la mort chez Ionesco
  Rosette Lamont   Entretien avec Eugène Ionesco
  Eugène Ionesco   Ecrire

BIBLIOGRAPHY: ESSAYS

1953

Robbe-Grillet, Alain. "Eugène Ionesco: Théâtre I." *Critique* 73:564-565, June 1953.

Humeau, Edmond. "Eugène Ionesco ou le théâtre de la contradiction." *Preuves* 32:84-86.

1954

Lemarchand, Jacques. "Le théâtre d'Eugène Ionesco." In: Eugène Ionesco, Théâtre I. Paris, Gallimard, 1954, pp. 9-12.

1955

Lemarchand, Jacques. "Spectacles Ionesco." *Nouvelle Revue Française* 36:1148-1153, 1955.

1957

Selz, Jean. "L'homme encombré d'Ionesco." *Les Lettres Nouvelles* 53:477-482, October 1957.

Reed, Muriel. "Ionesco, l'autore piu discusso del teatro contomporaneo." *Il Drama* 255:88-92, December 1957.

1958

Benmussa, Simone. "Les ensevelis dans le théâtre d'Eugène Ionesco." *Cahiers Renaud-Barrault* 22:197-207, May 1958.

Barbour, Thom S. "Beckett and Ionesco." *The Hudson Review* 11:271-277, Summer 1958.

Watson, Donald. "The world of Ionesco." *Tulane Drama Review* 3:48-53, October 1958.

1959

Brion, Marcel. "Sur Ionesco." *Le Mercure De France n⁰* 1150:272-280, June 1959.

Bosquet, Alain. "Commet se débarrasser du personnage." *Cahiers Des Saisons* 15:242-244, Hiver 1959.

Laubreaux, Raymond. "Situation de Ionesco." *Théâtre D'Aujourd'Hui* 9:42-44, January-February 1959.

Lamont, Rosette. "The metaphysical farce: Beckett and Ionesco." *The French Review* 32:319-328, February 1959.

Saurel, Renée. "Saint Ionesco, l'anti-Brecht." *Les Temps Modernes* 158:1656-1661, April 1959.

Pronko, Leonard. "The anti-spiritual victory in the theater of Ionesco." *Modern Drama* 2:29-35, May 1959.

Saurel, Renée. "Ionesco ou les blandices de la culpabilité." *Les Temps Modernes* 103:2286-2290, June 1959.

Girard, Denis. "L'anti-théâtre d'Eugène Ionesco." *Modern Languages* 15:45-52, June 1959.

1960

Doubrovsky, Serge. "Le rire d'Eugène Ionesco." *Nouvelle Revue Francaise* 86:313-332, 1960.

Schérer, Jacques. "L'évolution de Ionesco." *Les Lettres Nouvelles* 8ᵉannée (n 1):91-96, March-April 1960.

Fowlie, Wallace. "New plays by Ionesco and Genet." *Tulane Drama Review* 5:43-48, September 1960.

1961

Lamont, Rosette. "The outrageous Ionesco." *Horizon* 3: 89-97, May 1961.

Eastman, Richard M. "Experiment and vision in Ionesco's plays." *Modern Drama* 4:3-19, May 1962.

Knowles, Dorothy. "Ionesco and the mechanism of language." *Modern Drama* 5:7-10, May 1962.

Boatto, Alberto. "Il teatro di Ionesco." *Il Ponte* 17:888-197, June 1961.

Pucciani, Oreste F. "Où va Ionesco?" *French Review* 35:68-71, October 1961.

Dukore, Bernard. "The theatre of Ionesco: union of form and substance." *Educational Theatre Journal* 13:174-181, October 1961.

1962

Coe, Richard. "Le anarchistes de droite: Ionesco, Beckett, Genet, Arrabal." *Cahiers Renaud Barrault* 67:99-125, 1962.

Chambers, Ross. "Detached committal: Eugene Ionesco's *Victims of Duty.*" *Meanjin Quarterly* 22:23-33, March 1963.

Hughes, Catherine. "Ionesco's plea for man." *Renascence* 14:121-125, Spring 1962.

Murray, Jack. "Ionesco and the mechanic of memory." *Yale French Studies* 28:82-87, Spring/Summer 1962.

Schechner, Richard. "The enactment of the 'not' in Ionesco's *Les Chaises.*" *Yale French Studies* 28:65-72, Spring/Summer 1962.

Strem, George. "Ritual and poetry in Eugene Ionesco's theatre." *Texas Quarterly* 5:149-158, 1962.

Lamont, Rosette. "The hero in spite of himself." *Yale French Studies* 29:73-81, Fall 1962.

—. "The proliferation of matter in Ionesco's plays." *Esprit Créateur* 2(n°4):189-197, Winter 1962.

Hicksberg, Charles I. "Ionesco and the aesthetic of the absurd." *Arizona Quarterly* 18:293-303, Winter 1962.

1963

Kaiser, Joachim. "Ionesco 'politisches' theater (zu seinem neuen stuck Fusgänger der Luft)." *Theater Heute* 4:8-10, February 1963.

Wendt, Ernst. "Ionescos Jedermann." *Theater Heute* 4:8-16, March 1963.

Carat, Jacques. "Ionesco l'ancien et le nouveau." *Preuves* 146:71-73, April 1963.

Gelbard, Peter. "Interview with Eugene Ionesco (Paris: December 1962)." *Drama Survey* 3:27-32, May 1963.

Nores, D. "Itinéraire de Ionesco." *Les Lettres Nouvelles* 39:226-232, October 1963.

Cismanu, Alfred. "The validity of Ionesco's contempt." *Texas Quarterly* 6:220-235, 1964.

1964

Gaudet, Paul. "Ionesco, un drôle de tragiques." *Incidences* 4:25-45, January 1964.

Herviat, Paul. "Découoertes d'Eugène Ionesco." *Incidences* 4:8-18, January 1964.

Viatte, Auguste. "Le théâtre d'Eugène Ionesco." *La Revue De L'Université De Laval* 18:516-523, February 1964.

Ellis, Mary H. "The work of Eugene Ionesco." *The Southern Quarterly* 2:220-235, 1964.

1965

Lamont, Rosette. "Air and matter in Ionesco's plays." *French Review* 38:349-361, January 1965.

Vianu, Hélène. "Préludes Ionesciens." *Revue Des Sciences Humaines* 117:103-111, January-March 1965.

Lamont, Rosette. "Death and tragi-comedy: three plays of the new theatre." *The Massachusetts Review* 6:381-402, Winter-Spring 1965.

Cohn, Ruby. "Berenger, protagonist of an anti-playwright." *Modern Drama* 8:127-135, September 1965.

Goldstein, E. "Les précurseurs roumains de Ionesco." *Bulletin Des Jeunes Romanistes* 11-12:70-74, December 1965.

1966

Boisdeffre, Pierre de. "Plaidoyer pour Ionesco." *Les Nouvelles Littéraires* 2014:1, 13, April 7, 1966.

Lamont, Rosette. "Gestus versus image: A study of Brecht and Ionesco." *First Stage* 5:60-64, Summer 1966.

Cismanu, Alfred. "Ionesco the Rhinoceros." *The Laurel Review* 6(no2):33-42, 1966.

1967

Wegener, Adolph H. "The absurd in modern literature." *Books Abroad* 41:150-156, Spring 1967.

Cismanu, Alfred. "Ionesco's latest: *Hunger and Thirst.*" *The Laurel Review* 7 (no2):63-70, 1967.

Depraz-MacNulty, Marie-Claude. "L'objet dans le théâtre d'Eugène Ionesco." *French Review* 41:92-98, October 1967.

1968

Purdy, S. B. "A ready of Ionesco's *The Killer.*" *Modern*

Drama 10:416-423, February 1968.

Messenger, Theodore. "Who was that lady? The problem of identity in *The Bald Soprano* of Eugene Ionesco." *North Dakota Quarterly* 36:5-20, Spring 1968.

Toplin, Marian. "Eugene Ionesco's *The Chairs* and the theater of the absurd." *American Imago* 25:119-139, Summer 1968.

1969
Lamont, Rosette. "An interview with Eugene Ionesco." *The Massachusetts Review* 10:128-148, Winter 1969.

1970
Williams, Edith Shitehurst. "God's share: mythic interpretation of *The Chairs.*" *Modern Drama* 12:298-307, 1969/1970.

Sénart, Philippe. "Eugène Ionesco." *La Revue Des Deux Mondes,* March 1, 1970:518-525, 1970.

Mast, Gerald. "The logic of illogic: Ionesco's *Victims of Duty.*" *Modern Drama* 13:135-138, February 11, 1970.

Lamont, Rosette. "Number thirteen: visit to the Ionescos in Paris." *Town and Country* 124:81/90/93, September 1970.

Abirached, Robert. "La mort mise en scène—Ionesco et Genet." *Nouvelle Revue Francaise* 215:88-91, November 1, 1970.

Mambrino, Jean. "Carnet de théâtre (Jeux de massacre)." *Études* 1970:706-712, December 1970.

1971
Lamont, Rosette. "The topography of Ionescoland." *Modern Occasions* 1(n°4):536-546, February 11, 1971.

Craddock, George. "Escape and fulfillment in the theater of Eugene Ionesco." *The Southern Quarterly* 10:15-22, October 1971.

Heitmann, Klaus. "Das motiv der nahrungsaufnahme bei Ionesco." *Poetic* 4:60-68, January 1971.

Covaci, Vasile. "Procédés métalinguistiques dans les pièces d'Eugène Ionesco." *Revue Roumaine De Linguistique* 16:203-213, 1971.

Baciu, Mina. "Eugène Ionesco et le paradis perdu." *Conjunction, Revue Franco-Haitienne* 116:30-36, 1971.

Revzine, Olgaet Isaak. "Expérimentation sémiotique chez Eugène Ionesco." *Semiotic* 4:240-262, 1971.

1972

Lee, Vera. "Through the looking glass with Eugene Ionesco." *Drama and Theater* 10(n°2):63-68, Winter 1971/1972.

Wright, Jules N. "Caragiale, Ionesco and the bourgeois." *Drama and Theatre* 10(n°2):77-78, Winter 1971/1972.

Sandier, Gilles. "Caricature et vérité." *La Quinzaine Litteraire*, 16-19:27-28, February 1972.

Checroun, Sylvia L. "Philemon, Baucis et Sémiramis dans *Les Chaises* de Ionesco." *French Review* 45:116-122, Spring 1972 (Special Issue, n°4).

Ormesson, Wladimir d'. "Les propos." *La Revue Des Deux Mondes* 3:646-655, March 1972.

Witt, Mary Ann. "Eugene Ionesco and the dialectic of space." *Modern Language Quarterly* 33:312-326, September 1972.

Lamont, Rosette. "From Macbeth to Macbett." *Modern Drama* 15:231-253, December 1972.

1973

Baciu, Mira. "Eugène Ionesco et la quête de l'authenticité." *Présence Francophone* 6:44-53, Spring 1973.

Gerrard, Charolotte F. "Bergsonian elements in Ionesco's *Le piéton de l'air.*" *Papers on Language and Literature* 9: 297-310, Summer 1973.

Bonnefoy, Claude. "Ionesco ou l'étonnement." *Magazine Littéraire* 81:17-21, October 1973.

Brochier, Jean Jacques. "Ionesco: s'expliquer dans l'inexplicable." *Magazine Littéraire* 1:10-16, October 1973.

Braucourt, Guy. "Phantasmes en chair, en os, et en images." *Les Nouvelles Littéraires* 2407:20, 12-18, November 1973.

Vernois, Paul. "L'esthétique dramaturgique d'Eugène Ionesco." *Revue Des Langues Vivantes* 39:196-202, 1973.

Wurms, Pierre. "Eugène Ionesco: Le monde du dedans." *Neuren Sprachen* 12:649-658, December 1973.

1974

Chateau, Gilbert. "Ionesco toujours." *Nouvelle Revue Française* 255:119-121, March 1974.

1976

Suther, Judith D. "Ionesco's symbiotic pair: *Le Solitaire* and *Ce formidable bordel.*" *French Review* 49:689-702, April 1976.

THE TWO FACES OF IONESCO

Composed in IBM Selectric Composer *Journal Roman* and printed offset by McNaughton & Gunn, Incorporated, Ann Arbor, Michigan. The paper on which the book is printed is the International Paper Company's *Bookmark,* which is acid-free. The book was sewn and bound by Howard Dekker & Sons, Grand Rapids, Michigan.

The Two Faces of Ionesco is a Trenowyth book, the scholarly publishing division of The Whitston Publishing Company.

This edition consists in 1000 casebound copies.